LEGISLATING UNDEF

MW01230699

Parliament, Executive Power, and Rights

Legislating under the Charter explores how governments and Parliament justify limitations on rights when advancing laws that raise rights concerns or when responding to judicial decisions under the Canadian Charter of Rights and Freedoms.

Through an analysis of legislation concerning criminal justice policy, the approval of new safe consumption sites, sex work, and medical assistance in dying, the book provides a detailed analysis of the extent and nature of parliamentary deliberation about rights, the extent to which government initiatives are properly scrutinized, and the broader institutional relationships under the Charter. The authors draw from a host of qualitative data, including research interviews and examination of judicial decisions, various bills under study, Hansard debates from the floor of the House of Commons, committee and Senate scrutiny of legislation, bureaucratic advice and Charter statements by the department of justice, and news media coverage.

The book offers a set of concrete reform proposals to improve the transparency and accountability of executive and bureaucratic vetting processes, and to strengthen the role of Parliament in upholding constitutional values and holding the government to account. In doing so, *Legislating under the Charter* contributes to the broader comparative scholarship on models of judicial review, morality policy, policy change, and constitutionalism.

EMMETT MACFARLANE is an associate professor of political science at the University of Waterloo.

JANET L. HIEBERT is a professor emeritus of political studies at Queen's University.

ANNA DRAKE is an assistant professor of political science at the University of Waterloo.

Legislating under the Charter

Parliament, Executive Power, and Rights

EMMETT MACFARLANE,
JANET L. HIEBERT, AND ANNA DRAKE

UNIVERSITY OF TORONTO PRESS
Toronto Buffalo London

ISBN 978-1-4875-5244-2 (cloth)   ISBN 978-1-4875-5817-8 (EPUB)
ISBN 978-1-4875-5453-8 (paper)   ISBN 978-1-4875-5610-5 (PDF)

Library and Archives Canada Cataloguing in Publication

Title: Legislating under the Charter : Parliament, executive power, and rights /
    Emmett Macfarlane, Janet L. Hiebert, and Anna Drake.
Names: Macfarlane, Emmett, author. | Hiebert, Janet, 1960– author. |
    Drake, Anna, 1978– author.
Description: Includes bibliographical references and index.
Identifiers: Canadiana (print) 20220472386 | Canadiana (ebook) 20220472467 |
    ISBN 9781487552442 (cloth) | ISBN 9781487554538 (paper) |
    ISBN 9781487556105 (PDF) | ISBN 9781487558178 (EPUB)
Subjects: LCSH: Canada. Canadian Charter of Rights and Freedoms. |
    LCSH: Canada. Parliament. | LCSH: Judicial review – Canada. |
    LCSH: Judicial process – Canada. | LCSH: Constitutional law – Canada. |
    LCSH: Legislation – Canada.
Classification: LCC KE4248 .M33 2023 | LCC KF4483.J8 M33 2023 kfmod |
    DDC 347.71/12 – dc23

We wish to acknowledge the land on which the University of Toronto Press
operates. This land is the traditional territory of the Wendat, the Anishnaabeg,
the Haudenosaunee, the Métis, and the Mississaugas of the Credit First
Nation.

University of Toronto Press acknowledges the financial support of the
Government of Canada, the Canada Council for the Arts, and the Ontario Arts
Council, an agency of the Government of Ontario, for its publishing activities.

Canada Council   Conseil des Arts
for the Arts   du Canada

ONTARIO ARTS COUNCIL
CONSEIL DES ARTS DE L'ONTARIO
an Ontario government agency
un organisme du gouvernement de l'Ontario

Funded by the   Financé par le
Government   gouvernement
of Canada   du Canada

Contents

Acknowledgments

This book is the culmination of many years of research, writing, and thinking about institutional relationships under the Charter of Rights and Freedoms. As a collaboration of the three authors, it has evolved considerably since the idea of a book on our complementary research interests was first raised a decade ago. As a result, we are indebted to many scholars in the law and politics subfield for fruitful discussions over the years on topics addressed within the book, including Dennis Baker, Stéphanie Chouinard, Minh Do, Erin Crandall, Mark Harding, Matt Hennigar, Rachael Johnstone, Jim Kelly, Andrew McDougall, Eleni Nicolaides, Kate Puddister, Emma Richez, Troy Riddell, and Dave Snow. Additional thanks to Minh Do for her research assistance. We would also like to thank our colleagues at the Department of Political Science, University of Waterloo, and the Department of Political Studies, Queen's University for their support.

We are grateful to Dan Quinlan and the editorial team at the University of Toronto Press for expertly ushering the book through the peer review and production processes, and to the anonymous reviewers for their helpful comments.

Emmett would like to thank his parents, Don and Eileen Macfarlane, and his sister, Aingeal, for their continued support. As always, the love of his wife, Anna, is instrumental to his success (doubly so this time, since she is a co-author on the book!). Finally, to his daughter Thea, who is used to Mommy and Daddy writing books and feigns just enough interest to be polite about it.

Janet would like to thank Wayne for his unwavering love and support.

Anna would like to thank her parents, Peter and Karolyn Drake. She would also like to thank Emmett and Thea for their love, support, and patience, and her dog, Zoey, for the welcome distractions from work.

Introduction

In a landmark Charter of Rights and Freedoms case called *M. v. H.*, the Supreme Court ruled that Ontario legislation outlining spousal benefits for common-law couples, which limited the definition of "spouse" to opposite-sex partners, was an unconstitutional violation of the equality rights of individuals in same-sex conjugal relationships.[1] Although the Court's decision was limited to the specific benefits at hand, it prompted a flurry of legislative activity across the provinces and at the federal level on a host of benefits beyond spousal support. Parliament passed Bill C-23, which affected sixty-eight federal statutes including those implicating pension benefits, old age security, income tax deductions, bankruptcy protection, and the Criminal Code. The government took a clear cue from the Court's decision that benefit programs discriminating on the basis of sexual orientation were unacceptable. At the same time, however, the federal legislation left the definitions of marriage and spouse unchanged but expanded the definition of common-law relationships to include same-sex couples.

The Ontario government's response was similar, as it introduced a law amending sixty-seven pieces of legislation to accommodate the inclusion of same-sex couples, although Progressive Conservative Premier Mike Harris made it clear that he did not personally agree with the Court's decision.[2] Ontario's attorney general emphasized that "the only reason we are introducing this Bill is because of the Supreme Court of Canada decision. We would not introduce the legislation otherwise."[3] Most of the other provinces similarly viewed the decision as obligating a broad legislative response, incorporating changes to a substantial number of statutes dealing with common-law benefits rather than narrowly amending the spousal support policies specific to the case. By contrast, Manitoba was more minimalist in its approach. For example, where other provinces expanded adoption rights to include same-sex couples, the Manitoba government was criticized for limiting its legislative amendments to just ten provincial statutes on issues like alimony, pension, and death benefits.[4]

Few judicial decisions, even ones invalidating legislation on Charter of Rights grounds, result in such sweeping legislative action. Many Charter decisions result in no meaningful legislative response, leaving impugned legislative provisions as "dead letter" or repealed by the legislature, or they see governments introduce new legislation to comply narrowly with the courts' policy prescriptions.[5] Compliance of this sort is sometimes begrudging, as Ontario's response to *M. v. H.* certainly was. In some contexts, however, governments will sometimes push back against court decisions. They may pass new, differently crafted legislation to seek out their original policy objectives. In rare cases, they may even attempt to reverse the effects of a judicial decision.

Most legislation will never be subject to judicial review on Charter grounds; some laws may not raise rights concerns, others may be tailored to avoid litigation, and the application of some laws may take years before an individual circumstance arises such that a rights infringement becomes apparent. Litigation is also a costly affair, minimizing the likelihood of constitutional challenges. Regardless of the reasons, Parliament is often the only meaningful check on legislation when it comes to rights.

Yet the extent to which governments and parliamentarians consider Charter obligations when developing legislation has not received the academic attention that has been devoted to courts and judicial review. In contrast to our ability to assess jurisprudential developments and review the explicit reason-giving that courts engage in, much of the legislative process is hidden from public scrutiny. Cabinet confidence shields government discussions about legislation in development from public or media inspection. Similarly, governments rely on solicitor-client privilege to keep hidden the legal advice received from Department of Justice lawyers about the compatibility of legislation with the Charter. Only recently have the contours of this latter process come to light.

This book examines how governments and Parliament legislate under the Charter. The topic summons a number of core research questions, including: How do governments justify limitations on rights when advancing legislation that raises potential rights concerns or when responding to judicial decisions under the Charter? What is the extent and nature of parliamentary deliberation about rights? How do judicial norms about Charter rights and the requirements of the constitution influence the legislative process? Do governments or parliamentarians advance their own conception of the Charter's requirements, or do they equate judicial decisions with the meaning and scope of the rights at stake? Finally, what do the answers to these questions tell us about the inter-institutional relationships that govern policymaking under the Charter?

Our investigation incorporates analysis of a host of qualitative data, including the pertinent judicial decisions; the bills under study; comprehensive assessments of Hansard debate from the House floor on the government bills under examination; committee and Senate scrutiny of those bills, including witness testimony and submissions; where relevant, statements made in the news media from ministers or MPs that explain their position on bills; Charter statements issued by the Department of Justice (an innovation first introduced in 2016); and research interviews.[6] In chapter 2, we analyse the process for Charter scrutiny of legislation undertaken by the Department of Justice, as well as the justice minister's decision under a statutory requirement to report to Parliament when bills are inconsistent with rights. We then undertake case studies of the government and parliamentary debate surrounding key bills, in the context of newly developed legislation in criminal justice (chapter 3) and in responses to landmark Supreme Court decisions under the Charter on supervised consumption sites (chapter 4), prostitution (chapter 5), and medical assistance in dying (chapter 6). Finally, in chapter 7 we advance proposals for reform to enhance transparency and improve executive and legislative scrutiny of legislation for consistency with rights.

Our analysis contributes to significant issues animating the scholarly literature. Canada is the first Westminster system to incorporate a statutory bill of rights in the form of the 1960 Canadian Bill of Rights at the federal level, and later entrenching the Charter in the Constitution Act, 1982. Canada is thus the formative instance of the "Commonwealth model" of constitutionalism, which, in Stephen Gardbaum's words, reflects "an intermediate ground in between the two traditional and previously mutually exclusive options of legislative and judicial supremacy."[7] American-style judicial review stereotypically implies judicial supremacy in interpretation and effect – barring constitutional amendment or getting the Supreme Court to reverse itself (often through new judicial appointments), the Court's decisions are treated as authoritative and final. In contrast, the bills of rights enacted in Canada, the United Kingdom, New Zealand, and the state of Victoria and the Australian Capital Territory in Australia allow for judicial review but theoretically leave legislatures free to respond to, or avoid the effects of, judicial decisions on rights. Mark Tushnet describes the distinction as one between "strong form" and "weak form" review.[8] In his view, "weak-form judicial review provides mechanisms for the people to respond to decisions that they reasonably believe mistaken that can be deployed more rapidly than the constitutional amendment or judicial appointment processes."[9]

Within the Commonwealth model, Canada is the only country with a constitutionally entrenched bill of rights and whose judiciary holds the power to invalidate legislation on that basis. By contrast, the United Kingdom, New Zealand, and sub-national Australian rights instruments permit the courts to make only non-binding declarations of incompatibility or inconsistency (in New Zealand, inhabiting the weak end of the "weak form" judicial review spectrum, until recently the courts even avoided asserting this power).

Compared to its Commonwealth brethren, Canada looks very much like an American-style system of judicial supremacy in terms of judicial power, but structural features of the Charter itself put the Canadian system into the intermediate category. The most popular portrayal of judicial review of the Charter in Canada is the dialogue metaphor: thanks to these key features of the Charter, legislatures generally can still respond to court decisions such that the judiciary does not always have the final word on the policies implicated by rights.[10] The dialogue metaphor, the Commonwealth model, and the strong form versus weak form distinction all hinge on section 1 of the Charter, the reasonable limits clause, and section 33, the notwithstanding clause. The latter feature allows Parliament or the provincial legislatures to pass legislation "notwithstanding" the Charter – in effect, immunizing laws from the effects of judicial review. Section 33 applies only to certain sections of the Charter, and its use must be renewed in legislation every five years. Section 1 permits legislative responses to judicial rulings that tailor new laws with a new purpose or design, such that the legislature might achieve its policy objectives by advancing a successful proportionality argument under new legislation in light of any limitations of rights.

Yet we assert, as Gardbaum and Tushnet acknowledge, that Canada fits uneasily within the Commonwealth model or as a weak form system. Section 33 suffers from near obsolescence because the clause has been invoked only a handful of times outside of Quebec and never at the federal level (although a modest surge of recent cases at the provincial level is discussed in chapter 7). To the extent that section 1 permits legislative responses, some commentators overstate its distinctiveness; after all, legislatures in strong form systems are free to enact new, different legislation after suffering defeat before courts.[11] Moreover, the record suggests that in Canada the most common legislative response to judicial invalidation of statutes is to comply with the court decision, by leaving the legislation struck down, repealing it, or passing amendments that reflect judicial policy prescriptions.[12] The Canadian experience in practice, then, is one of strong form review, even as the structural features of the Charter keep it in its theoretical place of belonging in the Commonwealth model.

Much of the debate over, and analysis of, dialogue or different models of judicial review focus necessarily on courts and judicial policy prescriptions. While scholars have examined legislative responses to judicial decisions in previous studies, there are few book-length studies that centre on the legislative process, parliamentary debate, and government justifications for advancing policies that implicate rights.[13] We thus lack insight into the primary institutional locus of interaction that influences policy outcomes under the Charter, especially where frameworks like dialogue, as we explore in chapter 1, are deeply contested and found empirically and conceptually inadequate.

Our analysis eschews simplistic depictions of court-legislature interaction in favour of analysing highly salient cases in which governments have a strong motivation to pursue an ideological legislative agenda. Issue salience is a concept employed in political science and policy scholarship to identify matters of importance, often identified by issues that generate substantial media coverage or that are top priorities in public opinion polls.[14] Highly salient policy issues are more likely to receive public and media attention and are also more likely to be of importance to governing parties. By focusing our case studies on prominent cases, it is more probable that we can capture instances where governments are willing to depart from judicial policy prescriptions as well as be compelled to address the potential rights issues at stake.

We investigate criminal justice policies pursued under the Conservative government of Stephen Harper, and legislative responses by the Harper Conservatives and the Liberal government under Justin Trudeau to court decisions involving social or morality policies, including supervised consumption sites, prostitution, and medical assistance in dying. This necessitates an analysis that explicitly considers the nature of executive-dominance in the Canadian Parliament and the legislative process, and distinguishes the activities of government (i.e., cabinet and the prime minister), the bureaucracy, the governing and opposition parties, individual parliamentarians, and Parliament as an institution and its committees. We avoid an idealized assessment of legislative deliberation that assumes parliamentarians are simply autonomous representatives engaged in principled debate.[15] Instead, our analysis situates MPs as (typically) party members in an institutional setting where strong executive agenda-setting powers and high (even extreme) party discipline conditions deliberation over rights and legislation.

Understanding the Political Context in Which the Charter Functions

Before we look at how proposed legislation is evaluated, we emphasize the importance of understanding the institutional context and political setting in which a bill of rights operates. For Canada, this context is a Westminster-based parliamentary system. It was designed to function in a manner similar in principle to that of the United Kingdom (with important modifications to accommodate federalism and Canada's then colonial status) but has evolved to emphasize government and party-centric forces.

The relevant, modern "Westminster factors" that shape political behaviour include executive dominance of the legislative process, the introduction of legislation at an advanced stage of development, strong party discipline with its expectation that government members will generally resist parliamentary attempts to introduce substantial amendments that delay or distort the government's legislation agenda, the convention of responsible government (where the government must maintain support of the House of Commons to remain in power), and the centrality of strong, cohesive parties that organize how Parliament functions. The convention that government will resign if it loses a confidence vote has operated in Canada to encourage the strongest party discipline among Westminster systems, where defection from the preferences of party leaders is remarkably low.[16] Opposition parties' primary role is to demonstrate they are the best alternative to government, and like members of the government party, there is a strong tendency to vote as instructed by party leaders. Discipline is maintained not only by the culture of shared political commitments but also by privileges that leaders dispense, such as elevation beyond the backbench or, if in opposition, appointment to a shadow minister position. Discipline is also maintained by threats that leaders can exert such as demotion, expulsion from caucus, and withholding the ability to contest the next election as a party member.[17] Canadian backbenchers seem to lack the freedom of their counterparts in the larger UK House of Commons, and Canadian party leaders do not deal as frequently with internal party divisions as is apparent in Australia.

Our analysis of policy development in this book makes it clear that party discipline seems to prevail over concerns about Charter consistency, even in committee. The Standing Committee on Justice and Human Rights is the committee where Charter concerns most often arise in the House of Commons. However, the intense partisanship under which the committee operates means that if the government enjoys an electoral majority, it will also have majority status in the composition of the committee, and thus can usually be confident that the committee will not generally pose problems to the government's pursuit of its preferred agenda. A good example arose in 2013 when the Conservative government pressed its members to defeat an opposition motion to study the criteria for the justice minister's determination of whether legislation is consistent with the Charter.[18] The government subsequently tabled a document stating that the absence of a statutory report on Charter inconsistency (which is required under section 4.1 of the Department of Justice Act, as explored in chapter 2) "means that the Minister had concluded that the government bill was not inconsistent with the Charter."[19] A few months later, after one Conservative committee member resigned from the party, he acknowledged that intense pressure had been exerted on government members to defeat the motion and suggested that the opposition motion precipitated unprecedented activity between the minister of justice's staff and party whip, with committee members informed "unequivocally that the government doesn't want the study to be done."[20]

Cohesive party voting influences not only how the Justice Committee functions, but also how Parliament evaluates legislation when meeting as a committee of the whole. Second and third reading debates continue to be framed in binary terms: for or against the government, in which the position members take is dictated overwhelmingly by party affiliation. However, our research, along with earlier studies,[21] indicates that Charter compliance is not a particularly salient issue for opposition parties when evaluating bills. As we discuss in chapter 3, although opposition parties were extremely vocal about potential Charter violations associated with the Harper government's criminal law agenda, they promptly abandoned their resistance when it became apparent that pressures for amendments could thrust the parties into an unwanted election for which opposition parties were poorly prepared. In addition, the fact that Charter concerns arose in the context of the rights of those accused of crimes likely contributed to parties' willingness to stop pursuing Charter amendments, particularly in light of apprehension of fallout associated with the government's claims that they were soft on crime. In short, governments have had little reason to fear that rights-based concerns will be regularly marshalled to defeat legislation.

Our research reinforces the argument of Janet Hiebert and James Kelly in their evaluation of the relationship between a bill of rights and legislative behaviour in two other Westminster-based jurisdictions (the United Kingdom and New Zealand). The relevant question is not merely how a bill of rights affects legislative behaviour, but also how a Westminster-based political system affects the way a bill of rights functions politically.[22] Some might question the applicability of this observation for Canada because of the Charter's constitutional rather than statutory status, or because of far stronger judicial remedial powers than in the United Kingdom or New Zealand. However, our research suggests that, at least in policy areas of high political salience to the government of the day, neither apprehension of judicial censure nor attempts to mitigate this possibility are given priority over other considerations if doing so seriously undermines the government's ability to pass its preferred legislative agenda and/or avoid delays. Even in morality policy, where governments may permit a free vote, Charter rights do not seem to receive a robust appraisal from parliamentarians. Where the Charter is invoked, it is usually with respect to assurances or criticisms about adherence to court decisions rather than any independent assessment of how rights ought to be protected. The influence of judicial norms is apparent, but only in a superficial way and heavily conditioned by the ideological and partisan political contest at play. These findings therefore contribute to normative debates about judicial review and suggest we ought not be overly confident about the capacity of legislatures to give principled attention to the rights implications of legislation.[23]

We also find that the behaviour and attitude of the government and the legislature on Charter issues is somewhat independent of the interinstitutional interaction they have with the courts. Contrary to the overriding attention in scholarly studies to dialogue or models of judicial review, government willingness to pursue policy objectives with minimal regard to Charter concerns or to push back against court decisions does not particularly reflect whether the courts have the final say about the policies at stake. Consistent with Emmett Macfarlane's analysis of the supposed dialogic relationships under the Charter,[24] we find that even in the context of highly salient social policy issues where governments have a more combative or ideological disposition to the pursuit of their policy objectives, judicial policy prescriptions tend to win after subsequent rounds of litigation. *Legislating under the Charter* thus contributes to our understanding of Parliament, the concentration of power in the executive, inter-institutional relationships under the Charter, and the policy impact of courts and the constitution.

Policy Change under the Charter

One thing that makes investigation of the institutional relationships surrounding the Charter challenging – regardless of the lens of analysis used – is its complexity. A primary object of inquiry is ultimately about how policy change happens. This is sometimes framed as asking which institution enjoys the final decision on the policy at stake or who exercises a policy veto under the constitution. It is normally thought to be the courts, which most legal commentators argue hold interpretative supremacy on the constitutional limits at stake when policies are implicated by rights. Similarly, on specific policies challenged on Charter grounds, the systematic evidence suggests the courts' policy prescriptions are usually final.

Yet that is not the same thing as saying that judicial decisions do not leave open other avenues in the broader policy sphere. Indeed, sometimes the courts explicitly invite new legislative action while invalidating a specific policy or legislative provision. The 1988 *Morgentaler* case on abortion policy illustrates the importance of the legislative process in Parliament following a Supreme Court decision.[25] In *Morgentaler*, the Court struck down a Criminal Code provision requiring those seeking access to abortion services to obtain the consent of "therapeutic abortion committees" of accredited or approved hospitals. A majority of the Court found that the provision violated section 7's right to life, liberty, and security of the person because it was arbitrary and imposed harms on women as a result of serious delays and uneven levels of access. Even Justice Bertha Wilson's concurring reasons – the only set of reasons finding a full-fledged right to abortion under the Charter – were written with the presumption that Parliament would craft a new law governing access to abortion services, including limits, possibly based on stage of gestation or foetal viability.

The government of the day attempted to develop new legislation on abortion services, and a compromise bill famously died in a tie vote in the Senate in 1991.[26] For the present discussion, the details of this process are unimportant, except to note that they involved a deeply contentious, morally laden social policy issue that included intra-caucus divisions within the major parties, not unlike some of the policy issues explored in later chapters of this book. What resulted was a federal policy vacuum on abortion. This is not to say, as some critics suggest, that Canada has "abortion on demand"; indeed, the provision of abortion services is heavily regulated by the medical profession, and its availability is subject to the whims of the provinces in their jurisdiction over health care.[27]

The inability of Parliament to reach consensus and pass new legislation thus had a dramatic impact on the policy landscape. While it was the Court that "punctuated"[28] the policy status quo, the successive inaction of governments since the 1991 defeat of compromise legislation in the Senate has been a conscious choice of federal party leaders, including of the Conservative Party, which has many supporters who would instead prefer to impose criminal limitations on access. This federal inaction is not because the Charter is properly interpreted as prohibiting *any* limits on abortion or because elected representatives believe judicial norms would prevent any criminal regulation of the procedure. Instead it is driven by political calculations about the desirability of raising the issue. This is an autonomous political judgment that can be analysed independently of any inter-institutional dialogue or supposed seeping effect of judicial norms. Yet as a matter of attributing "policy impact" to a particular institution or actor, the 1988 *Morgentaler* case stands as a prime example of the conditional and complex interactions sometimes at stake. Simply put, the courts, governments, and Parliament are all responsible for the altered status quo in federal abortion policy. This is similarly the case when the legislature is able to pass new legislation that departs from judicial fiat or that sets out objectives not explicitly contemplated when previous policies were subject to judicial review.

The questions animating this book ask us to turn our attention to how governments and legislatures approach their own responsibilities for policymaking under the Charter, and what influence judicial norms might exert on that process. Thus, in addition to investigating institutional roles and relationships, this book contributes to our understanding of policy change under the Charter. Policy change as a discrete lens of analysis for the study of constitutions has been surprisingly rare. As Macfarlane writes, "This may stem from a silo effect in the academic literature: neither the constitution nor the courts receive significant attention in the broader public policy/policy studies literature in Canada. Scholars who study judicial impact tend to be scholars of courts or the Charter, rather than those who might otherwise identify, first and foremost, as public policy scholars."[29]

Even within the realm of Charter-focused studies, much of the policy-oriented work has focused on the impact of legal mobilization and has been heavily influenced by American studies and debates over the influence of litigation efforts and rights jurisprudence.[30] Studies in Canada have led to fruitful explorations, like Troy Riddell's analysis of official minority-language education policy[31] or Christopher Manfredi's work on feminist legal mobilization.[32] Recent work has built on these studies from an explicit frame of policy change – including Stéphanie Chouinard on language rights and Rachael Johnstone on abortion policy – but rights-based analyses focusing on the executive and legislative contexts are few.[33]

In *Legislating under the Charter*, we investigate policy change by assessing governmental and parliamentary justifications for policies that have implications for Charter rights or that emerge in response to court decisions under the Charter. The objective is to assess the influence of judicial norms on policymaking, as well as to identify whether parliamentarians or the government of the day assert independent judgment about existing constitutional constraints on policy or how legislative objectives might be constrained.

Morality Policy

The analysis in the later chapters of this volume also contributes to a growing sub-field of policy studies referred to as morality policy. Morality policy is a specific category of public policy in which questions of first principle are at stake. The study of morality policy includes issues like abortion, capital punishment, sex work, drug use, LGBTQ rights, and medical aid in dying. A common definition views morality policy as "no less than the legal sanction of right and wrong, the validation of a particular set of basic values."[34] Although many policy issues involve moral judgments, including most criminal law, what distinguishes morality policy as a discrete class of subjects is the existence of virtually irreconcilable differences between people within society over their resolution: "At least a significant minority of citizens has a fundamental, first-principles conflict with the values embodied in some aspect of a morality policy."[35] Morality policies thus "imply a zero-sum game where the values of a specific group get legitimated at the expense of others."[36]

In this respect, debates over morality policies involve "which basic values a policy ought to validate, not, as is usually the case, about what is the best way to achieve an agreed-upon policy goal."[37] In part as a result, morality policies usually involve highly salient issues and a higher than usual level of citizen participation. The literature has developed subcategories of morality policy, including "life and death" issues (abortion, euthanasia, capital punishment), issues involving sexual behaviour (prostitution, pornography), matters relating to addiction (gambling, drug use), and issues pitting individual freedoms against collective values (gun control, religious education).[38]

It is worth making a brief note on terminology: in this book we use the legal terminology employed (by legislation or by the courts) where appropriate. For example, we refer to supervised injection, assisted suicide, or prostitution when referring to the specific laws or decisions at stake and the terminology employed in them. Otherwise, we use the contemporary policy terminology, such as safe consumption sites, medical aid in dying, or sex work (recognizing that sex work is a broader umbrella term encompassing not only the selling of sex but other voluntary activities like pornography, erotic dancing, etc., and that recognizes the agency of the people in the sex work industry).

Our chapters on safe consumption sites, sex work, and medical aid in dying fall squarely within the classification of morality policy. Reflecting the discussion in chapter 1, these issues are noteworthy in comparative perspective for often dividing elected representatives within political parties, resulting in the relaxation of party discipline in favour of conscience voting.[39] At the same time, with respect to some morality policies, political party affiliation may nonetheless be the best predictor of legislative votes.[40]

Morality policy is also characterized as difficult to change, in part as the result of political avoidance and inaction. This is at least in part because the issues are morally contentious and divisive, so there is often a perceived political cost to tackling them. As Stephan Heichel and colleagues note, "Change in morality policies is more often triggered by various forms of judicial intervention.... The country- and field-specific impact of courts on morality policy change implies that the dependent variable is often heavily 'contaminated' by a factor that is actually outside of the realm of democratic politics."[41] Court decisions can act as major triggers or open policy windows[42] such that they result in broad social mobilization and political debate. Our analysis sheds light – in the Canadian context, at least – on what happens in these specific policy areas after judicial invalidation of the policy status quo.

The study of morality policy is complicated by conceptual and empirical issues. Given the basic definition at stake, the line between morality and non-morality policies is, perhaps unsurprisingly, not always clearcut. An important segment of the literature on morality policy relies on assessing how decision-makers frame policies to determine if they fit within the parameters of the classification, but framing is often strategic and multidimensional. For example, opposition to same-sex marriage has been found to not always emanate from the perspective of moralistic discourse but about social consequences or procedural arguments.[43] Similarly, we find, for example, that much of the parliamentary debate on medical aid in dying was about balancing the right of access with protections and safeguards for vulnerable persons. The core moral issue about whether medical aid in dying be prohibited had effectively been settled by the Supreme Court in its 2015 decision. Yet underlying the debates are fundamentally moral views supporting a more liberal versus a more restrictive approach to access. Our analysis of debates on safe consumption sites and sex work reveal that the moral question of conduct is even more pronounced, as reflected in the nature of the legislative response in those cases. As a result, these cases studies may help to shed further light on the distinctive aspects of morality policy and how legislative deliberation operates in that context.

Outline of the Book

This book consists of seven chapters. Chapter 1 situates the book in debates about the institutional relationships at the heart of legislating under the Charter. We explain why we eschew adopting a particular model of analysis, like the popular metaphor of dialogue between courts and legislatures, which suffers from serious empirical and conceptual contestation. The chapter similarly investigates other conceptions of legislative behaviour under the constitution, including coordinate interpretation. The competing theories surrounding institutional relationships are heavily normative. They may help explain a government or legislature's approach to specific cases but not others. We thus conclude that these frames do not provide a complete or accurate empirical understanding of the legislative or executive roles under the Charter. Nonetheless, our analysis may shed light on the extent to which legislative deliberations on the specific policy issues and Charter cases explored in the book might inform the operation of a coordinate model of interpretation or dialogic review. Chapter 1 then examines the nature of executive dominance of the legislative process in Canada, noting that any analysis of institutional relationships under the Charter must account for the roles of cabinet, party discipline, and intra-caucus disagreement. We conclude the chapter with a brief assessment of the relatively scarce literature on the behaviour of specific governments (as distinct from legislatures) under the Charter.

In Chapter 2 we review bureaucratic and political assessment of legislative initiatives, focusing on the process that has come to be known as "Charter vetting." The chapter investigates whether cabinet is receptive to bureaucratic advice about Charter compliance. One key area of interest in this process is the statutory requirement that the minister of justice reports to Parliament when government bills are inconsistent with rights. Yet the provision, section 4.1 of the Department of Justice Act, has never been exercised. Drawing on interviews and recently uncovered details about the section 4.1 process, we find that the Charter vetting exercise is premised on an extremely strong presumption against making a report, particularly given the perceived risks this would have for future litigation efforts and the obvious political costs of passing legislation that is recognized as infringing rights. We also examine the introduction of Charter compatibility statements under the

Liberal government in 2016. Our analysis finds that neither the bureaucratic scrutiny nor the recent innovation of Charter statements provides a useful context for parliamentary debate about legislation that is implicated by the Charter.

Chapter 3 examines the legislative process under the Conservative government of Stephen Harper's (2006–15) law-and-order agenda in criminal justice policy. The analysis focuses on two omnibus bills, one introduced under the government's first minority Parliament in 2007 and the other during its majority in 2011. These bills included a host of new mandatory minimum sentences for serious gun crimes, sexual offences, and drug offences, as well as changes to bail provisions and the pardon system. In our analysis of the government's justifications for the Charter compatibility of these measures, we explore the weak engagement with Charter norms and the parliamentary discussion of the minister's refusal to report inconsistencies under the section 4.1 process. We also find that, despite the rights-based concerns of experts and some parliamentarians, the government was able to leverage its position – even in the minority context – to ensure the bills' passage. Important political factors weakened parliamentary scrutiny of the Conservatives' law-and-order legislative agenda. Several key provisions of both bills were subsequently invalidated by judicial review.

The next three chapters examine legislative responses to landmark Charter decisions in several important social policy areas. Chapter 4 examines legislative responses by both the Conservative and Liberal governments to the Supreme Court's 2011 Charter decision in *PHS Community Services Society*.[44] The Court ruled that the federal minister of health's refusal to extend an exemption under the Controlled Drugs and Substances Act (CDSA) to Insite, a supervised consumption site in Vancouver, violated its clients' right to life, liberty, and security of the person under section 7. The Conservative government's response was to amend provisions of the CDSA, setting out a lengthy set of factors the minister must take into consideration before making a decision on future exemptions. Critics accused the Conservatives of setting up an excessively onerous process in order to prevent the approval of additional supervised consumption sites, but the government defended its legislation as consistent with the Court's decision. Upon forming government in 2015, the Liberals introduced their own bill, which scaled down the factors to the smaller number explicitly identified by the Court. Our analysis of parliamentary debate over both bills reveals little explicit assessment of the Charter's requirements. Instead, each government defended its bill as consistent with the Court's policy prescription. In short, there was little principled debate over rights.

Chapter 5 analyses the Conservative government's response to the Court's 2013 decision in *Canada v. Bedford* striking down provisions of the Criminal Code indirectly prohibiting prostitution.[45] The Court determined that laws prohibiting the keeping of a bawdy house, living off the avails of prostitution, and public communication for the purposes of prostitution violated the right to life, liberty, and security of the person. Each of these different provisions imposed harms, making an otherwise lawful activity more dangerous to sex workers. The Conservatives' legislative response, Bill C-36, prohibited the purchase of sex, re-established a modified ban on public communication for the purpose of prostitution, criminalized the advertising of sexual services, created a "material benefit" offence (with exemptions drawn from *Bedford*), and made it illegal to "procure" a person to offer or provide sexual services. Parliamentary debate focused on whether the new provisions were consistent with the Court's decision, clouded by the fact that the Conservative government outlined new legislative objectives, shifting the purpose of the old laws (in the Court's determination) from addressing the public nuisance associated with sex work to a stated objective in the new legislation of reducing demand for sexual services and protecting sex workers. While much of the parliamentary scrutiny addressed the potential harmful effects of the new law, there was little independent assessment by parliamentarians of the Charter's requirements. Bill C-36 has been subject to litigation in several cases, with two trial courts finding several provisions unconstitutional, and we examine the context under which the Liberal government has not taken action to make changes.

In chapter 6 we investigate Parliament's response to the Court's 2015 decision in *Carter v. Canada*, which determined that the criminal law prohibiting assisted suicide was an unconstitutional violation of the right to life, liberty, and security of the person under section 7. Where initially the Conservative government delayed any legislative response, the subsequent Liberal government introduced legislation setting out a threshold for access that was considerably more narrow than the one articulated by the Court. Although at first the government justified the legislation as consistent with the Court's decision, it eventually asserted an independent role for Parliament in interpreting the Charter's requirements, with opposition criticism focused on the divergence between the legislation and the Court's reasons. Although we note that the parliamentary debate reflected a clear partisan divide – with the opposition Conservatives opposing what they viewed as insufficient safeguards for vulnerable persons under the new legislation, and the NDP decrying insufficiently liberal access for those seeking medical aid in dying – there is also evidence of intra-party disagreement within the Liberal and Conservative caucuses, which may have contributed to the nature of the legislation the government advanced. The constitutional issue would eventually come to a head with a trial court decision invalidating a key aspect of the new legislation and the government's introduction of a new bill with further amendments to the medical assistance in dying scheme. We analyse these developments and find that the government's unwillingness to heed valid concerns about the constitutionality of its initial legislative response resulted in another round of judicial intervention and what appears to be further evidence that the courts will ultimately have the final word on policies implicated under the Charter.

Chapter 7 examines the book's findings for our understanding of the fundamental institutional relationships at stake in legislating under the Charter. While there is clear evidence that in these highly salient cases governments are willing to pursue policy objectives even in the face of existing jurisprudence – that is, a willingness in these contexts to do something other than merely comply with court decisions – the fate of many of these policies seems destined to rest in the hand of courts. Key features of the Conservatives' criminal justice policies were subsequently invalidated by courts. With regard to supervised consumption sites, the Conservative government's amendments to the Controlled Drugs and Substances Act were eventually replaced by Liberal legislation that almost perfectly matched the policy prescription set out by the Supreme Court. Criminal restrictions on prostitution brought in by the Conservative government have, in part, been invalidated by trial courts. Similarly, the Liberal government introduced legislation after a key part of its legislative response to the Court's medical aid in dying decision was invalidated by a trial court. This pattern further confirms systematic evidence that legislative responses that push back against court rulings are typically defeated in subsequent rounds of judicial review, further calling into question the supposed dialogue between courts and legislatures.[46] When government assertiveness under the Charter does make itself known, it seems doomed to failure.

A central issue is that executive dominance of the legislative process prioritizes the ideological policy objectives of governments and minimizes principled debate over rights and the meaning of the Charter. The opposition parties, regardless of party stripe, will tend to invoke Charter concerns from an explicitly court-centric point of view. There is little evidence that governments or parliamentarians engage in an independent assessment of rights. Instead, government and opposition members generally focus on the question of adherence to court rulings as the primary framing of debate when the Charter is invoked. Importantly, many of their statements about judicial norms are selective, if not amounting to outright cherry-picking. In chapter 7 we introduce a set of reform proposals that we believe strengthen the impoverished rights scrutiny taking place within the executive and in Parliament. These include separating the roles of attorney general and minister of justice, waiving solicitor-client privilege for advice governments receive from Department of Justice lawyers about the constitutionality of legislation, improving Charter statements released by the Department of Justice, and establishing a joint committee on Charter rights.

We conclude by briefly summarizing and explaining our findings, some of which are consistent with the phenomenon of judicialization – the tendency or willingness of elected actors to rely on courts to settle controversial social and policy disputes – and others that are explained by reference to partisan contestation, and electoral and ideological considerations. We also attempt to lead the reader through a short answer to the following question: What would a more robust culture of executive and parliamentary rights scrutiny look like? In our view, taking the Charter seriously requires legislators to consider issues that are related to, though not necessarily directly addressed by, judicial decisions, and more fundamentally to engage in deliberation about the full gamut of rights implicated by policies rather than focusing narrowly on Charter provisions that courts settled on to determine the constitutionality of previous legislation. Consistent with our reform proposals, governments and legislatures need to adopt a proactive approach to Charter scrutiny, not only to better protect rights, the policies implicating rights, and the legislative process itself, but also to mitigate, if only slightly, the problems associated with the concentration of power in the hands of the executive, the relative weakness of Parliament, and the increasingly troubling and impoverished state of transparency and accountability in Canadian politics.

1 Institutional Relationships and Executive Dominance

Any analysis of the role of Parliament and the government in legislating under the Charter needs to consider the inter-institutional relationships at stake. One primary question animating this book is the extent to which the legislative process is influenced by judicial norms about what the constitution requires to protect rights. This necessitates an investigation into how governments justify their policy choices, to what extent parliamentary debate reflects members' independent judgment about the Charter and its limits, and an analysis of the ways legislation that responds to judicial decisions invaliding previous policies adheres to, or departs from, the policy prescriptions advanced by courts.

Canadian scholarship on these questions tends to be judicial-centric. Most of the research and commentary on the Charter, especially in its first couple of decades, emphasizes judicial decision-making, judicial power, and debates about judicial activism.[1] Yet a body of work examining the inter-institutional relationships and the roles of government and legislatures under the Charter has developed. In this chapter we examine the debates that have emerged on these roles and relationships in an effort to situate our study and frame its contributions.

One objective of this chapter is to explain why we eschew adopting a particular model or frame of analysis. The leading understanding of institutional interaction under the Charter is one of a "dialogue" between courts and legislatures. Yet the dialogue metaphor suffers from serious empirical and conceptual contestation. It is also, by its nature, simplistic and belies the complexity at stake in the institutional processes and broader policy environments surrounding particular judicial decisions. In our view, this renders it an unsatisfactory approach for understanding how legislatures and governments approach rights issues in the policy process. Similarly, other approaches, like a coordinate constitutionalist conception of the role legislatures play in assessing Charter obligations, may occasionally fit certain relatively rare cases of legislative responses to court decisions, but not others. Thus, while the work of scholars employing these terms is useful for thinking about specific interactions, these theories do not provide a complete or accurate empirical understanding of the legislative process under the Charter. Indeed, our analysis may inform the limitations of those approaches in practice.

We also briefly explore the nature of executive dominance of the legislative process in Canada. We emphasize that any understanding of Parliament's role in assessing legislative activity under the Charter must account not only for the government (specifically, the prime minister and cabinet), but also the role of the bureaucracy, and the nature of party discipline. Parliamentarians do not function primarily as legislators but as actors to scrutinize and hold the government to account. In Canada, Parliament is generally regarded as a weak actor in this regard, and we briefly describe how this manifests and why it becomes a key factor in explaining government attitudes towards balancing Charter scrutiny with the pursuit of legislative objectives.

The chapter concludes with a brief explanation of the particular relationships specific governments can have with the courts. Few studies have analysed or compared the behaviour of governments of different stripes as it relates to the Charter itself, and those that exist emerged only recently and in relation to a perception that the Conservative government under Stephen Harper had a distinctly fractious relationship with the courts. This book's analysis, incorporating case studies under both the Conservative government and the Liberal government under Justin Trudeau, will shed further light on the role and behaviour of specific governments within the broader institutional relationships at stake.

Dialogue, Coordinate Interpretation, and Studies of the Legislative Role

The most prevalent conception of the inter-institutional relationships under the Charter of Rights is the dialogue metaphor. This particular understanding of constitutional dialogue was coined by Peter Hogg and Allison Thornton in a landmark 1997 article.[2] Initially envisioned as a response to democratic objections to the power of judicial review, the authors assert that criticisms of the undemocratic nature of judicial review are diminished where a legislature can respond by ordinary means to judicial decisions invalidating a law. The two primary mechanisms of this purported dialogue are section 33's notwithstanding clause and section 1, the reasonable limits clause, under which legislatures are afforded the ability to advance justifications for policies that implicate rights. In a context where the legislature can advance new grounds for policies that did not initially survive judicial review, it is possible, Hogg and Thornton note, to enact similar legislation without having to rely on either section 33 or constitutional amendment. In their initial study, Hogg and Thornton assert that dialogue "consists of those cases in which a judicial decision striking down a law on Charter grounds is followed by some action by the competent legislative body."[3] They thus find that dialogue occurs following 66 per cent of cases where legislation was struck down by the Supreme Court.

The dialogue metaphor's subsequent popularity – indeed, it was for a time adopted by different members of the Supreme Court itself, only to be abandoned when the judges seemed to disagree over its prescriptive significance[4] – flew in the face of a major scholarly debate about its empirical veracity and conceptual utility. Political scientists especially criticize the notion that the majority of Supreme Court invalidations under the Charter result in dialogue. First, with the notwithstanding clause rarely used,[5] and having all but fallen into desuetude at the federal level, where it has never been employed,[6] avenues for dialogue are less frequent than the initial Hogg and Thornton study implies. Second, and more fundamentally, Christopher Manfredi and James Kelly point out that instances where legislatures simply repeal offending legislation – counted as dialogue in the 1997 study – or where entire acts are replaced in response to judicial rulings amount to "Charter ventriloquism."[7] Hogg and Thornton themselves describe dialogue as instances of a judicial invalidation being "reversed, modified, or avoided by a new law," something their subsequent count did not appear to take seriously.[8] On this basis, Manfredi and Kelly find that instances of genuine dialogue constitute approximately half the proportion asserted by Hogg and Thornton, coming in closer to one-third of cases than two-thirds.

Emmett Macfarlane, in perhaps the most comprehensive study of legislative responses measuring dialogue, examines the substance of all legislative enactments following judicial invalidations under the Charter through 2009, and finds that the instances where legislatures simply enacted the policy prescriptions of the Court were even more frequent than previously thought. By his count, only 17 per cent of legislative invalidations were met with a genuine dialogic response.[9] Macfarlane also finds that the courts are unlikely to accept genuinely dialogic legislative responses when they are inevitably subject to judicial review or "second-look cases" (in contrast to earlier findings by Rosalind Dixon that judicial deference in second-look cases is significant[10]). This has important implications for the policy areas analysed in this book, particularly in the areas of medical assistance in dying and sex work, where response legislation has already been scrutinized and found wanting by courts at the trial level.

The basis for these differing empirical measures of dialogue is a fundamental disagreement between critics and proponents about the nature of the debate at stake. For dialogue to be meaningful, critics assert, the legislative response should evince independent judgment or disagreement with the Court's interpretation of rights.[11] By contrast, proponents of dialogue view the implication that legislatures can assert an independent *interpretation* of Charter rights as controversial, if not completely inappropriate. Kent Roach complains that both the Manfredi and Kelly study and the Macfarlane one do not count "agreement" as genuine dialogue.[12] As Matthew Hennigar points out, empirically speaking, "genuine agreement and grudging compliance 'look' identical."[13] Yet Hennigar and the other political scientists correctly conclude that "the appropriate course of action for researchers is to count as evidence of dialogue only those legislative responses which overtly signal government [or legislature] participation in a meaningful discourse."[14] This is the only way to determine the validity of Hogg and Thornton's original assertion that courts do not always have the final say on policies implicated by the Charter. Indeed, it becomes meaningless to assert that legislatures can respond to judicial rulings on the Charter, especially in the sense of "reversing, modifying, or avoiding" the effects of judicial review, if legislatures dutifully complying with judicial policy prescriptions are counted as dialogue.

In their efforts to empirically test Hogg and Thornton's claims, political scientists (as well as legal scholars[15]) have thus attempted to analyse the concept on the originators' own terms. The primary question from the perspective of analysing judicial influence on legislative decisions examines the judicial policy veto. Put simply, if judicial policy prescriptions generally win the day, then dialogue does not offer the renewed understanding of judicial review that Hogg and Thornton claim it does. Yet Roach is not wrong to complain that "simplistic binary categories of compliance or rejection are not well-suited to understanding the complex relationship between courts and legislatures."[16] He is also right to point out that judicial review sometimes results in governments and legislatures making policy changes not explicitly contemplated by the courts.[17] It is clear that a judicial decision can have knock-on effects that make governments reconsider a broader policy, but a particular policy – and sometimes a particular policy *objective*[18] – is often vetoed outright by the court and there is no meaningful response but legislative acquiescence. Thus dialogue is not a useful lens of analysis for either the simple question Roach dismisses *or* the more complex account of the policy impact of judicial decisions that he and many scholars – ourselves included – are interested in pursuing. For that reason, we generally eschew the dialogue metaphor in our own analysis in this book except to occasionally relay how relevant actors or commentators have invoked it in relation to specific cases.

Beyond this empirical disagreement, the broader *conceptual* utility of the dialogue metaphor is also subject to intense debate.[19] Many seem to adopt the concept as if it contains communicative significance. Yet this is rejected by dialogue's proponents, who argue that critics attack an "idealized" conception of dialogue, which should not be regarded as including "the ridiculous suggestion that courts and legislatures were actually 'talking' to each other."[20] As Robert Leckey describes, the metaphor has become imbued with normative, rather than just descriptive, significance, such that it is possible the concept itself "serves as an unacknowledged proxy for different preferences amongst the scopes of judicial activity and, especially, the judicial postures."[21] This may be true, although we reject Aileen Kavanagh's description of those who might oppose judicial finality in the dialogue context as "Charter haters."[22] The conclusion of Carissima Mathen that "the dialogue metaphor may obscure more than it enlightens" is thus another reason to avoid using it as a lens of analysis,[23] and we are not alone in abandoning it in this regard.[24]

An alternative vision of the institutional relationships surrounding the Charter, and one that is implicated by the debate over the dialogue metaphor, is coordinate constitutional interpretation. One issue implicated by the dialogue debate was judicial supremacy over interpretation. In short, proponents of the dialogue metaphor object to legislative assertions premised on alternative interpretative judgments about what the Charter requires. Thus, where critics see rare instances of genuine dialogue occurring when legislatures push back against judicial interpretation, proponents see a "dangerous" and unacceptable practice.[25]

Yet if dialogue does not actually mean the different institutions are engaged in a meaningful interaction about the Charter's requirements, then perhaps a coordinate understanding – each institution approaching policies with its respective understanding of the Charter in mind – is the more appropriate vision for the relationship. As Dennis Baker explains, "Coordinate interpretation means that each branch of government – executive, legislative, and judicial – is entitled and obligated to exercise what the constitution entails."[26] Importantly, this does not translate into legislative finality of interpretation any more than it means judicial finality. Instead, it assumes "an unfolding process of constitutional interpretation (in stark contrast to the unilateral 'lightning strike' of interpretative authority claimed by judicial supremacists). For the coordinate theorist, it is only through repeated inter-institutional exchanges that enduring constitutional principles emerge."[27] Baker's case is as much a normative project as a descriptive account, although his work brings to light a small set of cases that come close to matching what we might expect from the theory.[28]

This brief description of coordinate interpretation is necessary to shed further light on our animating approach to this study. As with dialogue, we do not propose to adopt a strictly coordinate understanding of institutional roles as the lens of analysis. Nonetheless, the concept may be useful for understanding how a government or a legislature conceives of its role in the context of a given case or policy objective. For example, the Liberal government appeared to invoke coordinate interpretative authority in defending its legislation governing the medical assistance in dying regime, as described in chapter 6. Understanding how the government and Parliament understand their respective roles under the Charter is central to this book's objectives.

Scholars have attempted to bring dialogue theory and coordinate interpretation together, reformulating certain categories of dialogue as either "court-centric" or "coordinate."[29] Similar to the distinction others make in terms of "compliance" versus "genuine dialogue" noted above, court-centric dialogue is thought to occur when legislative responses are consistent with judicial interpretations of the Charter as evident in the court decision, while coordinate responses occur when legislatures "test judicial commitment by acting on their contrary constitutional understandings."[30] Two of the most frequently cited examples of coordinate responses involve legislation enacted following rulings involving common law (judge-made) rules, both in the context of sexual assault cases.[31] In a case involving rules surrounding the disclosure of private records in sexual assault proceedings, the Supreme Court upheld Parliament's legislation despite the fact that it differed significantly from the common law regime the Court itself articulated.[32] In another context, Parliament enacted legislation to prohibit the use of the extreme intoxication defence in response to a common law decision by the Court to uphold it. Although the provision remained in place for well over two decades,[33] it was recently declared unconstitutional by the Supreme Court.[34]

In the context of statutory invalidations on Charter grounds, coordinate legislative responses are exceedingly rare. We are aware of only a single case in which a coordinate legislative response has been upheld by the Supreme Court in a subsequent round of judicial review. In that case, Parliament legislated a response to a previous Court decision that invalided the "public interest" criterion for denying bail.[35] The majority of justices in the initial case asserted that bail could be denied for only two reasons: ensuring an accused be present for trial and to prevent an accused from committing another serious offence (i.e., a public safety standard). Parliament's legislative response included a clause allowing bail to be denied to maintain the confidence of the administration of justice. As others note, "This new 'confidence' provision is arguably just as vague (or 'standardless') as the public interest wording it replaced. It was certainly intended to extend beyond [the majority's] two bail-denying circumstances, which were explicitly covered by other clauses in Parliament's legislative sequel."[36] Yet the Court upheld the new legislation, albeit with a stinging dissent that accused the majority of having "transformed dialogue into abdication."[37]

These rare occasions of coordinate responses are useful initiatives because they allow or encourage courts to reconsider past decisions and revisit their reasoning. In that sense, they might be truly dialogic in that they allow for productive exchanges between the institutions over constitutional meaning. They also demonstrate, according to some scholars, that dialogue proponents are wrong when they assert that coordinate interpretative authority "cannot exist" in Canada.[38] Yet as already noted, dialogue proponents question the legitimacy of these rare legislative pushbacks or "in-your-face" replies, asserting that if legislatures want to assert interpretative supremacy they should rely on the notwithstanding clause to do so.[39] Even Kelly and Hennigar, who in other contexts criticize the dialogue metaphor, refer to coordinate legislative responses as "notwithstanding-by-stealth."[40]

Our interest is less in the normative debate over the legitimacy of such replies as about the justifications made by governments and legislatures for their legislative decisions generally. As an empirical matter, we simply note that explicit defiance of court decisions, or attempts to effectively reverse them, are rare.

Another set of cases exist in the middle ground between coordinate legislative responses and simple compliance with judicial decisions, and those are legislative replies that may depart from specific aspects of the courts' policy prescriptions but not necessarily fly in the face of their reasoning. One such legislative sequel occurred in the context of prisoner voting rights. In 1993 the Court struck down a provision of the Canada Elections Act disqualifying prisoners from voting. It did so with only minimal reasons delivered orally but noted that the provision was "drawn too broadly and fails to meet the proportionality test" of section

1.[41] That single line of explanation might imply that a more narrowly tailored limit could meet constitutional muster, but Parliament was left with little guidance on what, if any, limits might be imposed and how they might be tailored under the Charter. The Court would revisit the issue in 2002, after the provision had been amended to limit voting restrictions to prisoners serving sentences of two years or more. In that decision, a divided Court found the provision unconstitutional, this time making it quite clear that any limit would fail to meet section 1's requirements, asserting that the restriction on voting was "not rationally connected to the goal of imposing legitimate punishment."[42] Commentators have pointed to this sequence of interaction between Parliament and the Court as further evidence of the vacuity of the dialogue concept, especially in light of the fact that the notwithstanding clause is unavailable in the context of legislation implicating voting rights.[43]

Many, if not all, of the legislative sequels examined in this book fall into the middle category of cases that are neither reflective of straight compliance with judicial policy prescriptions nor explicit attempts to overturn court decisions (although they arguably push the latter boundary – at least part of Parliament's legislative response to the Court's ruling on laws governing prostitution might reasonably be characterized as an "in-your-face" reply). They demonstrate why neither dialogue nor coordinate interpretation is an ideal empirical lens through which to assess such institutional interactions, even as those concepts may sometimes be reasonably applied to specific contexts.

Yet another framework, one not too dissimilar to coordinate interpretation, has been advanced by Janet Hiebert. In *Charter Conflicts*, Hiebert articulates a "relational approach" to describe the institutional relationships and mutual responsibilities for protecting Charter rights between courts and legislatures.[44] Eschewing the traditional focus on the judiciary, Hiebert examines Parliament's role and presents an analysis of the procedural and cultural changes effected under the Charter during the legislative process. As Hiebert noted at the time, however, her analysis was infused with a normative hope that Parliament could fulfil an independent role in a productive and good faith manner:

> Admittedly, this vision of shared responsibility for the reconciliation of legislative objectives and Charter values is very much an ideal rather than a general description of existing practices. Not all legislative responses can be described, by any stretch of the imagination, as thoughtful or principled attempts to reconcile Charter conflicts. Nevertheless, this ideal is worth pursuit. The normative goal is not that Parliament should aspire to ensure that legislation anticipates or replicates all judicial concerns, any

more than it is to encourage judicial deference towards Parliament's judgment without regard for how legislation affects rights. Rather, it is for each body to satisfy itself that its judgment respects Charter values, particularly when faced with the reasons for the other's contrary judgment.[45]

Writing two decades ago, Hiebert finds a mixed record in Parliament's ability to play an independent role. She criticizes a sometimes risk-averse approach epitomizing a judicial-centric attitude to reconciling policy objectives with Charter rights, expressing an optimistic view of Parliament's capacity to legislate while engaging in principled deliberation over rights issues. For an example of the latter, she points to Parliament's responses to judicial rulings in sexual assault trials, briefly described above.[46]

Kelly similarly eschews a judicial-centric analysis in his book, *Governing with the Charter*.[47] Kelly analyses cabinet's role in deciding how to respond to judicial rulings under the Charter and views it as reflecting a coordinate constitutional approach. Yet he notes that the prime minister's power contributes to the marginalization of Parliament, which he identifies as the "most pressing institutional limitation associated with the political response to the Charter."[48] Kelly also argues that the Department of Justice activity at the federal level, scrutinizing legislation for compatibility with the Charter – sometimes referred to more cynically as "Charter proofing" – "has greatly contributed to the improved quality of legislation in Canada."[49] Subsequent events, explored in the next chapter, call the quality of this bureaucratic Charter-vetting into question.

In recent work, Hiebert is more sceptical about the bureaucratic and parliamentary rights culture.[50] While noting that government lawyers are embedded in the policy process by assessing whether legislative initiatives are consistent with judicial norms, the risk of judicial censure has not weakened government resolve to assert policy objectives. Hiebert describes "Westminster factors" as the key drivers of legislative behaviour, which include the principle of parliamentary supremacy, executive dominance of the legislative process, and the centrality of strong, cohesive political parties.[51] The analysis coincides with a major study by Hiebert and Kelly of the experience of New Zealand and the United Kingdom with parliamentary bills of rights, where the authors find that neither experience has "functioned in a manner that substantially increases parliaments' willingness and capacity to hold governments to account for decisions that implicate rights adversely."[52] While the bills of rights in both countries resulted in procedural changes, enhancing bureaucratic attention to rights-compatibility and, in the United Kingdom, has spurred important scrutiny by the Joint Committee on Human Rights, executive dominance as a feature in policymaking has diluted the rights culture that might otherwise have emerged.

Canada presents unique tensions for analysis. On the one hand, executive dominance and party discipline are even stronger in Canada than in other Westminster systems. On the other hand, unlike the other major Westminster countries, Canada has a system of effective strong form review, if not judicial supremacy, in the courts' power to invalidate legislation as unconstitutional. The analysis in this book will shed further light on this context, and we now turn to the nature of executive dominance.

The Weak Legislature: A Brief Account of Executive Dominance

Executive dominance in the Canadian political system is a well-studied phenomenon. The centralization of power in the hands of the prime minister has been framed by the media as constituting a "friendly dictatorship."[53] The leading academic text advancing the centralization thesis is Donald Savoie's *Governing from the Centre*, which details the historical evolution of the Prime Minister's Office (PMO), the Privy Council Office (PCO) and other central agencies, and cabinet.[54] It argues that the role of prime minister, through growth in the PMO and the orienting of senior public servants across central agencies towards it, has strengthened an already impressive power base relative to Parliament and even cabinet itself. Parliament is presented as an institution that regularly fails to hold the government and the prime minister to account, especially in the majority government context. Cabinet is described as a mere "focus group" for the prime minister, who by virtue of the power of appointment and agenda-setting authority can roll roughshod over colleagues at a whim.

Legislating is a centralized enterprise too. Government bills presented to Parliament can often be regarded as a fait accompli, at least in a majority context. The drafting process is executive dominated, with parliamentary scrutiny in relation to a government that enjoys dominance over the House and its committees making major amendments relatively rare.[55] While a prime minister cannot be said to micromanage the entire legislative agenda, all bills of any import will have received serious scrutiny by the PMO. The content of significant legislation is unlikely to depart from the leader's preferences.

How does the prime minister's control manifest? A key source of power stems from a broad array of appointment authority, including to institutions that might otherwise be thought to serve as important checks on centralization, like the Senate. Through most of the modern period, the Senate has been largely regarded as an ineffective or weak and undemocratic institution, particularly when the party in government enjoys a majority in the upper house. This story, however, became much more complicated after 2016, when the Liberal government enacted a new "non-partisan, merit-based" appointments process that effectively eliminated traditional patronage appointments. As Macfarlane details in his recent book, *Constitutional Pariah*, this reform saw the Senate become increasingly activist in proposing amendments to government legislation.[56] Until this recent experiment, the Senate was perceived by some as a rubber stamp, with occasional – and controversial – stalemates with the lower chamber serving as a rare exception.

The prime minister's power to appoint cabinet members is traditionally viewed as creating the twin privileges of ensuring that the leader is more than "first among equals" at the cabinet table itself, and keeping the backbenchers – many of whom might hope to join the ranks of ministers one day – in line. Further, as party leader, the prime minister also enjoys the power over candidate selection. While many candidates are selected through an open riding-level selection process, the prime minister has the power to veto candidates or parachute hand-picked star candidates into specific ridings. One study by Royce Koop and Amanda Bittner finds that the prime minister's hand-picked candidates go on to serve in high-profile legislative positions compared to their locally nominated colleagues.[57]

Intense party discipline in the Canadian system, then, is a key driver of centralized power and contributes to the relative weakness of Parliament itself. This same phenomenon extends increasingly to the provincial legislatures.[58] Nonetheless, a number of scholars have pushed back on, or nuanced, the centralization thesis. Herman Bakvis argues that the prime minister as autocrat model is overblown.[59] Bakvis notes several modern examples of powerful cabinet ministers, as well as evidence that even when certain cabinet decisions seem pro forma, much has been worked out between the prime minister and ministers behind the scenes. While acknowledging Canada may be an outlier in many respects, particularly in a lack of significant checks on prime ministerial power, Bakvis's analysis raises important nuances. Similarly, J.P. Lewis's survey of cabinet ministers suggests that while cabinet members recognize the prime minister's powerful position – and are even empathetic and supportive of it – they also report that the actual operation of cabinet often reflects a healthy degree of ministerial autonomy and institutionalized collegiality.[60]

The idea that backbench and opposition MPs are completely without power has also been subject to careful scrutiny. In his study of the House of Commons, David E. Smith briefly describes a long-term trend in the modern period "towards greater influence by MPs over legislation and the order of Commons business."[61] His examples include the selection of the speaker by secret ballot, abolition of appeals to the speaker's rulings, committee selection of chairs, and the creation of the Standing Committee on Government Operations and Estimates, which has extensive oversight powers and is chaired by a member of the opposition. Smith concludes that "while far from total, members have greater control over their activities and more opportunity to influence legislation than at any time in the past century."[62] The committee work of Parliament, especially during minority governments, can compel important changes to bills. Yet, as Jean-François Godbout notes, these changes have occurred only after a longer-term trend of rule changes giving the government increasing control over the legislative agenda.[63]

Smith is less optimistic about the status of the opposition and its power generally. In a more recent study,[64] he notes developments that have weakened the relative status of the opposition as a force for holding the government to account, including the rise of independent actors like officers of Parliament, the diffusion of political views and activism through the internet (which makes it more difficult for the opposition to hold the spotlight as the government's primary antagonist), and the high turnover and change in the status of parties' respective positions that have arguably diluted the institutional memory that enables effective opposition.[65] Even these conclusions are subject to complex nuances. One study of the role of the conflict of interest and ethics commissioner, for example, finds scant evidence that this particular officer of Parliament does anything but supplement, rather than supplant, the role of the opposition.[66]

It is likely that the prime minister's own caucus often has more influence over legislation than the opposition. Key aspects of intra-caucus disagreement remain un(der)studied, at least in part because caucus secrecy reigns supreme. Despite their contributions to committee scrutiny, much of the impact of individual MPs on government legislation in highly salient bills occurs behind the scenes. Ian Brodie, who sat in on some caucus meetings when serving as chief of staff to Prime Minister Stephen Harper, describes caucus discussions as "serious, vibrant, and frank."[67] Caucus meetings are the key venue for backbenchers to have their say, and in Brodie's experience cabinet members tended to listen, not speak. There is a clear irony in the "unfortunate paradox of modern democracy that our elected representatives have to be off the record" to demonstrate most compellingly their principle and willingness to prioritize the views of their constituents.[68] Still, even after having had direct access to caucus meetings, Brodie acknowledges that "it is sometimes difficult to identify policy files where government backbenchers had influence."[69] He writes,

> There is little ammunition to rebut claims that government backbenchers are "trained seals" with no power. But a moment of reflection shows the implausibility of the idea that government backbenchers simply knuckle under to dictates from the prime minister and the executive branch. First, government backbenchers are in close physical proximity to Cabinet ministers and the prime minister when the House is in session. An ambitious MP could not possibly be that close to ministers and the prime minister without voicing views on public policy issues. Caucus members do not need to wait for formal caucus meetings to have influence.[70]

Brodie recounts how pressure from backbenchers got the Harper government to drop a bill that would give law enforcement and other agencies the ability to get information about online accounts from telecommunication companies and internet service providers without a judicial warrant.

Exit interviews with MPs conducted by the Samara Centre for Democracy tend to reflect great dissatisfaction with the extent of party discipline, but confirm Brodie's supposition that caucus meetings could be empowering, including the ability to change the leadership's direction on policy.[71] Yet even this was sometimes regarded as exceptional, with some MPs suggesting caucus meetings were more frequently used for the leader to provide briefings rather than submit to full deliberation or criticism from the caucus. Nonetheless, on highly salient bills – legislation that is likely to attract media attention or involve moral questions that animate individual MPs – there is reason to believe a leader who ignores caucus dissent is asking for trouble.

Government bills that plainly appear as compromise legislation or attempt to balance competing interests and concerns, particularly in majority governments, are likely influenced by intra-caucus discussions. One external indicator appears when party leadership allows free votes on bills, as increasingly seen in the context of morally controversial issues. The executive dominance of the legislative process, however, means that much of the compromise occurs before the formal introduction of the bill. As our analysis in chapter 6 suggests, caucus divisions within the governing Liberals likely contributed to legislation on medical assistance in dying that balanced Charter concerns with protections for vulnerable persons.

As Kelly Blidook writes, "MPs have, for the most part, acted principally as delegates of parties, with a national focus and a trustee style with regard to public preferences. MPs are seen as having relatively few opportunities to act as individuals."[72] Yet as Blidook notes, even as the academic literature focuses on the limited role for MPs in actual legislating, there is little attention to their broader roles as representatives and policy actors.[73] Blidook's study of private members' business (PMB) offers important relief to this broader context, even as it reinforces the idea that there are relatively few opportunities to observe individual MP behaviour and local effects. More recently, however, there is some evidence that even in PMB the government can exercise its influence over the legislative agenda. Kelly and Kate Puddister find that a significant amount of private members' legislation was enacted under the Harper government, including in criminal justice policy (the focus of chapter 3), which might have serious implications for rights because such bills do not receive legal scrutiny by the Department of Justice.[74]

The scholarly literature on intra-caucus disagreement over legislation tends to focus on analysing free votes. A landmark study by David Docherty notes that even in issues that involve free votes, where there should be a real possibility of loosening party discipline and what count as confidence issues – including gun control and gay and lesbian rights in the thirty-fifth Parliament – MPs reportedly recognize the importance of strong central leadership.[75] This is reinforced by studies on party discipline, which note that free votes remain rare.[76] One study of House votes on the Free Trade Agreement suggests legislators may benefit from strict party discipline because it allows them to depart from the wishes of their constituents without having to suffer direct blame for their individual votes.[77] Another study on free votes on abortion policy suggests that such voting "is never entirely removed from the pressures of party and, moreover, that votes are more likely to be 'free' if bills involving controversial subjects like abortion are sponsored by private members, not by the government."[78] However, a study on votes relating to the Civil Marriage Act, bringing in gay marriage, suggests a greater willingness among MPs to vote against party lines, particularly among Liberals, who were deeply divided on the issue.[79] A key takeaway of this study was that MPs who were more secure in their riding, and thus less dependent on their party, were more likely to vote freely.

The principles of party discipline and loyalty are traditionally maintained except in cases of strong moral or religious disagreement with a party's position, and while historically limited to issues of capital punishment and abortion,[80] more recently a movement to loosen these restrictions has prevailed, such that party leaders have declared votes on a broader array of social and moral issues to be free votes. Nonetheless, the evidence on party voting in practice is that the Canadian Parliament remains far from endorsing the view espoused by reformers like the McGrath committee, which suggested narrowing the definition of confidence solely to those of budget bills and other major pieces of legislation. MPs are expected to tow the party line on any legislative initiatives that reflect party campaign or platform promises, implicating a number of the policies examined in this book even while bills on other issues were conducted as free votes. Moreover, we see how governments can use the confidence convention to push legislation through, even in the minority context, such as when they declare that a bill will be treated as a confidence matter (as the Conservatives did on criminal justice legislation, explored in chapter 3). Tight control of the legislative agenda and messaging around it are explored at length in Alex Marland's recent book, *Whipped*, and underscore the extent to which party leadership exert substantial control over individual representatives.[81]

If the strength of the checks within Parliament are relatively weak overall, Savoie's landmark study – and many subsequent analyses – have given insufficient attention to perhaps the two most significant constraints on government decision-making: the Charter of Rights and Freedoms and the Supreme Court. The Charter does not appear in the index to *Governing from the Centre*, and the Supreme Court is referenced only once. Follow-up studies provide very brief reference to these institutions.[82] We agree with Vanessa MacDonnell that in studies of the Charter, far too much attention has been devoted to courts and legislatures and far too little to the role of the executive.[83] In a more recent work, Savoie notes that the rise of judicial power means that courts "can tell Parliament or provincial legislative assemblies to act and then specify how long they have to act."[84] A key goal of this book is to shed more light on the influence of judicial norms and the Charter itself within the government's and Parliament's legislative process. Key to understanding this is the work and influence of the executive in the legislative process.

The Executive–Judicial Relationship

Studies of inter-institutional relationships under the Charter have focused largely on the relationship between courts and legislatures.

Increasing attention has finally been directed towards the relationship between the courts and the executive. One natural area of scrutiny has been government approaches to litigation. Political scientists have scrutinized the specific arguments governments make in court via factums to investigate issues that include, for example, court receptiveness to provincial government arguments urging the recognition of federalism and provincial diversity in the face of national standards under the Charter.[85] Hennigar has examined decisions by the government to concede Charter violations, decisions to appeal lower court losses to the Supreme Court, and litigation strategies in specific cases.[86]

Two books, by Kate Puddister and Carissima Mathen, have recently examined executive decisions to pose reference questions to the Supreme Court or provincial courts of appeal.[87] The reference power is somewhat unusual in that it effectively allows the executive to pose hypothetical legal questions to courts, providing an opportunity not allowed in certain other jurisdictions, like the United States or Australia, in part as the result of separation of powers concerns. As Mathen writes, the reference power arguably privileges the executive at the legislature's expense, cutting it out of constitutional deliberations.[88] Strategic use of the reference power is also significant, although the true motivations for its use are often hidden from public (or academic) scrutiny. Puddister finds governments will use references to deal with hot potato issues, allowing them to engage in blame-shifting, to force negotiations between governments, or to simply seek assurance about the constitutionality of particular policies.[89] Mathen notes that the effect of political use of the reference power can result in "'democratic debilitation' – encouraging the legislature to withdraw from constitutional deliberation in favour of pronouncements."[90] While references have generated some of the most significant constitutional opinions by the Supreme Court, and they are one tool in the executive legislative toolkit, they are used relatively sparingly (about two to five times per decade at the federal level, since 1960).[91] Although the opposition parties occasionally called on the government to employ the reference power in the context of some of the bills in our study, the government consistently declined to do so.

Surprisingly rare among academic studies of the institutional relationships under the Charter are government-specific analyses, or studies that compare across governments of different stripes – a lacuna this book begins to fill. Only recently have analyses focused on the attitude of specific governments towards the Charter, and have tended to focus on the Harper government and its relationship with the Charter or the courts. This may reflect the extent to which the Harper government was perceived as distinctly antagonistic towards the judiciary relative to its predecessors. As Macfarlane writes with regard to conservative parties' (in reference to the federal Reform Party, the Canadian Alliance, and the Conservative Party) approach to the Charter itself, "As a result of the antipathy many of the parties' members occasionally express in regard to Charter enforcement – and specifically to the approach of the courts on a number of rights issues – respective leaders [Preston] Manning, Stockwell Day, and Harper each had to withstand attacks that they had a 'hidden agenda' to infringe rights."[92] As we discuss in chapter 3, the Harper government was also perceived as particularly ideological in its "law-and-order" policy agenda, which raised a number of rights implications. This is no mere topic of academic interest. There is evidence that public support of the Supreme Court is increasingly contingent on partisanship.[93] Given that the courts' authority rests on perceived legitimacy, understanding the relationship between the courts and specific governments carries important implications.

A few studies examining the Harper government's relationship with the courts present nuanced findings. Manfredi investigates a media narrative that the Harper period represented an "especially fractious relationship" with the Supreme Court, largely as a result of a handful of high-profile losses before the Court.[94] Manfredi notes that the majority of the government's losses involved policies passed by previous governments, leading him to conclude that the Conservatives' record before in Charter cases "did not differ significantly from that of the two other post-Charter governments."[95] Nonetheless, he also finds that the Conservative government adopted "a more consistently confrontational approach ... in its legislative responses compared to its predecessors," including in responses to invalidated legislation that originated with predecessor governments. In an examination of government arguments before the Court in Charter cases, Hennigar finds that the Conservative government also had a significant loss record in an area of utmost importance to it: criminal justice policy. Contra Manfredi, Hennigar concludes that this record indicates a Court "especially hostile" to the government's legislative agenda.[96]

In another study, Macfarlane compares the Conservative record before the Court with the record of the two other long-standing governments of the Charter period (the Progressive Conservatives under Brian Mulroney and the Liberals under Jean Chrétien). Applying the regime politics approach to the study of judicial behaviour, which regards the Court as largely preserving the policy agenda of the existing legislative majority, Macfarlane confirms Manfredi's broad finding on judicial invalidation of statutes: for all governments, a significant majority of defeats before the Court involved legislation passed by previous governments. However, Macfarlane adds important nuance to this finding. Deriving a proxy for issue salience, Macfarlane finds that the Harper government is the only government of the Charter period to have policies reflected in its campaign platforms invalidated or vetoed by the Court (no fewer than five major promises were implicated, compared to none for any other governments since the Charter was enacted).[97] The Conservative government is also the only government in Canadian history to effectively lose all reference cases it submitted to the Court.

These analyses of government records before the Court tell us only part of the story. The contribution of this book is to assess government approaches to legislating in a set of policy areas with obvious rights implications. Some of the policy issues assessed are advanced in the context of a government's preferred policy agenda. For example, our analysis in chapter 3 of key bills presented by the Conservative government on criminal justice policy provides insight to the approach the executive takes to legislative development in an area it considered to be highly salient. Other contexts involve responses to judicial invalidations of long-standing policies under which the government is effectively compelled to generate a legislative response. The Conservative government's efforts to replicate, in a different form, indirect prohibition of prostitution in response to the invalidation of existing provisions are explored in chapter 5. In a couple of instances, these policy issues straddle multiple governments and provide an opportunity to assess approaches to legislation by two different governments. Our analysis of supervised consumption sites in chapter 4 shows significant differences in the Harper Conservatives' and Trudeau Liberals' approach to the statutory scheme for granting ministerial exemptions under the Controlled Drugs and Substances Act, and with respect to the degree of adherence to the letter and spirit of the Court's decision. Similarly, in chapter 6 we examine how each government responded to the apparent need to establish a medical assistance in dying regime after the Court invalidated a long-standing prohibition on assisted suicide.

Our analysis focuses on the justifications advanced by the government for policies that have potential rights implications, the extent of the influence of judicial norms on those policies and justifications, the nature of parliamentary debate between the government and the opposition parties, and whether there is a meaningful attempt by the government to advance an interpretation of the Charter's requirements that are independent of the interpretations advanced by the courts. Some of this analysis sheds light on the utility and effectiveness of Parliament in protecting constitutional rights. Yet because the legislative process is executive dominated, and because it is the governing party's legislative agenda that is either at stake or implicated by new judicial rulings, investigating whether there are differences between the two governments' attitudes towards legislating under the Charter is an important part of our contribution.

Moreover, to the extent that previous studies, including of the regime politics approach cited above, confirm that courts rarely interfere with the *current* governing regime's policy agenda, it is useful to consider the potential fate of legislative responses when governments do assert a degree of independence or push back against judicial reasoning. Our analysis of highly salient social policies suggests legislative sequels of questionable constitutionality do not fare well, either because of subsequent legislation by successor governments reverting to the judicial policy prescription or because the courts once again have their say and find the new laws unconstitutional. In this respect, the institutional interaction between executives, legislatures, and the courts is an ongoing and iterative process – although not particularly dialogic – best viewed over a period of time.

Conclusion

The inter-institutional relationships surrounding policymaking under the Charter are inherently complex. This book eschews a focus on simplistic characterizations of "dialogue" between courts and legislatures or a focus on merely where legislation complies with judicial decisions. There is often considerable uncertainty around the Charter's requirements and even around Charter jurisprudence, especially as it relates to the values-intensive and policy-laden requirements of assessing the reasonableness of limits on rights.

Our goal is to enhance our understanding of these institutional relationships by focusing explicitly on government justifications for legislation, parliamentary debates pertaining to the Charter implications of bills before the House, bureaucratic assessments of legislation for Charter compatibility, and an assessment of the degree to which any of these demonstrate an independent political judgment about the Charter. This analysis requires recognizing the executive's role in establishing the legislative agenda. In highly salient and controversial social policy issues, this also necessitates sensitivity to the context around which issues are debated, including the potential for intra-party disagreement, whether the specific legislation emanates from the governing party's campaign platform, whether it is subject to free votes in the House, and the nature of partisan division and contestation over specific issues in terms of how parliamentary debate manifests.

We thus hope to contribute not only to scholarship on the Charter and the institutional interactions surrounding it, but also to enhance our understanding of the policy process, Parliament's role in scrutinizing legislation, and the centralization of power in the executive in the face of what is likely the most significant constraint on prime ministerial power: the constitution and the courts.

2 Charter "Vetting": Analysing Bureaucratic and Executive Assessments of Rights Compatibility

Assessing whether, how, or why judicial review of a bill of rights influences legislative decision-making is a complex and difficult endeavour. This task requires analysing legislative processes and evaluating the political and institutional factors that influence legislative behaviour. More specifically, and in Canada, it is necessary to determine if bureaucratic and political actors assess whether legislative initiatives implicate rights, whether ministers and their political staff are receptive to advice about Charter compliance (particularly if acting on this would delay or alter the government's preferred legislative agenda), determining what weight is given to prospective and previous judicial rulings when interpreting compliance, and assessing whether parliamentarians have the inclination and power to exert pressure on government to redress potential inconsistencies, especially where rights-compliant efforts may not be the popular position to take.

In this chapter we examine whether the political and institutional factors that shape legislative decision-making in the Canadian Parliament are sympathetic with and receptive to emphasizing legislative compliance with the Charter and/or justifying actions that are susceptible to successful constitutional challenge. The chapter begins by examining the origins and expectations of a statutory requirement under section 4.1 of the Department of Justice Act that the minister of justice reports to Parliament when bills are inconsistent with protected rights, and analyses the criteria now used for evaluating whether this reporting obligation for inconsistency is engaged with respect to the Charter of Rights and Freedoms. We then look at the Trudeau government's

---

This chapter draws heavily from Janet Hiebert, "The Charter, Policy and Political Judgment," in *Policy Change, Courts, and the Canadian Constitution*, ed. Emmett Macfarlane (Toronto: University of Toronto Press, 2018), 81–102.

introduction of a requirement to issue Charter statements and assess whether this practice addresses shortcomings that we associate with how the government informs Parliament about potential Charter problems. More specifically, we ask whether these Charter statements improve Parliament's willingness and capacity to ensure that legislation is consistent with judicial Charter norms or, alternatively, that legislation is justified in light of possible tension with judicial rulings and, hence, vulnerable to judicial invalidation.

Our analysis leads us to the troubling conclusion that neither the current section 4.1 reporting obligation for Charter inconsistency nor the introduction of Charter statements provides a useful context for parliamentary debate about the justification of legislation that conflicts with protected rights, at least as interpreted by the Court. More than that, these two provisions undermine rather than facilitate useful parliamentary deliberation about the merits and justification of legislation in light of its Charter implications because they confuse rather than clarify the issue of whether legislation will be upheld as constitutionally valid in the event it is subject to a Charter challenge. As our analysis reveals, both exercises may in fact give Parliament unwarranted confidence that particular bills pass constitutional muster.

Reporting Requirement for Consistency with Rights

The Department of Justice Act requires the minister of justice to report to Parliament when government bills are inconsistent with the Charter. The initial idea behind this reporting obligation was both innovative and ambitious. As it turns out, it was also naive.

The reporting requirement for inconsistency with rights originated in the 1960 Canadian Bill of Rights – the first ever bill of rights introduced in a Westminster-based parliamentary system. The very idea that a Westminster-based political system such as Canada's would adopt a bill of rights, even one whose status was statutorily based rather than constitutionally situated (and applied only to the federal level of government) represented a radical departure from prior assumptions that a Westminster-based system is not compatible with (or requires) a bill of rights. A key pillar of the constitutional framework at the time was the principle of parliamentary supremacy, modified initially for Canada's colonial status and later by judicial interpretations of federalism. Conventional wisdom had assumed that a bill of rights conflicted with this principle because if courts were to rule that legislation is inconsistent with rights they would also require the power to declare remedies. However, a remedial power that altered the legal status of legislation would interfere with the idea that Parliament has the final say on the legality of legislation (which in Canada also required legislative competence from an imperial and federalism perspective).

The Canadian Bill of Rights is noteworthy in another way. What was also unique about this bill of rights was its clear intent to make Parliament a more important venue for engaging in judgments about rights. Then prime minister John Diefenbaker's views differed from conventional ideas about the role and function of a bill of rights. Rather than design a bill of rights that relied exclusively on judicial review to protect legislation from rights infringements that have already occurred, which is a how bill of rights is typically defended, Diefenbaker thought it possible and desirable to use a bill of rights to improve the working of Parliament so as to strengthen its role as a custodian of civil liberties.[1] To that end, the Bill of Rights contained a reporting obligation requiring the minister of justice to alert Parliament when the government was introducing legislation or enacting regulations that conflict with protected rights.[2]

As initially conceived, this statutory reporting obligation in section 3 of the Canadian Bill of Rights was an experimental form of constitutional design. The idea was that by marrying a bill of rights with a statutory reporting obligation for inconsistency, this new form of rights instrument would interact in a way that would encourage bureaucrats, government ministers, and parliamentarians to examine proposed legislation from a different perspective. More specifically, the hope was that those proposing, promoting, or scrutinizing legislation would confront whether and how legislative bills implicate rights adversely, as a crucial element of reasoned judgment about the merits of legislation.[3]

However, this reporting obligation exerted little impact on bureaucratic, government, or parliamentary behaviour. Part of the problem was how judicial power was conceived, which led to judicial ambivalence about challenging Parliament, which in turn functioned as a disincentive for political change. The Canadian Bill of Rights referred to judicial remedial power in a vague and confusing manner. Section 2 provides that unless the Bill of Rights is explicitly set aside, every federal law shall "be so construed and applied as not to abrogate, abridge or infringe" the rights and freedoms set out in it. However, the Bill of Rights' silence on the issue of how courts should proceed if it is not possible to interpret or "construe" legislation in a manner consistent with rights, combined with the legacy of the principle of parliamentary supremacy in shaping judicial behaviour, led to a strong reluctance by the Supreme Court to take the Bill of Rights seriously as a new instrument for robust judicial enforcement.

The Supreme Court's decision not to interpret the Bill of Rights as imposing new norms for constraining uses of state power, but as recognition of the rights that already existed,[4] along with the validation of almost all federal legislation challenged, provided little incentive for policy and political officials to rigorously question the merits of legislative initiatives from a rights perspective. Interviews confirm that pre-legislative vetting did not introduce serious changes to how legislation was assessed or substantially increase pressure on departments to explain or justify decisions in terms of their potential implications for rights.[5] Only one report of inconsistency was ever made by the minister of justice under section 3 of the Bill of Rights Act. In 1975, the government introduced an amendment to the Feeds Act, which was returned from the Senate with a provision that presumed guilt. Upon its return to the House of Commons, the minister of justice reported that the Senate amendment was an infringement of the Bill of Rights and this section was deleted.[6]

Review of Legislation for Consistency with the Charter as Required in the Department of Justice Act

Despite the limited influence of the statutory reporting obligation under the Canadian Bill of Rights, in 1985 the Progressive Conservative government of Brian Mulroney extended the statutory reporting obligation to include the Charter, which is authorized in section 4.1 of the Department of Justice Act.[7] Section 4.1 provides as follows:

> 4.1 (1) Subject to subsection (2), the Minister shall, in accordance with such regulations as may be prescribed by the Governor in Council, examine every regulation transmitted to the Clerk of the Privy Council for registration pursuant to the *Statutory Instruments Act* and every Bill introduced in or presented to the House of Commons by a minister of the Crown, in order to ascertain whether any of the provisions thereof are inconsistent with the purposes and provisions of the *Canadian Charter of Rights and Freedoms* and the Minister shall report any such inconsistency to the House of Commons at the first convenient opportunity.

Little is known about the reasons for this decision, or the intentions or expectations of those who proposed and supported its applicability to the Charter. The most likely explanation is that then attorney general John Crosbie and others were troubled by the obvious inconsistency between having a statutory obligation to report when legislative bills are inconsistent with the Canadian Bill of Rights, and yet having no such requirement under the Charter.

At the time that this was being considered, it would have been difficult to anticipate the political and legal consequences of including this kind of reporting mechanism for the Charter. Specifically, what would the legal implications be if the minister of justice declares that government legislation is inconsistent with the Charter, particularly in light of a clear judicial remedial power that allows courts to declare offending legislation unconstitutional?

As jurisprudence evolved, it became increasingly apparent that making a report of inconsistency to Parliament could endanger any future attempt to defend legislation if subject to a Charter challenge. An obvious difference between making a report of inconsistency under the Charter, as distinct from the Bill of Rights, is that apprehension of having to make such a report is no longer directed primarily at the possibility of criticism in Parliament. The concern now also includes the actual survival of legislation that has been subject to a section 4.1 report of inconsistency if it is subsequently subject to a Charter challenge. It is unlikely that a court would be easily convinced by an attorney general's arguments to try to defend legislation as a reasonable limit under section 1 when the minister of justice (who also functions as attorney general) has already declared the legislation to be inconsistent with the Charter, and hence has engaged the section 4.1 reporting obligation.

As we began this project, we were curious about whether this difference in the scope of the Court's interpretive and remedial powers has influenced how legislative bills are evaluated as well as how it affects the legislative decisions made when Charter concerns arise. If a weak judicial approach led to minimal scrutiny of whether legislation was consistent with the Canadian Bill of Rights, would a more robust judicial approach when interpreting rights and stronger remedial powers have the opposite effect? Would Canadian legislative behaviour become more similar to what Alec Stone Sweet says occurs in Europe, where apprehension of judicial censure leads to legislative constraint?[8]

This does not seem to be the case. As we have already implied and will explain in more depth later, there is no obvious relationship between the strength of judicial remedies on the one hand, and risk-averse behaviour when passing legislation that has adverse Charter implications on the other.

Before discussing how the Charter influences the evaluation of bills prior to their introduction to Parliament, it is important to underscore the point we made earlier, that no report of Charter inconsistency has ever been made. Moreover, Department of Justice lawyers indicate that because there is such a strong presumption against reporting to

Parliament that a government bill is inconsistent with the Charter, they doubt a report of Charter inconsistency will ever be made.[9]

Processes and Criteria for Evaluating Charter (In)consistency

In the early years of governing under the Charter, department officials and ministers were said to be resistant to legal advice about possible inconsistencies between legislative initiatives and the Charter, and were also reluctant to act upon recommendations by Department of Justice lawyers about how to better insulate legislation from the possibility of a negative judicial ruling.[10] However, after a few early prominent Charter rulings that had serious policy implications, lawyers indicate there was greater reception by department officials to advice and suggestions about how to lower possible risks of judicial invalidation.[11]

An enhanced role for government lawyers in the policy process can be traced to a decision made in 1991, when Paul Tellier (then clerk of the Privy Council) alerted deputy ministers of the importance of Charter scrutiny in the early stages of legislative development.[12] Acting on the request of the Department of Justice, Tellier outlined steps to ensure Charter issues were identified and evaluated as a condition for new policy proposals to be considered by cabinet. This analysis was to include an assessment of the risk of successful challenge, the impact of an adverse judicial ruling, and anticipated litigation costs.[13] As James Kelly argues, the coordination of Charter review at the departmental level not only helped sensitize "policy exercises to the values and purposes contained in the Charter," but this Charter advice would also function as a potential constraint on the cabinet's ability to achieve its agenda.[14] This suggests that the centrality of Charter vetting in the policy process, along with the government's domination of the legislative process (a trait associated with the modern evolution of the Westminster model Canada has inherited) combine to ensure that the federal government is well positioned to exercise the kind of self-constraint Stone Sweet associates with European behaviour.

The Supreme Court's approach to the Charter influences how government lawyers evaluate proposed legislation for Charter consistency. The Court generally avoids imposing definitional limits when determining if an activity is constitutionally protected, and instead interprets rights broadly, subject to separate analytical consideration of whether legislation that restricts a right is justifiable. This increases the possibility that legislation will be found to implicate rights while also focusing considerable emphasis on whether the quality of the legislative scheme that restricts rights is nevertheless deemed to be a reasonable and justifiable infringement. As we discuss below, government lawyers' analysis of Charter problems reflects a risk-based approach to Charter consistency where risk is based on both the likelihood and consequences of legislation being declared unconstitutional. These assessments emphasize both the policy justification of legislation and also whether it is consistent with proportionality criteria along the lines developed by the Court.[15]

It is important to acknowledge the inevitable difficulties associated with attempts to ensure that legislation is consistent with the Court's interpretation of section 1. The development of legislation is fraught with imprecision and uncertainty, particularly in identifying and evaluating reasonable and proportional ways of pursuing a complex legislative objective in a rights-compliant manner.

Judgments about whether legislation will survive a section 1 analysis can lead to strong contestation for several reasons. First, the Charter context for evaluating the justification of legislative restrictions on rights is sufficiently broad and philosophical (the values of a free and democratic society) that reasonable people can disagree on whether the justification is reasonable. Indeed, the Supreme Court itself struggles with adhering to a consistent standard of reasonable limits analysis, and the attendant political values or ideological policy preferences at play are fraught.[16] Second, political parties have ideological differences that can result in contestation about core and relevant issues, including whether or why a bill of rights implicates the role of the state, the appropriate role of Parliament when interpreting constitutional requirements, or what responsibility government has to pursue perceived social problems or address substantive inequality in power or resources. Third, as Charter case law develops and changes to the composition of the Court occur, this increases the difficulty of predicting judicial outcomes based on earlier jurisprudence. Fourth, the task of imagining rational and minimally impairing ways of achieving legislative goals is extremely subjective because there are conflicting interpretations of scientific or other relevant information, differences about the relevance of experiences in other jurisdictions, speculative assessments and incomplete information about the benefits and shortcomings of alternative policy options, and differing judicial opinions about whether or how much deference is owed to Parliament. Thus it is misleading to characterize political judgment about what distinguishes consistent from inconsistent legislation as if this is analogous to a green/red light or on/off distinction. Consequently, we think it is preferable to frame the question of the significance of Charter vetting on government behaviour as the following: *To what extent do good faith efforts to comply with Charter norms drive how government leaders evaluate, pursue, and justify their legislative objectives?*

We rely on three different methods to evaluate the criteria used for Charter assessments of proposed legislation. These include interviews with then current and former government lawyers who have assessed and advised on the relationship between proposed legislation and its potential risks of constitutional challenge; analysis of committee hearings and the testimony of government lawyers when asked about Charter issues or questioned about compliance; and relevant department guidelines and descriptions of the process and criteria used for Charter assessments of proposed legislation, as made publicly available as a result of an unusual legal action.

What Justice Lawyers Have Said about the Processes and Criteria for Charter Vetting

In interviews we were told that government lawyers in the Department of Justice use case-driven, risk-based assessments of the likelihood that legislative initiatives will be successfully litigated, speculate about the policy and fiscal consequences should government lose, and suggest modifications to these initiatives to lower the risk of judicial invalidation.[17] We were also told that there is an extremely strong presumption against making a section 4.1 report of Charter inconsistency. Some suggest that if proposed legislation is close to or crosses the line, constituting an unacceptable level of risk, an intervention might be made from higher levels within the department to find ways to lower the level of risk to a more acceptable level.[18] If a department is determined to pursue an initiative that is considered extremely risky, in that it would likely fail the Supreme Court's interpretation of reasonable limits in section 1 of the Charter, the issue could move up the chain of command to the deputy minister and ultimately to the justice minister, who would have to judge whether the section 4.1 reporting obligation is engaged.[19]

Some of those interviewed suggest that the norm for determining if the section 4.1 reporting obligation is engaged is that the minister of justice is expected to make a section 4.1 report only if he or she believes there is no credible argument to justify the legislation in question, if subject to litigation. However, this reliance on a credible argument does not appear to be a substantial constraint. Reliance on a credible argument does not demand confidence that it will be a winning argument, only that it appear to be serious (or credible). Thus, the minister of justice might lack confidence that the government would win if the legislation were litigated, but he or she believes the arguments in favour of the legislation are credible, even in circumstances where a high level of risk is identified. One official characterizes the judgment on whether a section 4.1 report is necessary, even when high risk was identified, as based on "a straight-faced" test: the minister of justice and deputy minister must believe that legislation can be argued as justified under section 1 of the Charter.[20] What is telling in the comments of those interviewed was the distinction between an argument that can be made versus one that is likely to win.

Others interviewed point to the subjective nature of judgments about Charter inconsistency by emphasizing that decisions about whether to proceed with risky legislation, and whether this decision would be deemed to engage the section 4.1 reporting obligation, are highly dependent on the level of risk-tolerance the minister and government have when introducing legislation that is potentially vulnerable to a judicial ruling of unconstitutionality.[21] However, this reliance on risk raises several questions. How is risk defined? Is the interpretation of risk based only on an assessment of relevant jurisprudence and the implications for the stability of the legislative policy at issue of not being able to defend it in a Charter challenge? Or does risk reflect more political considerations? For example, is the risk interpreted as the impact of a section 4.1 report on undermining the government's ability to pursue its preferred legislative agenda, because of apprehension of pressure for amendments or concern about the ability to defend legislation if subject to a Charter challenge? Do risk-based strategies reflect strategic calculations of whether longer-term legal risks (the period it takes for the Supreme Court to deliver a judgment on the constitutionality of impugned legislation) are outweighed by shorter-term political benefits of passing the government's preferred agenda, and exploiting its accomplishments for political and electoral purposes? We will now elaborate on concerns about the dangers of political and partisan assessments of risk displacing good faith interpretations of the section 4.1 reporting obligation, and why these are amplified by the fact that the minister of justice also serves as attorney general.

New Insights into Section 4.1 Processes and Criteria

Although the role and influence that Charter assessments play for a government's legislative agenda are beyond public and parliamentary purview, an unusual legal action has provided greater clarity on the criteria used to determine if this section 4.1 statutory requirement is engaged. Edgar Schmidt initiated legal action in 2013 after serving for many years as a senior legislative draftsperson in the Department of Justice. The basis of his allegation was that the department was relying on an improper and unlawful interpretation of the statutory reporting obligation on Charter inconsistency.[22]

Schmidt had earlier expressed concerns within the department about what he considered to be an inappropriate standard for determining if the section 4.1 reporting obligation was engaged, and sought clarification and review to superiors as high up in the chain of responsibilities as the deputy minister. Not satisfied with the responses to his requests, he eventually sought assistance from the Public Sector Integrity Commission of Canada to obtain an interpretation of what would constitute an appropriate interpretation of this statutory reporting obligation. This request was denied in large part, in Schmidt's view, because of a misunderstanding of the question he was asking.[23] Contrary to how his request was interpreted at the time, Schmidt was not making an allegation that Department of Justice officials were subject to pressure to alter their advice in order to allow for a positive confirmation of Charter consistency. Rather, his argument was that the standard itself for interpreting if the section 4.1 reporting obligation was engaged was the problem.[24] He subsequently considered, but rejected, the idea of bringing this issue to Parliament. He decided his next and only option was to initiate legal action.[25] Schmidt filed his legal action on 14 December 2012. He was immediately suspended without pay for the purposes of an investigation into whether he had violated his duties as a public servant and was denied access to his office.[26]

The attorney general's immediate legal response was to try to have the case dismissed, characterizing the issue as a workplace dispute that lacked any public interest concern, and therefore was non-justiciable. Counsel for the attorney general also argued that the issue involved solicitor-client confidentiality and urged the court to strike out all the parts of the statement of claim that made factual assertions about the conduct of the department and what standard of examination department officials used.[27] Rather than rule the issue was non-justiciable, Mr. Justice Simon Noël instead directed the attorney general to provide four internal Department of Justice publications that Schmidt had relied upon in making his claim, after which he would assess their admissibility. The documents were to remain subject to a confidentiality order until the court decided the admissibility issue. Mr. Justice Noël expressed disapproval of the department's handling of Schmidt's allegations, stating, "It's unbelievable.... Your client has done everything it can to kill this thing. The court doesn't like that.... We see that in different countries and we don't like it.... Canada is still a democracy."[28] Counsel for the attorney general subsequently abandoned the motion to strike Schmidt's statement of claim or stay of action.[29] In so doing, the attorney general agreed to the public filing of the four relevant documents that were central to Schmidt's claim (albeit in a form that was heavily redacted).

Despite being heavily redacted, the information that is publicly accessible in the guidelines provides clear insights into both process issues relating to how legislative initiatives are evaluated under the Charter as well as the substantive criteria used when assessing Charter inconsistency for statutory reporting purposes under section 4.1. The subsequent factum of the attorney general in response to Schmidt's appeal of the ruling by the Federal Court (discussed below), elaborates more on the processes used.[30]

According to these guidelines, both the Legal Services Unit and the Human Rights sections in the Department of Justice work with other departments throughout the policy process as legislative initiatives are developed, approved, and transformed into draft legislation. Proposed legislation is subject to evaluations of the risk of a successful Charter challenge, the impact of an adverse judicial ruling, and anticipated litigation costs. When legislative proposals are included in a memorandum to cabinet, Charter considerations are included along with a range of other issues. Once a draft bill is in its final form it is subject to Charter "certification," where the drafter provides an opinion about whether the minister of justice's section 4.1 statutory obligation is engaged to report to Parliament if legislation is inconsistent with the Charter. After a draft bill has been tabled, it triggers the minister of justice's personal duty to determine if the section 4.1 reporting obligation is engaged – a decision that is said to be heavily influenced by the prior recommendation of the relevant legislative drafter.[31]

Two Different Streams for Charter Assessments

What became apparent in the Schmidt litigation is that Charter assessments occur in two separate streams. One functions as an advisory role for policy development and is to assist client departments and agencies when developing and refining legislative initiatives by identifying the risks associated with potential Charter litigation as well as the potential policy and financial impacts should the government lose. Assessments of Charter inconsistency range from very low to manifestly unconstitutional. If high risk is identified and the relevant department or minister does not follow legal advice, Department of Justice lawyers are advised that it may be necessary to take matters to a higher level, which may include the deputy minister. Yet Justice counsel are also instructed that in cases where high levels of risk have clearly been communicated to officials in a department or agency, they should accept that the final decision ultimately rests with that department or agency in all but exceptional cases.[32] Ministers are also informed when bills have adverse implications for rights, and the minister of justice is said to perform a critical advisory role in cabinet discussions where there are serious Charter concerns.[33]

A second form of Charter assessment is to advise whether the section 4.1 statutory reporting obligation for Charter inconsistency is engaged. This form of assessment is said to tolerate much higher levels of Charter risks when advising on whether legislation is consistent with the Charter than the above-mentioned assessment. Not only has no report of Charter inconsistency ever been made, but the consensus amongst those interviewed is that it is highly unlikely (some say completely implausible)[34] that there will ever be a section 4.1 report of Charter inconsistency.

Some of those interviewed offer pragmatic reasons for this overwhelming presumption against reporting that legislation is inconsistent with the Charter. They argue that not only would a section 4.1 report invite political and public criticism, it would endanger the government's chance of defending legislation if it is subject to a Charter challenge because it would be difficult for ministers of justice to argue subsequently in court that impugned legislation is a reasonable limit under section 1 if they have already declared it in Parliament to be inconsistent with the Charter. Thus some characterize this reporting obligation as a blunt instrument that is not well suited to the Charter, because of its authorization of strong judicial remedial powers.[35]

Questionable Standards and the Presumption against Reporting

One might interpret the absence of section 4.1 reports to Parliament, along with the presumption against making such a report, as an assurance that legislative bills introduced to Parliament have been subject to robust vetting, thus ensuring they are more than likely to be defended successfully if legislation is subject to a Charter challenge. In other words, by the time legislation has been introduced, the minister of justice is confident that all bills introduced to Parliament are consistent with judicial norms of the Charter, or at least that there is a stronger than not chance of successfully defending them in Charter litigation. Thus there is no reason to engage the section 4.1 reporting obligation.

Public and scholarly discourses refer to the notion of "Charter-proofing" legislation, which conveys an assumption that legislation generally has a clean bill of health from a constitutional perspective. Some political leaders have tried to foster this impression by arguing that if a bill is not subject to a section 4.1 report (again no bill has ever triggered such a report) it is safe to assume any Charter problems have been redressed. For example, as discussed in chapter 3, the Conservative government told Parliament explicitly that it should interpret the absence of a section 4.1 as an assurance that the minister of justice has concluded that legislation is constitutionally valid.

However, we are sceptical that this assumption is warranted. The cumulative weight of the following factors justifies a healthy dose of scepticism that federal legislative behaviour should be characterized as grounded in good faith attempts to ensure that legislation complies with Charter norms. These factors include acknowledgments in interviews that notwithstanding the nature of the legal advice given, the ultimate determination of whether or how to proceed with legislation depends upon a government's tolerance for risk when proceeding with legislation that may not survive a constitutional challenge; the acknowledgment that it is not safe to presume that the absence of a section 4.1 report means confidence that legislation will be successfully defended in Charter litigation; and the strong presumption against reporting under section 4.1 or invoking the notwithstanding clause, even in cases of government willingness to proceed with high-risk legislation. When we consider the weak standards for interpreting the statutory reporting obligation on Charter consistency, and the frequency in which the Supreme Court declares legislation an unreasonable and unconstitutional restriction on protected rights, despite the extensive resources employed for evaluating the nature and seriousness of potential Charter conflicts, we advise against the idea that the lack of a section 4.1 report means a government is confident about the constitutionality of any particular bill.

Risk Tolerance

Legal advice in the pre-legislative policy process is only advisory. Interviews confirm that the reliance of departments and ministers on and use of this information when developing legislation often depends on the level to which they are willing to engage in risky behaviour in approving legislation that could be subject to a successful Charter challenge.[36] Some of those interviewed also indicate that even when advised about less restrictive ways of accomplishing an objective, a department or minister might still approve of changes that embody high-risk means that are vulnerable to judicial nullification.[37]

Absence of a Section 4.1 Report Not Equated with Strong Judgment of Constitutionality

Interviews confirm that it is not appropriate to equate the absence of a section 4.1 Charter report of inconsistency with confidence that legislation is not vulnerable to a successful Charter challenge.[38] Officials were also asked if departments or ministers ever considered invoking the notwithstanding clause pre-emptively where there is little appetite to reduce the risk associated with particular high-risk measures. We were told the notwithstanding clause is not considered as a valid policy option, even when there is little willingness to abandon risky legislation.[39] Yet arguably the notwithstanding clause and the section 4.1 statutory reporting obligation share conceptual similarities in that both instruments embody a normative government obligation to announce when it intends to promote legislation that represents an interpretation of Charter principles that clearly contradicts relevant jurisprudence, and to explain the reasons for pursuing such actions. If a government is determined to proceed with a high-risk bill, where the minister of justice is fully aware that it is has a high level of risk of being nullified by the Supreme Court, it is difficult to imagine how a government that is committed to good faith efforts to abide by statutory principles and constitutional norms would systematically fail to consider not only whether the section 4.1 reporting obligation is engaged, but also whether the notwithstanding clause should be invoked. Yet neither instrument for acknowledging high-risk legislation appears to be seriously considered.

It is easy to understand the political resistance to either form of acknowledgment. Invoking section 4.1 or proposing use of section 33 would be extremely controversial and would press government to defend and convince Parliament and Canadians of the merits and justification of its judgment. This task would be made even more difficult by the Charter's popularity, public confidence in the Supreme Court's role interpreting it, and the tendency of many to equate political judgments that differ from the courts' as ignoring or "overriding" rights.

Although government leaders are reluctant to appear insensitive to the Charter (as interpreted by the Court), this reluctance does not seem to encourage risk avoidance in the Stone Sweet sense of minimizing conflicts with judicial norms. Instead, this reluctance is expressed in a more politically oriented form of risk avoidance: a refusal to acknowledge when government is aware that legislative bills contradict judicial norms and thus are vulnerable to judicial censure, and/or explaining why the government's contrary judgment is meritorious and justified. However, as this form of risk avoidance comes at the expense of a robust commitment to statutory and constitutional norms, we find it difficult to characterize it as a good faith form of Charter judgment.

Significance of the Credibility Standard

Although Schmidt was not successful in his legal actions at first instance or upon appeal, the reason for losing does not appear to be contestation about what standard is used for determining if the reporting obligation for Charter inconsistency is engaged. Instead, disagreement centres on what the appropriate standard should be.

Schmidt argued that the Department of Justice had "unlawfully transformed" the standards required for fulfilling the statutory obligation that the minister of justice report to Parliament when legislation or regulations are inconsistent with the Charter. His claim was that the section 4.1 reporting obligation permits two options. Either legislation is consistent with the Charter, and thus the reporting obligation is not engaged, or a bill is "more likely than not inconsistent" with Charter rights, in which a section 4.1 report is required.[40]

A core issue in Schmidt's legal challenge was his disagreement that interpreting whether the section 4.1 reporting obligation is engaged is based on the idea of a credible argument when defending impugned legislation. His concern was that the standard of a credible argument is extremely loose and envisages political or other considerations rather than an assessment that emphasizes the probability of winning or losing.[41] The Federal Court accepted the government's position that the section 4.1 reporting obligation is not engaged if a credible argument can be made to defend legislation, rather than Schmidt's argument that section 4.1 should be engaged when a bill is "more likely than not inconsistent" with the Charter.[42] The Federal Court of Appeal upheld this position, ruling that in light of the difficulty for the Department of Justice to conclude with certainty that proposed legislation complies with the Charter (as interpreted by the judiciary), section 4.1 need be invoked only when there is no argument to support the position that legislation complies with the Charter.[43]

In upholding the department's interpretation of the statutory reporting obligation, the Court also rejected the idea that the minister of justice bears such strong responsibility for ensuring that legislation is consistent with the Charter, as inferred from Schmidt's interpretation of credibility. One of the many arguments the court made was that Parliament itself must assume responsibility to ensure Charter rights are protected, and thus "must not place its duties on the shoulders of the other branches, notably on those of the Minister of Justice."[44] There appears to be no consideration of whether Parliament's capacity to assess legislation for Charter consistency is harmed by the weak reporting standard, something intrinsic to the purpose of the statutory requirement.

Notwithstanding the fact the court accepted the government's claims, the documents outlining guidelines for interpreting section 4.1 that the attorney general was compelled to provide appear to confirm Schmidt's allegations of the systematic use of low standards for determining Charter consistency. Indeed, these guidelines reveal that the standard used for determining if the section 4.1 reporting obligation is engaged all but guarantees no report of Charter inconsistency will be made. A report of Charter inconsistency is not deemed necessary if a bill is considered to be "not manifestly unconstitutional" and where a credible argument can be made to defend it. However, a bill is judged to be "not manifestly unconstitutional" even if it is identified as having an extremely high risk of being declared unconstitutional. The additional requirement that a credible argument can be made to support the bill is not particularly onerous, as "credible" is interpreted only as capable of being argued, as distinct from likely to be winnable. As the government argued in the Schmidt appeal, the mere fact that courts have not generally dismissed the government's previous arguments to defend legislation as frivolous justifies continued use of the credible argument standard, even though these arguments have not always succeeded and legislation has been declared invalid.[45] To characterize the standard used in quantitative terms, the reporting obligation is said to be engaged only at the far end of the highest category of risk (which is in the range of 81–100 per cent certainty of being declared unconstitutional).[46] Not surprising in light of these criteria, Department of Justice guidelines advise Justice lawyers that the statutory reporting obligation for Charter inconsistency "will only be triggered in rare cases."[47]

In defending this standard, the attorney general challenged Schmidt's characterization of the credible argument standard as being one of "faint-possibility of legality."[48] The attorney general's factum argues that this characterization is based on an incomplete reading of department guidelines on how to conduct the required assessments of Charter consistency.[49] In describing the process for whether the minister should be advised that the section 4.1 reporting obligation is engaged, the factum states that where an identified legal risk is significant these concerns are discussed and the "appropriate remedial steps" will be raised with the relevant department.[50] The formal review that is required for section 4.1 occurs at the end of policy development and legislative drafting. A memorandum is prepared for the chief legislative counsel, based on the bill as drafted. And at this stage, if inconsistency with the Charter is found, the memorandum would identify the inconsistencies.[51]

However, the attorney general's factum does not address what these "remedial steps" are, how often it is necessary to take them, what

differences they make in ensuring Charter consistency, or how often remedial advice is rejected. Although the factum rejects Schmidt's claim
that legal risk is calculated as a percentage, it does not explain why
the internal guidelines of the Department of Justice adopt categories or
bands of risks that are expressed explicitly in terms of percentages and,
more significantly, clearly state that the section 4.1 reporting obligation
is engaged only at the highest level of risk, which is in the 81–100 per
cent range of likelihood that the government would lose.[52]

In our view, Department of Justice guidelines for assessing Charter
consistency for section 4.1 statutory reporting raise doubts about the
extent to which the requirement constrains a government's legislative agenda. These guidelines for assessing Charter inconsistency bear
little resemblance to what is implied by a plain reading of the statutory reporting obligation to "report any such [Charter] inconsistency."
Charter inconsistency is deemed to occur only when no good faith,
reasonable argument can be made in favour of consistency.[53] However,
despite the apparent emphasis on good faith judgments, an argument
will be considered credible even when it is "reasoned with a minimum
level of strength or credibility."[54] This idea characterized departmental
practices between 1982 and 1991. This standard was reviewed in 1993,
which involved a consultation of Senior Committees of the Department
of Justice. Senior officials considered other options such as "more likely
than not consistent with guaranteed rights" but in the end maintained
the "no reasonable argument standard" but renamed it the "credible
argument standard." Despite the name change, the standards embody
the same substantive idea.[55] The same standard remains in place.[56]

Although Department of Justice documents suggest that reviewing
Charter risks for statutory reporting obligations use criteria different from those used for the day-to-day Charter evaluations (the legal
risk-management phase), the fact that such a low standard is used to
certify a bill's consistency with the Charter for the section 4.1 task in-
vites the following question: If the minister of justice and government
are committed to good faith efforts to pass legislation they believe is
more than likely to be upheld as consistent with the Charter, why is it
necessary to adopt such a low standard for judgments about Charter
consistency for statutory reporting? If policy processes are reasonably
characterized by good faith efforts to ensure bills are consistent with
judicial Charter norms, the necessary amendments should be made to
legislative initiatives to address Charter problems before bills are introduced, thus negating apprehension that a robust standard of reporting
inconsistency would frequently result in a section 4.1 report. Alternatively, the minister of justice would be prepared to issue a section 4.1

report where appropriate and explain the government's reasons for departing from judicial Charter norms. Interviews indicate that bureaucratic attempts to clarify and/or change this standard were blocked and government lawyers were pressed not to make trouble by raising this issue.[57]

Bureaucratic Advice as Distinct from Government (Cabinet) Decision-Making

It is important to note at this point that the standard to determine whether section 4.1 is triggered is distinct from the broader advice the Department of Justice may provide about the constitutionality of legislation. In other words, despite the weak section 4.1 standard, our claim is not that the bureaucratic advice cabinet receives from Justice lawyers is not substantial or nuanced. The general assessments of constitutionality involve much more than the specific section 4.1 assessment. Yet because this deeper advice is invisible to the outside world – indeed, shielded from the public by solicitor-client privilege – the lack of a section 4.1 report is the most visible indicator to Parliament and other actors about whether the executive views legislation as constitutionally sound. As a result, the problem is not merely that the section 4.1 standard is weak, but that the entire process risks misleading Parliament about the constitutionality of legislation.

Moreover, and as we noted in the introductory chapter of this book, it is also important to keep in mind the distinction between the bureaucracy, that is, assessments of constitutionality by Department of Justice lawyers and other public servants, versus decisions by the government (i.e., cabinet) of the day to heed or ignore that advice. This is especially important in that some governments may be more attentive and responsive to bureaucratic advice than others. Indeed, the Conservative government under Stephen Harper was often regarded as hostile to the public service, seeing it as more favourable to the Liberals, and with Harper himself even describing it as a potential "check" against a potential Conservative majority.[58] Coupled with a general antipathy towards the Charter, or at least the way the Charter is often interpreted and enforced by courts, it is likely that bureaucratic advice about legislation can instigate changes in some contexts and not others.

The Trudeau Liberals and Pressures to Revise Section 4.1?

Despite the concerns we discussed about political and bureaucratic interpretations of section 4.1, it is important to recognize that the Liberal government of Justin Trudeau did not incur strong pressure to revisit how section 4.1 is interpreted. While in opposition, Liberal members of the Justice Committee raised occasional concerns about the appropriate inferences to draw about Charter compliance from the absence of a section 4.1 report on inconsistency, or from a justice official's testimony that the bill as presented was not "manifestly unconstitutional." However, Charter compatibility was not a central focus of the Justice Committee's inquiries and, in any event, concerns of compatibility had little resonance for a majority of committee members or beyond the committee. Thus it is unlikely that the Liberal government incurred significant political pressure to revise the approach taken for interpreting the section 4.1 reporting obligation.

The most persistent critic of how the justice minister had interpreted section 4.1 under a Conservative government was then Liberal justice critic Irwin Cotler. However, Cotler did not seek re-election in 2015, and as a former minister of justice he had presided over a department that, according to its internal documents, used standards similar to those he criticized while his party was in opposition. Moreover, the Federal Court's ruling against Schmidt's appeal would have relieved the Liberal government of any immediate pressure to address the section 4.1 issue (if indeed such pressure existed). When Schmidt appealed the ruling, the Liberal attorney general did not concede the case but instead contested Schmidt's allegations. The federal government was ultimately successful defending these standards in Schmidt's appeal, a decision that reflects an extremely low standard for determining Charter compliance.[59]

Liberal Minister of Justice Retains Low Threshold for Section 4.1

In February 2016, the Standing Committee on Justice and Human Rights decided to undertake a study on the access to the justice system, which amongst other issues included section 4.1(1) of the Department of Justice Act. This would have been an opportune time to revisit the issue of how the section 4.1 reporting obligation is being interpreted, and to assess whether the standards used are consistent with the government's professed interest in transparency and ensuring its policy goals are achieved with minimal intrusion in terms of their implications for the Charter. However, the Liberal-dominated committee spent little time on this issue and members did not press the justice minister or her advisors to explain or justify the criteria used for determining when a report of inconsistency is not required under section 4.1.

Testimony in committee proceedings indicates the Department of Justice was not interested in altering the criteria for determining if the section 4.1 reporting obligation is engaged. This became clear in February 2016 when Laurie Wright, assistant deputy minister for the Public Law section, acknowledged the "long-standing" position that the minister is obliged only to report when there "is no credible argument to support the constitutional validity of the legislation,"[60] and indicated that no changes were required or contemplated, while expressing confidence in the process. As she stated, "We're quite satisfied that we have an entirely robust and well-functioning system in terms of how the advice is given and how it is reflected in the policy development process."[61] Another Justice Department spokesperson confirmed that the department is using the same standard for section 4.1 as it has used for years.[62]

Despite what we characterize as low standards for determining Charter consistency when determining if the section 4.1 reporting obligation is engaged, Wright equated the absence of reports with the practice of attaining Charter consistency in legislation. As she stated, "It's a mark of success with respect to adjustments that are made to policy proposals as they're developed that we have never come to that impasse where a minister would be at odds with cabinet colleagues with respect to the constitutionality of legislation."[63] When questioned about whether the Justice Department has ever had cause to think that a report should have been made, she replied that it is "the minister's decision" about how to respond to the advice received, and that the department "has a good track record of managing to work with clients in order to address those risks before it would get to that stage."[64]

Wright characterized the section 4.1 assessment as a challenging exercise because of the nature of how proportionality considerations are interpreted and because jurisprudence is "constantly evolving."[65] She also acknowledged that different approaches could be taken to interpreting this reporting obligation. She implied that if a more robust standard were used than was current practice, and therefore on occasion it was deemed necessary to engage the section 4.1 reporting obligation, Parliament would be denied the opportunity to debate or pass the legislation in question. As she stated, the idea behind the standard used is that "it's only in the clearest of cases that you would want, essentially, the executive to prevent Parliament from being able to have a debate on whether it wishes to go forward with a certain piece of legislation representing a certain policy solution to a problem."[66]

However, this explanation is unconvincing. It suggests there should not be any opportunity or scope for parliamentary debate about whether or not government should pursue legislation that the minister of justice believes or acknowledges has serious implications for protected rights, or to push for amendments where there is contestation about Charter compliance or the justification of legislation that contradicts or challenges judicial norms of compliance. Yet, as discussed above, government lawyers admit in interviews that legislation has been introduced that is quite risky in terms of the potential for judicial invalidation or other remedies, and this possibility is verified by the department's own guidelines that no section 4.1 report will be made even in cases where there is significant risk that legislation could be successfully challenged. Fundamentally, Wright's statement ignores a principal purpose behind the section 4.1 reporting obligation, which is for parliamentary scrutiny of bills where judgement about the implication for rights is contested.

When in opposition under the Harper government, Liberal members of the committee (albeit individuals different from those on the committee when Wright was testifying), along with other opposition members from the NDP and BQ, raised concerns about a lack of transparency about the legal standards or advice used to claim that a bill was consistent with the Charter and therefore no section 4.1. report was required. They also expressed concerns about the lack of substantive explanation for why the minister of justice had concluded the reporting obligation was not engaged, particularly when contrasted with testimony by non-governmental members who raised serious concerns of Charter infractions. Nevertheless, Liberal members in 2016 did not pursue the issue of the standards used by the Liberal justice minister for deciding the reporting obligation is not engaged, or ask about the relationship between Charter vetting for approving legislation, as contrasted with deciding whether the section 4.1 reporting obligation is engaged. Murray Rankin, the lone NDP on the committee, was the only member to contest this claim about the functioning of the section 4.1 standard and suggested that the amount of money spent by the government when it has not been able to successfully defend legislation suggests that if the current approach used is to represent a check on government or Parliament, the claim that it is working is "wildly counterintuitive."[67]

The committee did not seek additional information on the standards used for determining that a section 4.1 report of Charter inconsistency is not required. Thus while the justice minister testified before the committee that the government would "provide explanations to Canadians about the thinking and considerations that have gone into legislation, as well as the considerations or risks in terms of the [C]harter that may or may not exist,"[68] she was not asked about whether the current emphasis on a credible argument is adequate, or how the government will facilitate conversation within Parliament if it continues to rely on low standards of Charter consistency as the basis for determining if the section 4.1 reporting obligation is engaged. The committee has not indicated it will spend any more time on the section 4.1 issue.

Introduction of Charter Statements

Soon after the Liberals won a majority government in 2015, newly minted Minister of Justice Jody Wilson-Raybould introduced Charter statements to explain the government's thinking about the justification of legislation that implicates protected rights. Adding to this perception of increased sensitivity to Charter constraints was the content and public release of the initial mandate letter of the minister, which emphasized that an overarching goal of the government would be to ensure that legislation respects court decisions and the Charter and to ensure that it fulfils its policy goals with the "least interference with the rights and privacy of Canadians as possible."[69]

In this part we query whether the introduction of Charter statements redresses the concerns we associate with how Charter consistency is being interpreted. More specifically, are Charter statements conceived of as a way to facilitate parliamentary deliberation about whether legislation is justified in light of its potentially adverse implications for the Charter? Do they overcome the reliance on low standards for determining Charter inconsistency? Or do they convey to Parliament the misleading message that Charter-inspired amendments or debate are unwarranted in light of the strong possibility that courts may declare legislation unconstitutional?

As noted above, the original normative intents of the statutory reporting obligation for reporting inconsistency were to confront whether and how legislative initiatives implicate rights adversely; to discourage government from intentionally promoting legislation that is inconsistent with rights without at least explaining or attempting to justify these decisions; and to focus Parliament's attention on whether legislation is compatible with rights so as to either impose pressure on government to accept rights-friendly amendments or justify decisions that implicate rights adversely.

In April 2016 Wilson-Raybould introduced a Charter statement as part of the background information that accompanies proposed legislation. Seven additional statements would follow for bills Wilson-Raybould sponsored before she introduced a bill that would require a Charter statement for every government bill. This new requirement for Charter statements for every bill was not the subject of its own bill, but was included in Bill C-51, which introduced significant amendments to the Criminal Code to clarify laws about sexual assault, repeal provisions of the Criminal Code that have been found unconstitutional by courts, and remove obsolete or redundant offences. Perhaps not surprisingly, given the significance of how the law deals with sexual assault, committee members did not focus on the issue or implications of Charter statements.[70]

No public statement or other information available explains the genesis of this initiative. It did not flow directly from the Minister's mandate letter, although a link can be inferred from the stated goals of transparency and fulfilling the government's policy goals "with the least interference with the rights and privacy of Canadians as possible."[71]

Charter statements constitute part of a broader background document explaining the bill and can also be found on the Department of Justice website. These explanations were initially referred to as potential Charter impacts, or Charter considerations, and now are referred to more generally as Charter statements. Charter statements open with an acknowledgment that the minister has evaluated the bill for its consistency with the Charter as required in section 4.1 of the Department of Justice Act. The statements do not state explicitly whether the section 4.1 reporting is engaged; this is an inference that must be drawn from the lack of a section 4.1 report. The statements discuss potential Charter rights that are engaged and offer the policy justifications the government relies upon to approve the bill.

The stated intent of Charter statements is to reflect the government's commitment "to be open and transparent" and to ensure that Canadian laws conform to the Charter. The department's website says that if rights are limited, there must be "a very good reason" for so doing, and that Charter statements will help "inform Parliamentary and public debate about proposed legislation by identifying a bill's potential effects on *Charter* rights and freedoms and by explaining how any limits on these rights or freedoms could be considered constitutional."[72]

Charter statements made to date share several features in common. The stated intent is to facilitate conversation or dialogue within Parliament, the public, and between Parliament and the courts. Readers are reminded that assessing Charter compliance requires more than recognizing a prima facie rights violation but also must consider if the bill is consistent with section 1 (the general limitation clause).[73] Statements raise relevant Charter principles, with some adding a brief discussion of judicial interpretations or caselaw of relevant issues. Potential Charter rights implicated are identified, whether they occur adversely or whether the legislation upholds a particular right. Analysis of potential Charter implications is qualified by an explicit disclaimer that the legal information provided should not be construed as constituting a legal opinion about the constitutionality of a bill.[74] Although the stated intent is to facilitate conversation, this conversation is not strictly constitutionally oriented; instead, it focuses on the justification of the policy rationale for the government's decision, as distinct from a conversation about whether the legislation satisfies judicial criteria under section 1 for upholding legislative restrictions on Charter rights. There is no explicit explanation of whether the government anticipates serious difficulty convincing a court about its legislative justifications. The statements do not discuss alternative legislative options in terms of their practicalities or implications for protected rights, or explain why the government has chosen the option it has and rejected other perhaps less restrictive measures.

Do Charter Statements Redress the Deficiencies in How Section 4.1 Has Been Interpreted?

The Department of Justice and minister's explanation for Charter statements asserts three purposes. These statements are said to provide a rationale for the government's thinking about how to proceed with its legislative initiative; they are to inform parliamentary and broader assessments of proposed legislation; and they are to contribute to greater transparency. There is nothing inherently objectionable about these objectives.

However, despite purporting to alert Parliament of possible Charter concerns, Charter statements do not explain the reasons or assumptions for the minister of justice's judgment that legislation complies with the Charter. Charter statements do not address the level of risk that the government would lose if litigation arises, or outline the criteria used for concluding that legislation is more likely than not to be upheld as a reasonable limit under section 1, if subject to a Charter challenge. In other words, there is no obvious connection between these statements and the reasons or criteria one might associate with a good faith interpretation of whether the section 4.1 obligation to report Charter inconsistency is engaged. We explore the Charter statements issued in relation to medical assistance in dying legislation in chapter 6.

To be effective, we believe these Charter statements require an explanation for ministers' judgment that legislation is consistent with the Charter and/or why the legislation is justified even if it is highly vulnerable to judicial invalidation. This is a judgment that must be informed by an assessment of Charter compatibility and not simply by a broad list of possible questions that might arise, devoid of context for evaluating the bill in terms of whether it is likely to be upheld or rejected by a court. This is important because Parliament should be aware of whether the legislation it passes is vulnerable to judicial censure, so as to satisfy itself whether legislative amendments are appropriate or that the legislation is warranted.

The policy rationale the Justice Department provides is useful for understanding the government's assumptions about how it conceives of the best way to pursue its policy agenda. However, it is not enough on its own for Parliament to assess whether legislation is consistent with the Charter. These Charter statements fail to facilitate a meaningful assessment of whether a compelling legislative objective that implicates rights adversely will likely be deemed a reasonable limit under section 1.

Instead of explaining assumptions or providing an analysis of why the minister believes the legislation will likely survive a Charter challenge, or why a bill should be considered justifiable even though it is vulnerable to judicial invalidation, Charter statements provide a scattergun approach – a shopping list of the reasons the government believes the legislative objective in the bill is warranted, and a list of rights that are engaged but is devoid of a proportionality-based analysis of why a bill should be considered valid. Yet, even by the Department of Justice's own admission, the Charter statements acknowledge that a prima facie rights violation is inadequate for determining constitutionality without assessing whether the limitation will likely be upheld as reasonable under section 1. Thus, while the Justice Department recognizes this to be the case, Charter statements neither reflect this position nor provide sufficient context for Parliament when grappling with the issue of whether the bill complies with the Charter or whether amendments are appropriate.

For Parliament's purposes, Charter statements neglect the most important questions Parliament should address when evaluating legislation that implicates Charter rights in an adverse manner: Is the legislative objective important enough in light of the deleterious nature of the rights infringement? How serious is the rights infringement? Is the bill likely to accomplish its legislative objective? Was there an obvious, effective, and less restrictive way of accomplishing the legislative objective? Does Parliament believe the legislation is justified even if it departs from judicial norms and thus is vulnerable to invalidation? If so, does the nature of this conflict justify invoking the notwithstanding clause?

The problem with the Charter statements as currently conceived is not simply that they do not direct such considerations or conversations, but also that they send out contradictory information. They are premised on the assumption that the minister of justice has performed the necessary section 4.1 review. While they make no explicit mention that no report is forthcoming, this fact must be inferred from the absence of a report. However, there is no explanation for whether this judgment will be contested, or how the subsequent discussion of Charter considerations affected this judgment. Rather than facilitate these conversations, Charter statements confuse rather than enlighten parliamentary assessments of Charter compatibility. It is not unreasonable for Parliament to infer from these statements that the minister of justice, who occupies the dual role of attorney general, is offering his or her best judgment about whether legislation complies with the Charter. Parliamentarians have legitimate reasons to interpret this as a legal opinion about whether legislation complies with the law and not simply a government's wishful thinking that the legislation might survive a Charter challenge.

Some might balk at our suggestion that Parliament should engage in discussions about whether proposed legislation is consistent with the Charter. Criticisms might reflect the position that all but the last of our suggested questions resemble legal analysis that is beyond parliamentarians' general capacity, and also that such an approach risks distorting policy objectives by subjecting them to judicial norms.

We reject this characterization and criticism for several reasons. Proportionality considerations are often portrayed as being legal or juridical because they are performed by judges and associated with an important part of judicial review in many jurisdictions, and certainly in Canada. However, at heart, these are policy-laden inquiries into the importance and justification of pursuing a legislative objective that implicates rights adversely, the merits of different ways of pursuing these objectives, and the rationality and sensitivity of the legislation in terms of the relationship between legislative goals and the means used to achieve them. As such, they provide a useful framework and discipline for evaluating proposed legislation, whether this is by those developing and proposing legislative initiatives or those who evaluate them, including parliamentarians. As such, proportionality assessments should be considered a valuable dimension of any policy exercise that seeks to confront how proposed legislation affects rights and to redress these potential problems, and not simply for those who prefer a heavily risk-avoiding strategy to minimize the likelihood of judicial censure. It is difficult to imagine how Parliament could take seriously the proposition of passing legislation that complies with the Charter without engaging in this form of analysis (most likely in committee in its detailed review of a bill).

As for the second concern, policy distortion, some might argue that it is inappropriate for Parliament to adopt legal perspectives to resolve social and political conflicts. One reason for taking this position is apprehension that a focus on judicial criteria could discourage pursuing legislative objectives if it cannot be demonstrated that the relationship between the legislative objective and means is rational, or where it cannot be proven that the means used will actually redress the intended goal without imposing overly harsh restrictions on rights. Mark Tushnet warns that if legal views of constitutional norms have too much influence on the law-making process, legal perspectives will replace legislative considerations that may be more relevant.[75] Similarly, Robert Nagel suggests that a legal orientation for political decision-making is inappropriate because legislative decisions depend on "trusting and honoring the reactions of the public to the experience of being governed." The dignity and importance of political involvement is not measured by the formulation of neat intellectual solutions but consists in trying, failing, and learning.[76] As he argues, while the legislative process "works imperfectly and looks worse," attempts to evaluate its integrity and the quality of its outcomes in terms of "unconstrained standards of constitutional rationalism undermine much of the usefulness of legislatures in a democracy."[77]

We have already discussed why we reject the equation of proportionality criteria with legal norms. We accept that policy distortion can be a legitimate concern if legislative decision-making is informed by extreme examples of risk aversion; for example, by approving only bills that obviously or patently comply with judicial norms as can be derived from earlier jurisprudence and ruling out all others simply because they do not allow for certainty of their survival if subject to a Charter challenge. This extreme form of risk-averse behaviour would result in an overly cautious approach for evaluating the government's legislative agenda that would have a chilling effect on legislative development and unduly cede to courts sole responsibility to contribute to judgment about the meaning of protected rights or the scope of permissible limitations on rights under section 1.[78] Judicial norms might be in flux, either because of disagreements amongst judges or because the law has not been adequately or thoroughly developed on the subject in question, or Parliament may believe it has a valid opinion that is different from that of the courts and wishes to persuade courts of the merits of its judgment.

We are not advocating a transformation of Canadian legislative decision-making to rely on jurisprudence as a rigid template for assessing the merits or justification of legislation. We recognize that government and Parliament may differ from courts in their respective judgments about whether legislation complies with the Charter. Consequently, we do not equate Charter compliance with strict adherence to what government lawyers have necessarily gleaned from relevant jurisprudence when assessing whether and how proposed legislation complies with judicial rules. Developing legislation is fraught with imprecision and uncertainty, particularly when identifying and evaluating reasonable and proportionate ways of pursuing a complex legislative objective. Moreover, the government's own legal advisors may themselves differ on interpretations of how relevant jurisprudence addresses the proportionality issue or its implications for new legislation.

However, we believe it is important that those developing and scrutinizing legislation confront whether and how legislation implicates rights. The purpose of so doing should not be to scrap any bill that has a chance of failure before the courts, but for Parliament to satisfy itself as to whether modifications are warranted and/or that the legislation is sufficiently meritorious to proceed, despite its potential vulnerability to judicial censure. Moreover, in those circumstances where government leaders knowingly support and promote legislation that is clearly inconsistent with judicial norms, and for which they have been apprised stands an overwhelming chance of being declared constitutionally invalid, they should respect the statutory mechanisms intended to support their political judgments to knowingly proceed by informing Parliament via the section 4.1 reporting obligation for inconsistency. This decision might also entail consideration of whether the notwithstanding clause should be introduced. Any of these actions will be controversial, but we believe they appropriately impose a burden on government to explain and justify its decisions, and also impose a burden on Parliament to satisfy itself that the legislation is warranted, particularly if it has adverse implications for rights. Thus, while sympathetic to concerns of an excessively risk-averse approach, we nevertheless believe there is a significant and important difference between "good faith" interpretations of Charter compliance and actions that appear to be more akin to rolling the dice by pursuing legislation for which the minister of justice has been fully apprised contradicts judicial norms to such a high level that it has a very strong chance of being declared invalid, particularly in situations where case law is reasonably settled.

In short, we believe it is important for Parliament to be advised when legislative bills are fundamentally at odds with judicial Charter norms, particularly where the chances of their being subject to strong judicial remedies are substantial. However, Charter statements do not provide the appropriate context for Parliament to satisfy itself that legislation is consistent with the Charter, or to pressure the government to explain its reasons for pursuing high-risk legislation. Moreover, we don't believe it makes sense to ask Parliament to assess

Charter statements that are divorced from the broader section 4.1 exercise, which was founded on the idea of acknowledging when legislation is inconsistent with the Charter so as to facilitate more critical evaluations with the bureaucracy, amongst cabinet, and in Parliament on whether amendments are required. To return to a variation of the criticisms made earlier by Cotler, we think it is inappropriate that Parliament should be placed in the position of unknowingly passing legislation that stands a strong chance of being declared unconstitutional. This has the effect of effectively passing the burden for enforcing Charter norms to citizens, which is both costly and time consuming. It is also a prescription for a considerably more restricted scope of rights protection because even if citizens are willing or can afford to litigate, only a small portion of the legislation Parliament passes will ever be subject to judicial review.

Conclusions

Our analysis suggests that the prevailing approach to deciding whether to issue a section 4.1 statement risks discouraging or confusing Parliament's assessment of whether legislation is consistent with the Charter. It is all too tempting for government to exploit the absence of a report to not only send out misleading assurances that legislation is consistent where no section 4.1 report has been made, but also to mute or dismiss opposition arguments about the importance of Charter-inspired amendments. In addition to the lack of respect for Parliament, which is the message conveyed regularly by how this section 4.1 obligation is exercised, the use of low standards for determining Charter consistency presents several other serious concerns. One is the potential to blur the lines between a principled or reasoned judgment about whether section 4.1 is engaged as distinct from more political and partisan justifications for passing risky legislation. The latter might include factors that have very little to do with Charter compliance. This concern is enhanced by the non-transparent and non-accountable way in which the minister exercises this statutory responsibility.

A related concern is respect for the law. The minister of justice wears two hats, also serving as attorney general. The attorney general is responsible for ensuring that government acts in a manner consistent with the rule of law. To the extent that he or she is willing to interpret a statutory obligation in a manner that ignores its clear purposes and common-sense construction, this leads to serious apprehension about the fidelity to law: a concern amplified by the minister of justice's dual function as attorney general. We discuss this further in chapter 7.

We argue that the section 4.1 reporting obligation places a high premium on good faith interpretations of what constitutes a compelling and reasonable interpretation of the Charter, an expectation that the justice minister will exert a certain level of autonomy from prime ministerial and cabinet pressures, and also that he or she will not compromise professional judgment about Charter consistency for political purposes. The strong – and what appears unequivocal – presumption against making a report of Charter inconsistency, the absence of any history of reporting Charter inconsistency in the four decades in which this obligation has been in place, and the fact no minister of justice has ever resigned over this issue, almost certainly influence how "warnings" of Charter problems are interpreted when legislation is being developed. These factors also combine to convey a clear message: the goal is not to develop Charter-compliant ways of implementing the government's legislative agenda, but to construct arguments to justify limiting rights, even when risk levels are exceptionally high and it is not at all obvious that courts will accept these arguments to uphold the legislation in question.

We do not believe the introduction of Charter statements as presently conceived redress problems with how the statutory reporting obligation on Charter inconsistency is interpreted. If the minister of justice is not prepared to engage in more robust interpretations of section 4.1 it would be better to propose that Parliament repeal this reporting obligation rather than continue a practice that risks misleading Parliament that government legislation complies with the Charter. Instead of acting as a disincentive for introducing rights-offending legislation or as a stimulus for parliamentary and political pressure to redress rights violations, this reporting requirement has been interpreted so restrictively that government is shielded from acknowledging Charter inconsistencies, contestation about its judgment, or the level of apprehension or risk of vulnerability to judicial invalidation or other remedies.

3 The Legislative Process and Charter Rights: Criminal Justice Policy and the Harper Government

Notwithstanding the supremacy of Canadian constitutional principles as interpreted by the Supreme Court, only a fraction of the legislation Parliament passes will actually be litigated. Thus, a cavalier or dismissive attitude by Parliament about whether legislation complies with the Charter offloads responsibility to citizens to check legislation for constitutional compliance, requires expensive litigation to challenge legislation that is believed to violate constitutional norms, and undermines the normative ideal of governing in a manner that respects rights.

Concern about legislative compliance with the Charter is particularly salient when the rights at stake are those of minorities or others lacking electoral clout and whose claims may alienate or divide political parties' electoral bases. A particularly good example appears when politicians exploit concerns about public safety by advocating "tough on crime" measures without adequate consideration for their impact on the legal rights protected by the Charter or systemic effects like the over-incarceration of Indigenous and Black people in Canada. The rights of criminal suspects seldom garner sympathy from political parties or the Canadian public more generally, and this is reflected in a tendency in political discourse to present public safety and respecting the legal rights of suspected or convicted criminals as if one occurs at the expense of the other. Debate on criminal justice policy often takes a more populist turn emphasizing victims' rights and/or public safety, a discourse sometimes referred to as "penal populism"[1] in which political parties often compete to present themselves as the best safeguard of public safety.[2]

This chapter examines what the Conservative government's law-and-order legislative agenda and the record of parliamentary deliberation reveal about the extent to which Charter considerations guide legislation. Our analysis centres on two significant omnibus crime bills – one in 2007 during the Harper government's period of minority rule, and the second introduced by the Harper majority government in 2011.

In our analysis we ask three questions: To what extent did the minister of justice explain or attempt to justify assessments that the proposed legislative measures comply with the Charter? How did the minister of justice address the section 4.1 statutory reporting obligation under the Department of Justice Act to apprise Parliament when bills are inconsistent with the Charter? What other factors affected Parliament's willingness and/or ability to hold government to account for its legislative choices in the face of parliamentary and extra-parliamentary arguments that many provisions may not survive a Charter challenge?

As we argue below, the minister of justice did not explain or justify reasons for concluding that the legislation complies with Charter norms or explain why it was unnecessary to report Charter inconsistency under section 4.1, despite arguments of legal scholars and concerns of some parliamentarians that key aspects of the government's legislative agenda were vulnerable to judicial invalidation. This reporting obligation was interpreted in a manner that confused rather than clarified questions of Charter consistency, and the decision not to report was used by the government to deny the necessity of amendments proposed by the opposition to address Charter concerns. The ensuing parliamentary debates emphasize constraints political parties incur when they lack the power to defeat amendments. They also reveal the low priority given by opposition parties to try to pass Charter-friendly amendments if they fear that doing so will be unpopular and/or undermine their party's political agenda.

Background

"Tough on crime" measures characterized much of the legislative agenda of Stephen Harper's Conservative government from 2006 to 2015 and comprised a core part of each of the four national election campaigns over that period. The Harper government presented its legislative agenda as constituting a distinct departure from what party officials alleged was the "dangerous, ideology-driven criminal justice" position of the then opposition Liberal and NDP parties. By its own account, the Harper government introduced and passed more than sixty pieces of legislation during its nine years in office that purported "to help keep criminals behind bars, protect children, put the rights of victims ahead of criminals, and crack down on drugs, guns and gangs."[3] This included the support of a significant number of private member's bills introduced by backbench CPC parliamentarians – bills that did not receive Department of Justice scrutiny as government bills do.[4] The opposition either lacked the numerical strength in Parliament to defeat the bill or, where the combined vote could have defeated the government's legislation, lacked the willingness to oppose measures similar to those they had earlier supported, fearing political fallout from the inevitable political taunts of worrying more about criminals than victims or public safety. In some cases, this support for Harper's criminal justice agenda occurred despite opposition members' acknowledgment that they were failing their parliamentary obligation to avoid passing legislation they believed was unconstitutional.[5]

The Harper government sought not only to distinguish its position from that of the opposition parties, but also from the courts. Anticipating judicial difficulties in the event of Charter challenges, the Harper government tried to revamp the judicial appointment process to ensure that its legislative efforts to "crack down on crime and make our streets and communities safer" would have a better chance of surviving Charter litigation.[6] One change made was to place a representative of law enforcement on panels for recommendations for judicial appointments despite the strong objections of Beverley McLachlin, then chief justice of the Supreme Court, as well as the Federation of Law Societies of Canada and the Canadian Judicial Council.[7] As Harper explained his reasons to the House of Commons, "We want to make sure that our selection of judges is in correspondence with [the government's law-and-order] objectives."[8] The assumption was that judicial candidates supported by law enforcement were more likely to uphold the constitutionality of contested provisions. Yet there is little evidence that the Harper government transformed the judiciary via its appointments. Emmett Macfarlane, writing about Harper's inability to mould the Supreme Court to his way of thinking, notes that the "culture of appointments in Canada, particularly the extent to which it has tended to avoid explicit partisan contestation, complicates this narrative. Importantly, constitutional experts have noted there were few 'like-minded' judges for the Conservative government to choose from."[9]

As it turned out, key elements of the government's criminal law policies were subsequently declared unconstitutional by the Supreme Court, including mandatory minimum sentences for drug offences[10] and the government's decision to limit the credit that convicted criminals receive for time served in pretrial detention.[11] In addition, lower courts have declared that several other aspects of the Conservatives' tough-on-crime reforms are inconsistent with the Charter, including the retroactive abolition of early parole review and other mandatory minimum sentences.[12]

The Harper Minority Government and the Tackling Violent Crime Act (2007–8)

In the 2006 election the Conservative Party campaigned on an agenda that emphasized the need to protect communities from crime by creating tougher sentences for serious and repeat crimes and by tightening eligibility for parole. In its campaign platform the party promised to create mandatory minimum prison sentences for serious drug trafficking offences, weapons offences, crimes committed while on parole and for repeat offenders; end conditional sentences for serious crimes; create a presumption of dangerous-offender designation for anyone convicted and sentenced to three violent or sexual offences (popularly known as "three strikes you're out"); ensure that criminals convicted of multiple crimes are given consecutive rather than concurrent sentences; repeal the practice of allowing prisoners to obtain parole after serving two-thirds of the sentence; create a reverse onus for bail hearings for anyone charged with an indictable firearms offence; and pursue a constitutional amendment to deny prisoners in federal institutions the ability to vote in elections.[13]

In trying to sell its message to the public, Conservative Party strategists exploited the highly publicized and tragic gang-related shooting in Toronto on Boxing Day 2005 that resulted in the death of high school student Jane Creba. Party leaders hoped they could use this incident to gain more support for the Conservative government's campaign commitment to "crack down on crime" and to "fix our criminal justice system."[14] As then adviser Tom Flanagan said of this political strategy, "Our internal polling had already established criminal justice as the issue area where we had the strongest lead over the Liberals, and Jane Creba's tragic death helped to make our position more salient to voters."[15]

Upon winning minority government status in 2006, the Harper government introduced the first of several new laws requiring mandatory minimum sentences for certain firearms offences. Initially, the government's proposal was subject to substantial revisions by the Justice Committee. The government's minority status was reflected in the composition of the Justice Committee and prevented the government from dominating proceedings and blocking amendments. In speaking of the need to amend the bill, NDP member Joe Comartin argued the importance of retaining judicial discretion and reducing the use of mandatory minimums. He warned that the legislation would not likely survive a Charter challenge if amendments were not made. Moreover, he emphasized the importance of parliamentarians ensuring legislation is consistent with the Charter. As he stated, "It [behooves] us as a committee, as legislators, that we don't pass laws that we know in advance are not going to survive [a Charter challenge]" and that failure to revise the legislation "would be irresponsible on our part."[16]

The opposition approved amendments to remove mandatory minimum penalties, with the exception of offences with maximum penalties of life imprisonment. However, the bill died on the order paper (along with several other crime-related initiatives) when Harper decided to prorogue Parliament early (15 September 2007) to begin a new session.

When the second session of the thirty-ninth Parliament began, the government again introduced mandatory minimums but this time they were included in an omnibus bill (Bill C-2, also referred to as the "Tackling Violent Crime Act"). Bill C-2 included measures that had earlier been introduced in five separate bills before the earlier parliamentary session was prorogued.

Despite the Harper government's continued minority status, it was now in a considerably stronger political position to resist opposition pressure for amendments. Stéphane Dion's tenuous stature as leader of the Liberal Party and Liberal losses in a by-election in Quebec (previously an area of electoral strength)[17] weakened Liberal resolve to challenge legislation if doing so would trigger a confidence vote. This strong political reluctance to precipitate an early election call was consistent with an earlier and unusual political occurrence: the Liberal Party leadership's decision to whip abstention for voting on the government's 2007 Throne Speech.[18]

Non-parliamentary critics and opposition members argued that the omnibus bill presented serious Charter difficulties. However, Parliament's assessment of whether aspects of the bill were vulnerable to judicial invalidation was seriously hampered by Department of Justice explanations about why the bill should be considered consistent with the Charter – an explanation influenced by how the section 4.1 reporting obligation was interpreted by the department and minister (as we discuss in more depth below). This does not mean that justice lawyers were not advising the government about the constitutional risks some of the provisions presented, but as noted in chapter 2, this broader advice is invisible to the public and Parliament, as is the extent to which the government takes such advice into consideration. Instead, as we show below, senior lawyers appearing in committee adopted the weaker section 4.1 standard – that the provisions were "not manifestly unconstitutional" – when questioned about the constitutionality of the bill, while refusing to make public predictions about whether the provisions would survive before the courts.

A particularly contentious element of the bill was its variation of the controversial American practice of "three strikes you're out" penal policy. Under the bill, anyone convicted a third time for a primary designated offence could be found to constitute a dangerous offender, and would then bear the burden to prove on a balance of probabilities that he or she does not present a threat to the life, safety, or physical or mental well-being of others. With this reversed onus of proof, the accused could be found to be a dangerous offender "notwithstanding any reasonable doubt as to his or her dangerousness or the risk of recidivism."[19] Such a finding would result in an indeterminate sentence unless the court is satisfied by the evidence that there is a reasonable expectation that a lesser measure would protect the public.

The bill also created two new firearm offences with escalating mandatory sentences of imprisonment; introduced stronger bail requirements for those accused of serious offences involving firearms and other regulated weapons; increased penalties for impaired driving; and raised the age of lawful consent for sexual activity from fourteen to sixteen years.

Rather than send the bill to the Justice Committee that normally examines legal issues, including Charter concerns, it was sent to a committee established to examine this particular bill (the Legislative Committee on Bill C-2). This committee was given an extremely short time for review (less than a month) despite the vast range of provisions included.[20] The combined effects of such a short period for review and the sheer size of the bill undermined both the committee's ability to conduct a thorough review as well as potential witnesses' capacity to assess it and make presentations before the committee. Moreover, unlike the amended versions of these bills in the earlier parliamentary session, which occurred through opposition pressure, these provisions now appeared in their original form.[21]

Then justice minister Rob Nicholson appeared before the committee and testified that he was satisfied the provisions were fully constitutional.[22] He did not elaborate on the basis for his judgment. Witnesses who subsequently appeared before the committee challenged his claim of constitutionality, suggesting that a Charter challenge was extremely likely and that lawyers "will be chomping at the bit" to initiate a challenge.[23]

Particularly telling about the committee's Charter deliberations was the confusion generated by how the minister of justice and Department of Justice approached the issue of Charter consistency. As discussed in chapter 2, a low standard of determining Charter compliance is used for deciding that the section 4.1 statutory obligation is not engaged to alert Parliament that a bill is inconsistent with the Charter. Despite the systematic reliance on a standard that permits high-risk legislation to escape reporting Charter inconsistency for section 4.1 purposes, the minister equated the absence of a section 4.1 report with the assurance that the bill complies with the Charter. The equation of these two different judgments confused rather than clarified Parliament's attempts to ascertain whether elements of the proposed legislation were vulnerable to judicial invalidation for violating the Charter, particularly in the face of arguments of non-governmental legal experts that contradicted these assurances of constitutionality.

Committee deliberations revealed a sharp division between Conservative and opposition members on whether the bill had serious Charter deficiencies. Opposition members were concerned about a number of Charter issues, particularly after hearing critical assessments from legal experts. Liberal MP Brian Murphy characterized the principal job of the committee as the determination of whether the bill violates the Charter. He indicated that while he was initially satisfied by what he heard from Department of Justice lawyers on Charter considerations, witness testimony generated serious doubts.[24] After hearing from witnesses who argued that key aspects of the bill would not likely survive a constitutional challenge,[25] in particular its limits on judicial discretion and reverse onus provisions,[26] opposition members tried to gain a better understanding of the legal arguments that had influenced the bill. Specifically, they wanted a better understanding of why the minister of justice's claim that the bill was indeed constitutional was so strongly contested by non-governmental legal experts. The ensuing proceedings left committee members with serious questions about whether the bill complied with the Charter.

Opposition members questioned explicitly the basis for the justice minister's earlier assurances or his judgment that no section 4.1 statutory report of Charter inconsistency was required. Liberal member Marlene Jennings proposed that the committee have access to the legal opinions upon which the minister of justice had relied, on a confidential/in camera basis. Conservative members rejected this idea, arguing it would implicate client confidentiality, despite assurances that this information would not be made public and that parliamentarians would respect confidentiality.[27]

BQ member Réal Ménard acknowledged he was troubled by witness testimony that the bill was inconsistent with the Charter[28] and expressed his intent to table a motion that the minister of justice must provide a letter verifying the bill is constitutional. Ménard also challenged the explanation for denying the committee access to Department of Justice legal advice, disputing the opinion that the minister should be viewed as a client. He argued that since the committee had heard from nine witnesses advising that the bill was not constitutional, the committee should be able to obtain written assurance from the minister that the bill is constitutional. Ménard also warned the chair that if the committee did not get the written information it requested, he would table motions for adjournment, adding that "if we do not have the information we require, we will not vote on the bill."[29] As with the case of Jennings's earlier motion, this motion was defeated with all Conservative members voting against (along with one Liberal member), with all other opposition members voting in support.

Although the minister of justice did not reappear to address opposition questions about why the bill had been presented as being consistent with the Charter, members had an opportunity to question a senior Department of Justice lawyer, Stanley Cohen. Cohen was asked explicitly if the provisions on dangerous offenders would withstand a Charter challenge. What emerged appeared to be a careful attempt by Cohen to distinguish his opinion that the bill complies with the Charter from assurances that the legislation would withstand a constitutional challenge. He testified that the bill would not have been introduced "if any opinion had been issued to the effect that the legislation in question was manifestly unconstitutional and could not be defended by credible arguments before a court."[30] However, a careful reading underscores that Cohen did not actually state that he was confident the legislation would be successfully defended if litigated.

Not persuaded by Cohen's response, Ménard asked for clarification about the "verification mechanisms" used by the minister of justice to declare that legislation is constitutional.[31] In response to this pointed challenge, Cohen testified that neither in this situation nor in any previous appearance before a committee had he "offered an opinion" that legislation "will be upheld by the court," suggesting instead that his statement on Charter consistency reflected the department's view that "the legislation in question is not manifestly unconstitutional" and that if required, the arguments the government would present to defend the legislation "are capable of being accepted by the courts."[32]

As this parliamentary review occurred several years before the Schmidt case (which, as discussed in chapter 2, precipitated publication of the departmental guidelines used for determining if the section 4.1 reporting obligation for acknowledging Charter inconsistency is engaged), committee members were unaware of the systematic reliance by the Justice Department and minister on the concept that a bill "is not manifestly unconstitutional" to justify a decision not to report Charter inconsistency under section 4.1, even if a bill is assessed as having a high risk of being declared unconstitutional. As discussed in chapter 2, the guidelines for the reporting obligation indicate this reporting requirement is engaged only for a bill that is said to occupy the far end of the highest category of risk (which is in the range of 81–100 per cent certainty of being declared unconstitutional). Committee members were also unaware that the minister's judgment that it is unnecessary to engage the section 4.1 obligation to report Charter inconsistency does not require confidence that the legislation will be successfully defended if challenged, as became evident in court proceedings of Schmidt's legal challenge.[33]

Despite this important discrepancy between the minister of justice's views of Charter consistency and the testimony of non-governmental legal experts that the legislation was extremely vulnerable to a successful Charter challenge, Conservative committee members revealed considerable trust in the legal opinions of the minister and Department of Justice. As one Conservative member stated, "This bill wasn't drafted on the back of a napkin in an afternoon; it was drafted with the assistance of the finest legal and constitutional minds the Minister of Justice can find. When they signed off on it, they signed off with an understanding that it may face a constitutional or charter challenge in the future and they signed off with the complete confidence that this bill withstands any constitutional or Charter challenge."[34] The committee chair ruled that several proposed opposition amendments were out of order because of procedural rules precluding amendments after second stage reading if these have the effect of altering the purpose of the bill. However, as Charter concerns arose from the intent(s) of the bill, this rule seriously constrained members' abilities to address perceived Charter problems. These proposed amendments included attempts to reintroduce judicial discretion on mandatory minimums; remove the reverse onus dimension for determining a dangerous offender; and remove some of the less serious crimes from the list of those that would be considered for mandatory minimum sentences.[35] The bill was ultimately reported without amendments.

When the bill returned to the Commons, opposition members who had served on the committee confirmed that they were uncertain about how to interpret the Department of Justice's position that the bill is "not manifestly unconstitutional"[36] in response to their pointed question about whether the bill was vulnerable to being declared inconsistent with the Charter. NDP member Joe Comartin proposed an amendment to remove the reverse onus element on the dangerous offender provisions.[37] In urging the House to support this amendment, Comartin emphasized that with the exception of the minister of justice, every legal expert appearing before the committee testified that the reverse onus section would not survive a Charter challenge.[38]

Although Nicholson tried to assure the House he would not have lent his name as minister of justice to the bill if he was "not convinced that it complied with the Charter,"[39] he subsequently employed a more forceful and ultimately effective way to defeat pressure for reforms. Nicholson threatened that if the NDP's amendment was to pass, the government would interpret this as a confidence measure, and warned that the government was prepared to fight any ensuing election by emphasizing it is "serious about fighting violent crime."[40] This threat was almost certainly influenced by the knowledge of the Liberal Party's weakness at the time and its reluctance to force an election on this or any other issue in the near future. Moreover, by including the contentious provisions in omnibus legislation, it was more difficult politically for the opposition to defeat the bill, particularly given the prior election commitments by the Liberals and NDP to increase mandatory minimum penalties for certain firearm-related offences.[41]

Nicholson's threat had a direct impact on parliamentary voting. None of the opposition parties appeared anxious to force an election. The NDP acknowledged that despite its serious concerns of Charter inconsistencies, it was not prepared to oppose this bill if doing so would trigger an election. As Comartin characterized the NDP's dilemma, on the one hand it was aware that the reverse onus provision on dangerous offenders offends the Charter and therefore would likely be declared unconstitutional. Yet, on the other hand, if the party were to oppose this provision, it effectively would have to give up "the rest of the bill." Given this dilemma, he said the NDP would support the bill, but acknowledged that in so doing, members would be abdicating their responsibility as legislators to pass proper legislation.[42] Comartin subsequently indicated that Parliament will have to rely on the courts to strike down the reverse onus provision.[43]

Liberal and BQ members also indicated that the combined effects of the threat of a confidence vote and the omnibus character of the bill prevented their parties from basing their vote on Charter concerns. Liberal member Robert Thibault acknowledged that despite lingering Charter concerns that were not allayed by Cohen's testimony that the bill is not manifestly unconstitutional, his party would support the bill.[44] Similarly, although the BQ had been critical of the bill in committee and believed the NDP amendment would be an improvement, the BQ indicated it would vote against the amendment for pragmatic reasons because it did not want the disagreement to trigger a confidence vote.[45] The Conservative-dominated Standing Senate Committee on Legal and

Constitutional Affairs reviewed the bill and did not recommend any amendments.[46]

The parliamentary debate on these bills demonstrates that a number of factors had a significant influence on the outcome of the legislation. Initially, the minority status of the government allowed the committee to propose Charter-friendly amendments. However, the government's decision to prorogue Parliament early (15 September 2007) meant all bills died on the order paper. Upon the resumption of Parliament (16 October 2007), the Harper government's decision to reintroduce previous bills in an omnibus form complicated the task of evaluating Charter issues, particularly given the short time frame for parliamentary scrutiny and hearing from relevant witnesses. The minister of justice equated the decision that it was unnecessary to report Charter inconsistency for section 4.1 statutory reporting purposes with an assurance that the legislation was consistent with the Charter, despite weak standards used for the former. Committee members were unaware of the low standards used for evaluating Charter consistency and deciding it was unnecessary to report Charter inconsistency under section 4.1. Committee members were also unaware that when the minister and Department of Justice conclude that the proposed legislation is "not manifestly unconstitutional," this does not necessarily reflect confidence that the legislation will be defended successfully if subject to Charter litigation. It requires only that an argument that is capable of winning be provided, not one that reflects confidence it will likely convince the court of constitutionality. Opposition calls for amendments to address Charter concerns were ruled out of order because they affected the intent of the bill. By threatening that any amendment would transform the vote into a confidence issue, the government was able the exploit the Liberal Party's weak status and realization that opposition parties were not willing to trigger an election call. Although opposition parties had the numerical strength to defeat the bill, they were not prepared to give primacy to the Charter over aspects of the legislation they supported. This refusal to defeat the bill occurred despite the acknowledgment of some that they were knowingly passing legislation they suspected was unconstitutional.

The Harper Majority Government and the Safe Streets and Communities Act (2012)

Several criminal justice bills were before Parliament when the minority Conservative government failed to win a vote of confidence in 2011, triggering a new election. In the ensuing election campaign, the

Conservatives promised that if re-elected they would give priority to law-and-order issues by passing sweeping legislative changes within 100 days of taking power.[47]

Upon re-election with a strong majority (the first majority it had held since taking office in 2006) the Harper government quickly introduced a large omnibus crime bill: Bill C-10 (better known by its short title, the Safe Streets and Communities Act), which included nine bills introduced in the previous Parliament. The wide-ranging proposals sought to establish new mandatory minimum penalties for sexual offences against children under sixteen; create new mandatory minimum penalties for drug offences carried out for purposes of organized crime or targeting youth; double the maximum penalty for the production of marijuana (from seven to fourteen years); provide higher maximum penalties for date-rape drugs; reorient the principles of the Youth Criminal Justice Act to emphasize the protection of society; expand the definition of a violent offence and require the Crown to consider adult sentences for youth (fourteen to seventeen) convicted of serious crimes (this, after long-standing reverse-onus provisions were struck down by the Supreme Court in 2008);[48] restrict the use of conditional sentences such as house arrest for certain crimes; allow warrantless arrests of any offenders who appear to be violating their conditions for release; replace the concept of a "pardon" with a "record suspension"; add new criteria for the minister of public safety when deciding if a criminal should be granted a transfer back to Canada; permit victims of terrorism to sue the perpetrators or supporters of terrorism; and allow the denial of work permits to foreign nationalists who are presumed vulnerable to abuse or exploitation, such as exotic dancers, low-skilled labourers, and victims of human trafficking.[49]

Government leaders equated their decisive electoral majority victory with strong authority to pass Bill C-10 swiftly – a prospect enabled by the imposition of tight time constraints on parliamentary deliberation and limited opportunities for non-parliamentary witnesses to prepare and present their assessments.

In his appearance before the Justice Committee, Minister Rob Nicholson reaffirmed the government's electoral promise to pass the legislation within 100 sitting days of the new Parliament, and urged committee members to "work with the government" to ensure this happened.[50] As is often the case for omnibus legislation, the sheer complexity of the legislative bill made assessments more difficult than usual, particularly with the addition of severe time restrictions on committee deliberations and the short time given for intervenors to prepare and make oral submissions. Not surprisingly, opposition members expressed strong concerns about their ability to conduct adequate scrutiny.[51]

Witnesses who appeared before the Justice Committee criticized the bill for having been influenced by the "politicization" or "ideological response" to concerns of youth crime rather than driven by research or "on-the-ground experienced professionals."[52] They also chastised the government for its failure to engage in necessary consultations, deliberation, and accountability when relying on "legally illiterate" materials that were "hastily convened and ignored 150 years of correctional history" and without reference to the Charter or to decisions of the Supreme Court.[53] Critics argued that aspects of the bill were inconsistent with Supreme Court jurisprudence and would not likely survive a Charter challenge.[54] Critics also argued that the measures would transform the country's legal landscape[55] by imposing a massive policy shift towards expanding the Canadian prisoner system that would cost millions of dollars to implement, send thousands more to prison,[56] and contribute to the persistent problem of over-incarceration of Indigenous peoples.[57]

Although not asked to appear as a witness, the Canadian Bar Association presented a comprehensive and stinging rebuke of the bill in a written submission to the Justice Committee. The CBA identified several potentially rights-offending provisions, including restricting the availability of conditional sentences, restrictions on prosecutorial and judicial discretion to depart from mandatory minimum sentences, restrictions on judicial discretion when sentencing on drug offenders and drug trafficking, inattention to human rights principles within prison, and the potential for arbitrary and inconsistent refusals to transfer Canadian offenders back to Canada.[58]

The Conservative government demonstrated a distinct lack of interest in addressing Charter concerns, despite the CBA's submission to Parliament and its critical analysis of the bill in an elaborate press release.[59] At no time did Nicholson explain why he or the department had concluded that the legislation complied with the Charter and/or why it was unnecessary to issue a report of Charter inconsistency under section 4.1 of the Department of Justice Act.

Neither the CBA's submission nor criticisms from witnesses about potential Charter breaches appear to have had an obvious influence on government committee members' assessment of the bill. A series of opposition-led amendments were defeated by the Conservative-dominated committee.[60] Opposition committee members indicated they were subject to "inappropriate comments" from Conservative members who "ridiculed us if we did not speak in favour of the bill."[61]

Nicholson did not respond to the urging of Irwin Cotler, a previous Liberal justice minister, who implored the minister of justice to revisit the bill and conduct a comprehensive review to ensure it was not inconsistent with the Charter and to amend or repeal any provisions that risked breaching the Charter.[62]

When the bill returned to the House, Cotler again pressed the minister of justice to justify his judgment that the legislation was constitutionally sound. Cotler criticized what he interpreted as the government's reliance on its professed mandate to legislate on crime legislation to deflect questions about Charter compliance. He advised members that the legislation had a series of Charter deficiencies, including its contribution to prison overcrowding and the effects this would have on cruel and unusual punishment, and its use of disproportionate and prejudicial mandatory minimum sentences. Cotler reminded Parliament that the minister of justice had not complied with requests to table constitutional opinions that the government received so as to satisfy Parliament that the legislation complies with the Charter.[63] Cotler also argued that the government had demonstrated its "contempt for the necessary deliberations of Parliament," as evident in its use of omnibus legislation, short time allocations for witnesses at the committee stage, the rejection of all proposed Charter-friendly amendments, and time allocations at the report stage that denied substantial debate.[64]

Cotler's concerns about Charter deficiencies and what he considered inappropriate attention to the minister's statutory obligation to report on Charter inconsistency had little impact on the outcome. Other opposition members raised concerns with the bill that focused on issues other than Charter compliance.[65] In any event, the Conservative majority was sufficient to ensure passage of the bill, by a 154–129 vote.

Much of the focus in the Senate was the bill's potential to exacerbate the overrepresentation of Indigenous peoples in jail. Justice officials appearing before the Standing Committee on Legal and Constitutional Affairs were asked for assurances that the bill complied with the Charter. Officials testified that although they expected there would be constitutional challenges, Department of Justice lawyers would "defend" the provisions to the "full extent possible."[66] Perhaps not surprisingly, they did not provide assurances these provisions would survive a Charter challenge. The Senate made several amendments to the bill, but they were not directed at previously raised Charter concerns.[67]

The government effectively exploited its recent election victory as a mandate to pursue its criminal legislative agenda and avoid focusing on Charter issues. Reliance on omnibus legislation and serious time constraints undermined effective parliamentary scrutiny and also undermined the ability of witnesses to appear and/or present their analysis of the proposed measures. The government's majority status shielded the justice minister from having to explain and justify assessments of Charter compliance, despite their being contested by prominent extra-parliamentary opinions, such as that of the Canadian Bar Association. Only a handful of parliamentarians were prepared to, or saw it necessary to, address Charter concerns in their assessment of the bill.

How the Harper Government's Criminal Justice Policy Fared in Court: Implications for Legislative Assessments of Rights

Several provisions of the Harper government's legislative agenda on criminal justice were subsequently found unconstitutional by the Supreme Court and lower courts. These include provisions in the two major pieces of legislation analysed here. Reverse-onus provisions concerning the police use of Breathalyzers contained in the Tackling Violent Crime Act were invalidated in the 2012 case *R. v. St-Onge Lamoureux*.[68] In *R. v. Nur* three years later, a majority of the Court found the mandatory minimum sentences created under the Tackling Violent Crime Act unconstitutional because, in some "reasonably foreseeable" cases, they constitute cruel and unusual punishment under section 12 of the Charter.[69] A mandatory minimum sentence brought in under the Safe Streets and Communities Act was similarly struck down by the Court in *R. v. Lloyd*, not long after the Conservatives were defeated in the 2015 federal election.[70] Another mandatory minimum under the latter Act, for sexual interference, has been struck down fourteen times by lower courts across the country.[71]

Other Harper government policies have also been invalidated, including the retrospective abolition of early parole under the Abolition of Early Parole Act in 2014's *Canada v. Whaling*,[72] and changes to regulations affecting the use of medical marijuana in *R. v. Smith*.[73] In a more recent decision, the Court invalidated the mandatory victim surcharge brought in under the Conservatives.[74] Similarly, the Court has narrowed the Conservative government's attempt to eliminate enhanced credit in sentencing under the Truth in Sentencing Act.[75]

These judicial rebukes stand as a significant, though far from total, veto of the Conservatives' criminal justice agenda. What do they tell us about the government's and Parliament's assessment of the rights compatibility of these policies? Scholars have differed on the degree to which the Court has been especially antagonistic to the Conservatives' legislative agenda. Christopher Manfredi, for example, argues that the

Conservative "record in Charter cases has not differed significantly from that of the two other post-Charter governments," pointing to the fact that 75 per cent of its Charter losses involved legislation passed by previous governments.[76] In short, in the Charter period, government losses have proven inevitable, regardless of partisan stripe. By contrast, Matthew Hennigar notes that within the realm of criminal law the Harper losses were much more significant, leading him to conclude that "the Court was hostile to the signature component of the Harper government's 'law and order' policy agenda."[77] Macfarlane's analysis notes that the government's record before the Court stands apart from its predecessors' when issue salience is considered. While the Court rarely invalidates laws passed by the sitting government, a point also emphasized by Manfredi, Macfarlane finds that the Conservative government is the only government of the Charter period to have policies that were in its various election platforms blocked by judicial review on Charter grounds, including several of the criminal justice policies examined here.[78]

Hennigar raises the prospect that some of the legislative initiatives subject to invalidation were simply poorly crafted, noting that this "is arguably a predictable outcome of heavily concentrating power in the Prime Minister's Office, as Canada has experienced in recent decades, and the concomitant weakening of careful legislative scrutiny in the House."[79] Our analysis suggests there is some veracity to this claim. Indeed, then minister of justice Peter MacKay's reaction to the government's loss in *Nur* largely reflected an ideological commitment to tough-on-crime policy rather than any reflection on the Charter rights implications of the decision, as he noted, "Our government will continue to be tough on those who commit serious crimes and endanger our communities."[80]

Nonetheless, it is worth briefly noting that in each of the cases of *St-Onge Lamoureux, Nur,* and *Lloyd,* several justices dissented and would have upheld the impugned laws. In the case of mandatory minimum sentences, Puddister notes that the courts until *Nur* had been largely deferential to Parliament's choices in sentencing policy, with the Supreme Court having invalidated a mandatory minimum only once under the Charter, all the way back in 1987.[81] Further, in both *Nur* and *Lloyd,* the Court relied on "reasonable hypotheticals" to justify striking down the mandatory minimum sentences, not the facts in the cases before them, something the dissenting justices noted was a "departure from the Court's jurisprudence."[82] On these particular policies, then, we caution against a reliance on the benefit of hindsight to declare that the provisions at stake were clearly unconstitutional at the time they were crafted. However, scant attention was devoted to scrutinizing the rights-compatibility of the legislation, and the overall quantity and quality of legislative debate was poor.

Conclusions

Parliamentary deliberations about a wide range of law-and-order measures introduced by the Harper government demonstrate that rights-inspired concerns may not be given high priority by legislative decision-makers if the potential rights claimants lack political influence and political parties are apprehensive that pro-Charter positions can be used to undermine their electoral support. The parliamentary record also reinforces the serious political constraints that the Canadian variant of a Westminster-based political system presents for effective parliamentary scrutiny and assessment of Charter concerns. These constraints arise from the ability of government to introduce comprehensive measures in the form of omnibus legislation that make parliamentary and extra-parliamentary scrutiny of potential Charter (and other) problems more difficult; impose strict time limitations that undermine a committee's ability to hear from witnesses and evaluate opinions that contradict the minister of justice's implicit or explicit affirmations of Charter compliance; dominate parliamentary committee business in cases of majority or where the opposition is in a weak position to defeat Charter-inspired amendments; and use political threats to transform a vote into an issue of confidence, thus changing the dynamics of debate.

As discussed in chapter 2, the original intent of the section 4.1 statutory obligation that the minister of justice report to Parliament when government is introducing legislation that is inconsistent with protected rights was to discourage government from unknowingly introducing rights-offending legislation, ensure government leaders are prepared to acknowledge and justify the merits of such inconsistent legislation, and facilitate Parliament's ability and willingness to hold government to account for legislative decisions that infringe upon rights. However, these ideals have not been able to overcome the political dynamics of how Canada's parliamentary system functions.

Far from improving transparency and accountability for legislation that implicates rights adversely, the record of parliamentary scrutiny of Harper's tough-on-crime agenda underscores worrying indications that the bureaucratic and political manner in which Charter assessments are made and the section 4.1 statutory reporting obligation is interpreted hinders rather than improves Parliament's ability to pressure government to explain or justify decisions that implicate rights. This reporting obligation is functioning in a manner that routinely sends parliamentarians the misleading message that if there is no report of Charter inconsistency under section 4.1 they have no need to question whether a bill complies with the Charter. In effect, this political context is leveraged to provide false assurances of Charter consistency and masks very low standards used for affirming Charter consistency.

An additional obstacle for parliamentary scrutiny has been the government's reliance on the idea of "client confidentiality" or solicitor-client privilege to withhold from Parliament the legal advice upon which it relies, and to refuse to explain or justify the assumptions used for concluding that legislation is consistent with the Charter, even when these are strongly contested. However, the premise of this claim, that the government is a client and thus legal opinions about Charter compatibility must be treated as confidential, is not only inconsistent with the public interest but is also challenged by practices elsewhere, such as New Zealand, which has a statutory reporting obligation modelled upon Canada's section 4.1 requirement and where legal advice is published along with the name of the author of the opinion.[83]

Finally, the fact that key provisions of the Conservative government's legislative agenda were struck down or narrowed by the courts adds context to our analysis that the government did not take Charter issues as seriously as it might have. We stop short of suggesting judicial invalidation is itself proof that the government knowingly introduced legislation that was likely unconstitutional. For one thing, jurisprudence can change, as is evident in the context of mandatory minimum sentences. For another, we take the position that courts can get it wrong: Charter interpretation is a political and values-laden exercise, and the courts are not always well equipped to deal with the complex policy issues that come before them, especially in assessing and balancing proportionality concerns. Yet this is all the more reason it is incumbent on Parliament and the government to take their constitutional obligations under the Charter seriously and to engage in robust and independent deliberation about the rights implications of legislation. The fact that many of the critics' concerns about the Harper government's criminal justice policies bore out is thus relevant to any analysis of whether they did so here, and adds further support to our conclusion that these processes are impoverished.

4 Legislative Responses under the Charter: Harm Reduction and Drug Policy

In 2008 the federal minister of health refused to extend an exemption under the Controlled Drugs and Substances Act (CDSA) to Insite, then Canada's only supervised drug injection facility. Three years later, in *PHS Community Services Society*,[1] the Supreme Court determined that this decision constituted a violation of Insite's clients' section 7 right to life, liberty, and security of the person under the Charter of Rights and Freedoms. This chapter examines Parliament's legislative responses to the decision. Specifically, it explores parliamentary debate to examine the extent to which the government and parliamentarians assessed the policy response in light of their own considerations of the Charter or what they believe judicial policy prescriptions and judicial norms about the Charter requires. Analysing the legislative debates also uncovers differences between the government and the opposition's approach to debating the merits of policy objectives and the degree to which they articulate a desire to comply with, or depart from, the dictates of the Court's decision.

Following the Court's decision, the government decided to develop a policy to establish how ministerial exemptions would be provided for the proposed creation of new supervised consumption facilities. As described below, the Court's decision laid out a set of criteria the minister must consider when making a determination, but beyond that left the CDSA's provisions permitting ministerial discretion intact (indeed, the Court upheld the CDSA itself in part because of the availability of a ministerial exemption).[2] The Conservative government's legislative response, in the form of Bill C-2, relied on this part of the Court's decision to establish a lengthy list of specific criteria that critics argued would make it exceedingly onerous for jurisdictions that want to open a facility. The government defended the legislative scheme on the basis that the criteria it established were based on those identified by the Court itself. When the Liberals later formed government, they introduced Bill C-37, repealing the Conservative legislation and amending the CDSA to model the ministerial exemption provisions more precisely on the five criteria identified by the Court.

Our analysis of the parliamentary debates over both bills finds that there is very little explicit analysis by either government that focuses on Charter considerations. Each government defended its legislation as compatible with the Court's reasons in *PHS*. Each legislative scheme reflected the respective government's policy objectives: the Conservatives were generally hostile to supervised injection as a harm-reduction strategy, and the Liberals generally supported approving new facilities for jurisdictions that applied for them. We find that policy objectives and at least the appearance of compliance with the Supreme Court are the relevant factors motivating decisions by governments in this case, with little apparent independent consideration of rights or the Charter itself, even on aspects of the policy where potential rights implications remain unaddressed by the Court. Further, when rights are invoked by opposition members, it is usually in the context of asserting a particular interpretation of the Court's decision rather than asserting an independent vision of what the Charter requires. We conclude the chapter with an exploration of the implications these findings might have for both policy development and implementation and for future rights litigation.

Background

The supervised injection site in Vancouver's Downtown Eastside (DTES) neighbourhood emerged as a product of a multilevel governance agreement between the federal government, the province of British Columbia (BC), the city of Vancouver, and non-governmental organizations. This cooperation was a response to the health crisis experienced within the DTES as reflected in interconnected problems of crime, mental illness, and poverty.[3] The Vancouver Agreement, established in 2000, outlined collaborative strategies to improve the economic and social situation of the DTES. Broad health policy objectives included stabilizing the crisis by reducing preventable deaths and the spread of infectious diseases, such as HIV/AIDS.[4] An important element of this health policy is a comprehensive substance misuse strategy, including reducing harm and deaths associated with substance misuse.[5]

Insite is a supervised injection site that represents one component of the harm-reduction strategy within the Vancouver Agreement's larger policy framework. The facility operates under an exemption of

the CDSA (thus ensuring that staff and clients are not subject to criminal law prohibitions on the possession of otherwise illegal drugs).
At the time Insite was established, section 56 of CDSA stated that the
federal minister of health can grant an exemption from the Act if it is
"for a medical or scientific purpose or is otherwise in the public interest."[6] The exemption for Insite was initially granted in 2003 and was
extended twice. However, the Conservative government determined
that a further exemption would not be granted past 30 June 2008. This
prompted PHS Community Services Society, a non-profit society that
co-manages Insite, two Insite clients, and the Vancouver Area Network
of Drug Users (VANDU) to launch a legal challenge. The BC Supreme
Court and a majority of the BC Court of Appeal both found that the
discretion permitted under the CDSA to provide exemptions created a
violation of Insite's users' right to life, liberty, and security of the person
under section 7 of the Charter.[7]

On appeal, the Supreme Court delivered a unanimous decision that
the health minister's decision to close Insite, despite evidence that
Insite provides life-saving treatment, violates section 7.[8] Although section 7 rights were engaged, the Supreme Court stopped short of finding that the prohibitions in the CDSA were unconstitutional or that the
provisions permitting ministerial exemption contravened the Charter.[9]
Rather, the Court ruled that the minister's specific decision to refuse
an exemption to Insite was arbitrary and grossly disproportionate to
its goals of balancing public safety and health.[10] The only remedy the
Court found satisfactory was for the minister to grant an exemption for
Insite as long as the facility continued meeting its objectives of promoting public health and safety.[11]

Having left the legislative scheme for the provision of exemptions under the CDSA intact, and limited its decision to the minister's refusal to
extend the exemption for Insite in this instance, the Court minimized the
potential policy impact of its decision. The chief justice, writing for the
unanimous Court, explicitly stated that the ruling "is not a licence for
injection drug users to possess drugs wherever and whenever they wish.
Nor is it an invitation for anyone who so chooses to open a facility for
drug use under the banner of a 'safe injection facility.'"[12] What the Charter requires, the Court stated, is an exercise of discretion under the CDSA
that is not arbitrary and that does not impose grossly disproportionate
harm on those suffering from addiction when balanced against the potential benefits of maintaining a prohibition on possessing illegal drugs.[13]

The standard articulated by the Court is clear as it applies to Insite,
but less so as it applies to what a Charter-compliant policy governing
the creation of new safe consumption facilities in other parts of Canada

ought to look like. Moreover, the rights implications of the Court's minimalist approach in this case are complex. The Court has avoided imposing any positive duty on the federal government or provinces to open new consumption facilities where there might be demand, although its decision prevents any government from closing Insite so long as demand remains, because doing so would threaten the lives and security of the person of its clients. In effect, those suffering from addiction in Vancouver have a constitutional right of access to a health service while those in other parts of the country do not. This tension in the logic of the decision is a by-product of an approach to section 7 of the Charter that is rooted in a "negative rights" context – where rights are perceived as protecting individuals from state interference – as opposed to protecting "positive rights," which would require the state to fund or provide rights like a right to health care.[14] The Court has thus far refused to read section 7 as providing for positive rights,[15] and it is beyond the scope of our analysis to engage in the normative debate about whether it should.

What we want to briefly point out, however, is that a consequence of the Court's approach is that there was less clarity for the federal and provincial governments on the constitutional standard by which to approve or seek the creation of new safe consumption facilities. At the time, the evidence relied on by the Court to arrive at its conclusions regarding the health and safety of Insite's clients depended heavily on the particular circumstances of Insite and the problems endemic in the DTES of Vancouver. Indeed, as a pilot program established to support research, Insite provided a unique context for the Court to make its decision. Those seeking to open new facilities had the burden of demonstrating a need where there might not be as acute or evident a drug problem as there was in the DTES of Vancouver.

Things have since changed, particularly in light of an ongoing opioid crisis and a change in government that views harm reduction as an important component to dealing with it. There is now much more evidence about the effectiveness of supervised consumption sites generally, and there are, at the time of writing, forty-five approved sites across the country, in five provinces.[16] Our analysis, however, is on the immediate policy response to the Court's 2011 decision, when the evidence focused on the context of the DTES of Vancouver and the constitutional threshold for when a ministerial exemption might be required was not clear as a result of the Court's narrow focus.

In that context, even the fact of Insite's existence – that the federal government was attempting to shut down a facility that was already operating – marks an important distinction from subsequent attempts to seek a CDSA exemption to open *new* facilities. As a result, the Court's minimalist approach in *PHS* arguably diminishes the clarity of the decision as it regards future policy decisions on new facilities. On the one hand, this is problematic to the extent that it could lead to the asymmetrical rights protection and policy implementation described above. On the other hand, the Court left the door open for Parliament to develop its own guidelines on future decisions on exemptions under the CDSA regime. We explore the governments' and Parliament's response in the next section.

The Conservative Government's Response: Bill C-2 – The Respect for Communities Act (2015)

The Conservative government's response to the Court's decision came in the form of Bill C-2, the Respect for Communities Act. Its provisions would require anyone applying to open a new supervised consumption facility to provide the minister of health with a plethora of information that, in turn, serve as principal criteria for the minister to determine whether or not a proposed site would receive an exemption under the CDSA. The bill lists no fewer than twenty-six criteria, including scientific and medical evidence demonstrating the benefits of the proposed site; letters from the provincial ministers of health and public safety outlining their opinions, as well as from the local government, head of the local police force, and local health officials; data, including trends, on the number of drug users, crime rates, overdose deaths, and diseases in the vicinity of the proposed site, including coroner's reports; and a report of "consultations held with a broad range of community groups" and responses to any concerns they might express. The requirements also include "any other information that the Minister considers relevant." The bill specified that the minister is permitted to make a decision only once all of these pieces of information are submitted.

The Canadian Medical Association and other critics of the bill argued that the federal government was creating "unnecessary obstacles and burdens" to prevent the creation of new supervised injection sites.[17] The new CDSA provisions imposed significant requirements on any applicants seeking to open new facilities, but it is not clear whether they failed to reflect the standard articulated by the Court. On the one hand, the criteria listed in Bill C-2 are generally consistent with the sort of factors the chief justice identifies in her decision:

> [The Minister's] discretion must be exercised in accordance with the *Charter*. This requires the Minister to consider whether denying an exemption

would cause deprivations of life and security of the person that are not in accordance with the principles of fundamental justice. The factors considered in making the decision on an exemption must include evidence, if any, on the impact of such a facility on crime rates, the local conditions indicating a need for such a supervised injection site, the regulatory structure in place to support the facility, the resources available to support its maintenance, and expressions of community support or opposition.[18]

On the other hand, and despite the above, it remains unclear when factors like crime rates or "expressions of community support or opposition" outweigh the harms associated with not providing users with a facility. As noted above, the Court carefully limited the scope of its decision to Insite – an instance where the facility had already been operating and on the basis that shutting it down would create unjustifiable risks to the lives and health of its clients. The justices expressly avoided imposing broader policy implications, such as a positive right requiring governments to provide services where they are not already available.

Regardless of whether Bill C-2 lives up to the requirements imposed by the Charter, how are we to assess the government's response to the Supreme Court's decision in *PHS*? In the remaining sections of this chapter we focus on parliamentarians' understandings of their own obligations under the Charter on the rights and policy objectives at stake. We eschew an investigation of whether the legislative response constituted a "dialogue" for an approach that focuses on the role conceptions legislators have of their place as policymakers in relation to the constitutional requirements imposed by the Charter and the Court. This permits a richer assessment of Parliament's response to a Court decision than one reduced to investigating whether there was mere compliance with the judicial ruling.

In the next section we analyse legislative debate over Insite and Bill C-2 to discover the extent to which government and opposition MPs consider what the Charter requires and which constraints are imposed by the Court's decision. This analysis considers the discrete issue of whether parliamentarians articulate their own understanding of what the constitution requires, as distinct from the Court's interpretation; whether there is evidence that their primary consideration is adherence to the Court's ruling; or whether there is little consideration of either of these things. Although this helps to address the question of whether there is judicial finality on the policy at stake, our examination of the debate permits a broader enquiry: Are rights considerations central to the legislative debate on the policy response, or is the focus on maintaining the original policy objectives at stake irrespective of considerations about constitutionality? On the latter question, is there a clear distinction between how the government and opposition members approach these issues? As such, how do we assess the policy change that ultimately results from the inter-institutional interaction over the Charter?

Parliamentary Debate: Insite and Bill C-2

From its initial decision to refuse to extend the CDSA exemption for Insite, the federal Conservative government maintained that the scientific evidence did not unequivocally support the effectiveness of a harm-reduction strategy that includes supervised consumption. The health minister at the time, Tony Clement, described research on the effectiveness of supervised injection facilities as "mixed," noting that "more than 95% of injections occur outside Insite and less than 10% of addicts used Insite for all of their injections."[19] The government's narrative in advancing and defending Bill C-2 was consistent with this view. As noted above, while the Supreme Court's decision in *PHS* does not make clear whether Bill C-2's onerous provisions for approving CDSA exemptions meet constitutional muster, the government's defence of the new law clearly reflects an effort to ensure enforcement of the CDSA and to mitigate the expansion of consumption sites in other jurisdictions.

In parliamentary debate on Insite, the government repeatedly emphasized that there was divided public opinion on supervised consumption. While there was consensus among scientific experts on Insite, there were groups and individuals who opposed the facility. From the outset of the legal challenge in 2008, the government highlighted the Canadian Police Association's concerns about the model of harm reduction through safe consumption sites to show there was not "unanimous approval" for them.[20] The government also brought forward a petition by the Canadian Alliance for Social Justice and Family Values Association. The alliance, based in Vancouver, opposed any continuation of Insite.[21] The government leveraged these statements in an attempt to show that other actors were pressing it to adopt an alternative approach to addiction.[22] Legislative debates prior to the Supreme Court's ruling in 2011 centred on realizing the most effective drug policy with little explicit concern regarding Charter rights.

The government's position remained consistent after the BC Supreme Court declared unconstitutional the minister's decision to withhold a further exemption. Expressing "respectful disagreement" with the Court decision, Clement further stated the government's intent to reassert its legislative objective to promote drug prevention because "injection is not medicine [that] heal[s] the addict."[23] The government also warned that safe consumption sites are not supported by stakeholders in other cities. Conservative MP Steven Fletcher quoted the chief medical officer in Toronto as saying that "a facility similar to Insite would be ineffective and that other proven strategies are working well to help Torontonians get off drugs."[24]

There was scant engagement by the government with the trial judge's reasoning that the minster's decision violated Insite clients' section 7 rights; the government's "respectful disagreement" was reflected by the pending appeal of the decision. After the Supreme Court decision, the government stated it would comply with the ruling but reasserted its position that "the system should be focused on preventing people from becoming drug addicts in the first place."[25] For their part, the opposition parties emphasized the Court's findings that Insite saves lives and that closing it violates the rights of its clients. Others went further, suggesting that respecting "the intent and effect" of the Court's decision meant that under the Charter, and specifically section 7, exemptions must be granted.[26]

When Bill C-2 was first tabled, the government framed the legislation as respecting "the high bar set by the Supreme Court for supervised consumption sites" while also achieving its commitment to ensure that "communities have a say in any decisions made."[27] The government also pointed to the Court's decision to justify the way it structured the new approval process for exemptions under the Act. The long list of factors and evidence that communities wishing to establish safe consumption sites are required to supply to the minister for an exemption, the government argued, builds directly upon the criteria articulated by the Court.[28] The government stressed that the Court's decision was rooted in Insite's life-saving treatment taking place within the unique and exceptional circumstances of Vancouver's DTES. It thus follows, from the government's perspective, that future exemptions be subject to strict conditions to ensure "that exemptions to undertake activities with them should be limited to rare or unique circumstances."[29] The rigorous set of criteria was also justified on the basis that it was in accordance with the Court's assertion that its decision should not be interpreted as allowing "anyone who so chooses to open a facility for drug use under the banner of a 'safe injection facility'" to do so.[30]

The five factors articulated by the Court that the health minister must consider when granting an exemption are "evidence, if any, on the impact of such a facility on crime rates, the local conditions indicating a need for such a supervised injection site, the regulatory structure in place to support the facility, the resources available to support its maintenance, and expressions of community support or opposition."[31] As noted above, Bill C-2 considerably expanded the Court's criteria, and it is not obvious how a minister should weigh the various pieces of information.

The opposition criticized the bill as arbitrary and as providing the minister with too much discretion to refuse an exemption if there was community opposition to a supervised consumption site, contrasting the bill's wording, which notes that the minister "may" grant an exemption, with the Court's statement that an exemption "should generally be granted" if a safe consumption site saves lives.[32]

The opposition generally expressed a view that the Court had declared a Charter right to access life-saving treatment for drug users. While some statements focused explicitly on Insite's clients enjoying a right to treatment,[33] others went further, suggesting that since section 7 rights are guaranteed to all individuals, all drug users have a right to access treatment.[34] Opposition members also criticized Bill C-2 for failing to demonstrate balance between the considerations of public safety and public health when making determinations about exemptions. They argued that because the bill made no mention of the benefits of supervised consumption, the government over-emphasized concerns for public safety[35] in a manner that departs from the Court's direction that the minister must "strike the appropriate balance between achieving the public health and public safety goals."[36] There was also speculation from the opposition benches that "the government is hoping it can do an end run around, or even circumvent, the Supreme Court judgment by downplaying, in the new amendments to the CDSA, references to the positive health effects of a system like the injection site system and to public health, despite the fact that public health remains one of the two purposes of the CDSA."[37]

NDP MP Craig Scott linked the government's decision-making to the weak section 4.1(1) process, even citing the Edgar Schmidt case that we explore in chapter 2:

Here I would like to believe that the Minister of Justice has had thorough advice from his officials on the constitutionality of the bill so as to exercise the duty he has under section 4.1(1) of the Department of Justice Act. Regrettably, we have all come to learn in the last year that the standard of review that goes on in the Department of Justice these days, and perhaps for longer than we realize, borders on the farcical. A whistleblower has come forward to tell us that instructions have been sent to lawyers to say that if there is a 5% chance that a provision or law would pass muster in the courts under the charter, then it is fine to recommend that it go ahead as being constitutional from the perspective of introducing the law. I have no confidence at all that the mere fact that this is before the House means that some kind of analysis has been undertaken that suggests that it is presumptively constitutional. Under the current government, that is not the case.[38]

For its part, the government asserted Parliament's role in the policy process and questioned whether elected representatives should rely on speculation about what the Court may or may not say about the constitutionality of legislation introduced in the House:

I am fascinated by the member presuming what the Supreme Court will or will not say. If we follow his logic to its logical conclusion, we should not even have the debate and just go straight to the Supreme Court, but the fact is that Parliament will vote on this legislation. As we are all representatives of the people of Canada, the people of Canada would agree that the preamble of the bill, which I have read in part already, is sound and important for public safety and communities. We are putting communities and families first and we do have additional programs, other than being complicit in the illicit drug trade. Why does the member want to be complicit in the illegal drug trade?[39]

Taken to an extreme, this statement implies that questions of constitutionality are not relevant in Parliament's consideration of a bill on the merits. At the very least, it reflects the government's general attitude in defending Bill C-2, which involved virtually no direct engagement with the Court's section 7 analysis regarding decisions to grant exemptions. Instead, the main focus of the government was the pursuit of its policy objectives of health and community safety.

The Standing Committee on Public Safety and National Security's deliberations on Bill C-2 largely reflected the debate from the House floor. Opposition NDP member Libby Davies argued that even the choice of committee reflected the government's ideological approach to the issue, noting "the fact that it's coming to the public safety committee, not health, is a very clear signal about the government's biases."[40] Davies pushed then minister of health Rona Ambrose on whether she believed that drug users have a right to access safe consumption sites. Ambrose essentially refused to say, responding that "what I will say is that my obligation when considering an exemption for proposed section 56 is now clearly laid out by the Supreme Court of Canada."[41] The minister also emphasized the government's commitment to treatment and its funding for prevention and treatment. In answering questions from other opposition members on the committee about the success of "prevention" models, Ambrose repeatedly cited her adherence to the Court's ruling and balancing the criteria outlined by the Court. As she did from the House floor, Ambrose also repeated the line from the Court's ruling that it was not "an invitation for anyone who so chooses to open a facility for drug use under the banner of a 'safe' ... [consumption] facility."

There was little discussion about whatever rights users might actually hold under the Charter. Then public safety minister Steven Blaney was even more direct about his considerations focusing on community opinion and safety before the committee, noting,

> Why I'm here today is to fully support Minister Ambrose, who is abiding by the law and the court decision and also making sure that a community that could potentially be impacted by such a facility would be consulted. I think as a democrat you would certainly agree that it is more than obvious that, if I were to have the prospect of such a facility facing my neighbourhood, I would be involved in the process and it would not be left to others to decide what my neighbourhood would look like in five or ten years.[42]

Blaney's answers reflected a framing that privileged the interests of people living in the vicinity of a potential consumption site, with no apparent consideration of the potential Charter rights at stake.

The committee heard from twenty witnesses, including the two ministers, senior members from the Departments of Health, Justice, and Public Safety, the RCMP, several police associations, the Canadian Drug Policy Coalition, and the Pivot Legal Society, among others. Some of the witnesses, including those from the Drug Prevention Network of Canada, REAL Women of Canada, and Safer Ottawa, spoke out against supervised consumption sites. Several of the police-affiliated witnesses refused to enter into the debate about the merits of supervised consumption sites, either emphasizing that decisions about establishing sites should balance public health and public safety concerns and should involve local input (thus supporting the general aims of Bill C-2) or appearing to provide context about local efforts to combat drug use and associated ills.

By contrast, other witnesses were heavily critical of the bill. The witness for the Pivot Legal Society, Adrienne Smith, argued Bill C-2 "will likely not withstand constitutional scrutiny" and "will result in needless human suffering for some of the most vulnerable Canadians." She argued that the Court's decision means that "when there is not evidence of a public safety threat, exemption must generally be granted...."

What Bill C-2 does is a significant departure from that. It answers the requirement that exemptions generally be granted, which the court directed, with a presumption in the bill that exemptions will generally be withheld."[43] The Canadian Drug Policy Coalition criticized the bill on the basis of the "extremely onerous extra layer of work" it adds to a community wishing to bring in harm-reduction measures and for "advocating a focus on public safety at the expense of public health."[44] The Conservative majority on the committee were not swayed by this testimony, and the bill was returned to the House with no amendments.

In sum, both the government and opposition interpreted parts of the Court's ruling to fit their preferred narratives during debate over supervised consumption facilities. While some opposition members may interpret the scope of the Court's decision too broadly by suggesting it pronounced a general right of access to safe consumption facilities, their focus on the spirit of the decision by invoking and emphasizing rights concerns was evident. Whether this was strategic or reflected a genuine concern about rights is difficult to discern. By contrast, the government framed the Court decision as presenting particular barriers to legislative objectives that must be met in a way that best complemented their initial objectives. So long as these specific restraints were met, in a narrow sense, there was no perceived need for the government to participate in a broader debate about the Charter rights implicated.

Assessing the Bill C-2 Debate

Our analysis thus far has focused on how the Supreme Court and Parliament have treated the policy and rights issues at stake in relation to Insite. The Court did not directly engage with the question of whether those suffering from addiction have a right to health services, but the decision clearly raised implications of a positive right to access,[45] particularly in the eyes of some members of the opposition. The Conservative government, for its part, failed to address the primary rights question emanating from the case and instead seized on the caution expressed by the Court on how its decision should be interpreted. The Court made great effort to avoid having its decision interpreted in a way that supported a positive right to access for drug users, even though, in effect, the result ensured precisely that for those with addiction in Vancouver. In the result, the justices' reasoning was vague with respect to what rights implications flowed from their decision for future proposals for supervised consumption facilities. The government's failure to explicitly frame policy objectives with the rights implications at the forefront, and the Court's carefully circumscribed reasoning, arguably left a vacuum in which drug users' access to life-saving treatment depends on where they live in the country.

By engaging directly with the Court's rationale as it applies to Insite, some opposition members seemingly inferred that all drug users have a positive right to supervised injection facilities under section 7. This interpretation of the ruling could also be strategic: opposition members were highly critical of the government's approach to harm prevention, and the Court's decision armed them with a point of attack. The opposition was interpreting the Court's ruling to fit their own policy preference to establish more supervised consumption sites across the country.

House debate also reveals how Parliament has at least some capacity to engage in questions of constitutionality and Charter rights in the course of its legislating and particularly in the opposition's efforts to hold the government to account. However, our analysis reveals that the debate was ultimately not a wide-ranging or comprehensive assessment of rights. On balance, rights questions were raised as points of criticism, and the government's unwillingness to engage on those terms limited the opposition's capacity to shift the focus to the Charter or its interpretation by the Court.

Parliamentary debate over Bill C-2 and future supervised consumption facilities took place in the context of a unique decision by the Court. As such, the analysis thus far does not permit generalizable conclusions about the nature of judicial-legislative interaction over the Charter. Nevertheless, as a landmark decision on section 7, the case stands as an important potential model for evaluating Parliament's considerations of its constitutional obligations, particularly on Charter cases that demand policy responses. The Insite case reveals a government willing to address the unconstitutional elements of its previous policies (in a narrow fashion, at least) while ignoring or downplaying the broader rights implications of its new legislation.

The case also exposes the extent to which Parliament can fail to seriously consider the Charter implications of its legislation and its constitutional obligations to protect rights. While the opposition members emphasized in a more substantial way the Court's section 7 analysis, parliamentary debate over Bill C-2 was far from a robust debate over the policy from a rights-protecting perspective.

The Liberal Government and Repeal of Bill C-2

The Liberals formed government in 2015 and introduced amendments to the Controlled Drugs and Substances Act in late 2016 in the form of Bill C-37. Among the amendments were provisions to replace the onerous approval process established by Bill C-2 with one that exclusively focuses on the factors identified by the Supreme Court in *PHS Community Services*. Applicants would no longer face a list of twenty-six criteria and instead would be expected to provide information on five matters, if any evidence was available: the impact of the site on crime rates; the local conditions indicating a need for the site; the administrative structure in place to support the site; the resources available to support the maintenance of the site; and expressions of community support or opposition. The legislative description of the criteria matches almost exactly the language the Court used in outlining relevant factors for consideration.

In defending the decision to establish these five factors in parliamentary debate, the health minister stated,

> [The] legislation would simplify and streamline the application process for communities that want and need to establish supervised consumption sites. It would replace the current 26 application criteria with the five factors outlined in the Supreme Court of Canada 2011 decision regarding Insite. In fact, the criteria in the proposed legislation are exactly those written in paragraph 153 of the Supreme Court decision.[46]

This talking point, citing adherence to the Supreme Court's policy prescription, was repeated by the government side throughout debate about Bill C-37. For example, when CPC MP Michelle Rempel argued that it was not necessarily clear from the legislation how the criteria were defined or what information would be required to meet them, Liberal MP Raj Grewal's response was to simply cite the Court: "Does the hon. member agree with the Supreme Court of Canada's 2011 ruling on Insite? In that ruling, the Supreme Court laid out five criteria for safe injection sites. I would like her comments on that, and specifically whether she agrees with the Supreme Court."[47] Rempel responded that Parliament had its own responsibility to craft legislation, regardless of whatever prescription the Court might make: "I reject the notion that the Supreme Court of Canada defines everything we do in this place. It is our responsibility as legislators to come up with the best possible legislation, and I still argue that the health minister has not defined these criteria in here. Just because the Supreme Court says something does not mean that we have to abdicate our responsibility to come up with legislation that makes sense and is clear."[48] Far from suggesting Parliament was free to outright defy the Court, Rempel's statement is consistent with the Conservative position that legislation can build upon or fill in specifics rather than merely and narrowly match judicial policy prescriptions. By contrast, the Liberal position was that given Bill C-2 established an overly onerous and therefore constitutionally suspect process, the best solution was to mirror the Court's policy pre-scription as closely as possible.

Nevertheless, the Charter itself was almost never mentioned as a fac-tor supporting the amendments. There is no evidence in the parliamen-tary record that suggests the Liberal government made an independent assessment of what a Charter-compatible approval process for future sites should look like. How should the various factors be weighed to ensure a rights-compatible decision-making process? What measures are necessary and connected to the potential harms at stake to ensure outcomes are not arbitrary? Rather than engaging on these questions with explicit consideration of the rights at stake, the government re-lied on adherence to the five factors outlined in a single paragraph of the Court's ruling – a list that was not necessarily intended to be com-prehensive. Further, although the minister of justice began releasing Charter compatibility statements on government legislation in 2016, no compatibility statement was issued for Bill C-37.

Two broader components of parliamentary debate over Bill C-37 are worth noting. First, most of the debate was framed in light of an on-going opioid crisis that had resulted in 2,861 deaths in 2016 alone, ac-cording to the government of Canada.[49] The vast majority of questions and comments to the minister of health in reference to Bill C-37 were about the opioid crisis and other policies and resources to address that problem.[50]

On the specific question of approving future supervised consump-tion sites, however, the Conservative opposition stuck firmly to the po-sition they held while in power:

> Under the previous Conservative government, we took steps to ensure there was a robust consultation process which included residents, local law enforcement agencies, and elected officials to be on board with an in-jection site in their community. Bill C-37 proposes to significantly change those requirements. While the expression of community support for op-position is a requirement, the specific requirements have been removed to allow the Liberals to easily change them as they see fit. This is a way to completely avoid parliamentary oversight. The minister's attempt to avoid community approval will fail.[51]

To the extent that Conservative members raised rights issues, it was the "rights of communities to provide their input" in any approval process.[52]

By contrast, NDP MP Don Davies arguably adopted the opposite extreme, characterizing the Supreme Court's ruling on Insite as suggesting that "other supervised consumption sites *must* be granted a section 56 exemption from the Controlled Drugs and Substances Act because they 'decrease the risk of death and disease, and there is little or no evidence that it will have a negative impact on public safety.'"[53] In fact, while the Court stated that the minister should *generally* grant exemptions where those factors are indicated, it explicitly grounded its decision in relation to the minister's exercise of discretion regarding Insite and cautioned against the notion that its reasoning fettered the minister's discretion on future decisions.[54] Moreover, the entire point of establishing criteria by which future decisions are made implies that evidence pertaining to those criteria can affect the outcome of any application, on a case-by-case basis.

A second key element of the debate occurred in relation to three amendments proposed by the Senate. Senate Conservatives proposed a minimum of forty-five days for the public to comment on new supervised injection sites, the establishment of citizen advisory committees to write annual reports on public concerns about the presence of sites in their community, and a requirement for doctors at sites to offer substitute pharmaceuticals to drug users as an alternative to the drugs they bring in off the street. The government accepted the forty-five-day consultation period, rejected the citizen advisory committee as an unnecessary burden on supervised consumption facilities, and altered the wording of the third proposal by making the decision to offer alternative pharmaceuticals optional (replacing the words "shall offer" with "may offer"). None of the debate over the Senate amendments invoked Charter considerations. Bill C-37 received royal assent on 18 May 2017.

Policy Impact: Lessons for Constitutional Assessments?

Bill C-2 was criticized for defying the Supreme Court's *PHS* decision by making the approval process for supervised injection sites overly burdensome. The Conservative government's legislation was framed by the opposition as an attempt to prevent the establishment of any new sites. In defending the bill, Conservatives argued that the plethora of criteria applicants had to meet under the process included (and largely reflected) the criteria outlined by the Court. It is far from certain that the legislative scheme would have been found unconstitutional had it been subject to judicial review. The legislation left the minister of health with the ultimate discretion to weigh the criteria and make a determination about approval. In fact, the Liberal minister of health approved two new supervised injection facilities for Montreal under the Bill C-2 scheme. Further, several more facilities whose applications were largely developed under the old scheme (two in Surrey, BC, one in Toronto, and another one in Montreal) were approved less than a month after the new Liberal legislation, Bill C-37, received royal assent. At the very least this suggests that the Bill C-2 legislative scheme did not remove ministerial discretion entirely or preclude the possibility of approval.

The Liberal government defended its repeal of the Bill C-2 approval process on the basis that streamlining the requirements would make it more efficient and in order to more directly follow the criteria established by the Court. Since the new scheme was enacted (not counting the seven sites granted exemptions that were effectively processed under the old statutory regime), thirty-eight new supervised consumption sites have been approved (in Alberta, Ontario, British Columbia, Quebec, and Saskatchewan).[55] At the time of writing, a further ten applications for exemption are open. It is impossible to definitively assess whether all of these approvals would have occurred under the old system, but however burdensome an administrative process Bill C-2 imposed, the legislative requirements largely left ministerial discretion intact on the final decision. Whether there were twenty-six factors or five, it is unlikely that a Conservative health minister would weigh the criteria in the same way as a Liberal one, given the parties' positions on the utility of supervised consumption sites generally.

Does the discretion available to the minister under either legislative scheme make them arbitrary? Critics of Bill C-2 argued that the scheme did not provide sufficient protection against arbitrariness, in part because it did "not indicate what level of information, research, opposition or support would result in an application being accepted or denied."[56] This is no less true of the new approval process laid out in Bill C-37. Likely a court would allow for some discretion in the weighing of various factors. A decision to refuse an application could be upheld so long as the minister's decision rested on some evidence indicating strong community opposition, public safety concerns, or calling into question the need for a facility. Nonetheless, the goal of this analysis is not to argue whether either legislative scheme holds up to Charter scrutiny. Instead, there are important conclusions to be drawn about how the two governments approached the policy issue and about the nature of parliamentary deliberation over Bill C-2 and Bill C-37.

The most immediate conclusion to draw from this analysis is that there is little evidence of serious, independent government assessment of the compatibility of the legislation with the Charter. Similarly, debate in the House of Commons rarely explored what a Charter-compatible process should look like. In relation to each bill, both governments cited the Supreme Court's decision in *PHS* in support of their legislative scheme. Yet as noted above, the Court's decision provides little guidance about future ministerial decisions under the CDSA. The governments' reliance on the Court's prescription ultimately leaves myriad constitutional questions unanswered. These include perhaps the most pertinent question of how the minister should weigh the criteria to avoid an arbitrary decision under the Charter to the more fundamental rights-related question of whether there might be a Charter right to supervised consumption sites.

One fundamental issue virtually absent in parliamentary debates on legislative responses to judicial decisions is that there is often more than one Charter right implicated by specific policy issues. The Supreme Court will often rest its decisions on a single provision of the Charter – in this case, section 7 – and in instances where laws were deemed unconstitutional the justices will often find it unnecessary to address other Charter arguments. Yet consistency with the rest of the Charter ought to remain a crucial consideration in the development of new legislation. In the context of supervised consumption sites, one obvious right implicated by access to the service is the section 15 equality rights of those suffering from addiction. Properly regarded as both a health issue and a disability, a failure by the state to provide adequate health services for those suffering from addiction is arguably discriminatory on the basis of disability under the Charter.[57] Yet because of their focus on the Court's decision rather than the Charter itself, parliamentarians and the government fail to attend to equality rights or other rights considerations in drafting and scrutinizing the legislative responses. This oversight seriously weakens the extent to which we can have confidence that the legislative process suitably protects rights.

Governments have a strategic interest in remaining within the dictates of the Supreme Court's written reasons, even where the Court has not been clear or specific in its policy prescription. If the Court's decision provides ambiguity or latitude within which a government can pursue its preferred policy objectives, then engaging in a serious consideration of how best to meet Charter standards – or indeed, to define what the Charter standards should be in relation to a particular policy – only risks creating an impediment to meeting its preferences.

Consider an unsettled constitutional question that arises from the Court's own decision in *PHS*. The Court stated that the minister should generally grant an exemption in cases where there is evidence that a facility will decrease the risk of death and disease and there is little to no evidence of an impact on public health and safety. Nevertheless, the Court also identifies community expressions of support or opposition as one of five criteria a minister must consider in making a determination. Assuming the other factors supported granting an exemption, would a ministerial decision denying an exemption on the basis of strong community opposition withstand constitutional scrutiny? The Court's reasons do not tell us. On the one hand, such a decision might be regarded as arbitrary, given the section 7 rights at stake. On the other hand, it is unclear why the Court would list community public opinion as a relevant criterion for consideration in the first place. Public opinion should be a largely irrelevant determinant of whether individual rights are protected and yet for some reason the Court decided to list it as one of the criteria for consideration.

It is this sort of ambiguity that Parliament and successive governments had opportunities to address through careful, independent consideration of what the Charter might require. Both the Conservative and Liberal versions of the legislative scheme effectively leave the resolution of such questions to the discretion of the minister, without having enquired into whether denying exemptions in such cases would be consistent with the Charter. For the current government, this is unlikely to have constitutional implications – the resulting policy achieves the objectives of streamlining the process to ensure efficient approvals for new sites. Yet because the legislative process paid little heed to potential Charter issues beyond the Court's reasons, future governments run the risk of facing further litigation if applications are denied, even if they are, as the government itself emphasizes, based on the very criteria established by the Court. These questions are further raised when provinces seek to close safe consumption sites after they have opened, a context that emerged in Alberta in 2021.[58]

Conclusions

Our analysis of the Conservative government's legislative response to *PHS* mirrors our findings in the preceding chapter on criminal justice policy. Legislative development was executive-dominated. With the benefit of its majority in the House, the government did not need to pay much heed to the constitutional and policy concerns of health experts, advocates for people suffering from addition, or legal experts. The legislative debate was far from a rigorous discussion about rights and the Charter. Given that the government could point to part of the Court's decision to support the inclusion of a set of criteria for making determinations about exemptions under the CDSA, it is not surprising that no section 4.1 statement by the minister of justice was forthcoming. It is far from certain that the legislative scheme as crafted in Bill C-2 would have been found unconstitutional. We are less certain, however, that particular ministerial decisions would necessarily pass muster under the statute, given the lack of clarity over how certain criteria ought to be balanced. This is just as true under the amended scheme brought in by the Liberal government in Bill C-37.

The influence of the judicial decision in parliamentary debate over Bill C-2 was apparent, but only to the extent that the government and opposition parties emphasized aspects of the reasons that were advantageous to their preferred policy outcome. Arguably both sides of the debate suffered from cherry-picking in this regard. The Conservative government's emphasis on the fact that the Court laid out criteria for the minister to consider before granting an exemption accompanied scant attention to the underlying rights concerns expressed by the Court. By contrast, in simplifying the set of criteria assessed by the minister, the Liberal government's legislative amendments under Bill C-37 simply adopted the language of the Court wholesale. Rather than grappling with how to balance the criteria in a rights-protecting manner, the government – and, as a corollary, Parliament – failed to engage in a robust Charter discussion at all.

5 Legislative Responses under the Charter: Sex Work Policy

In its 2013 decision in *Canada (Attorney General) v. Bedford* (2013),[1] the Supreme Court struck down three Criminal Code provisions prohibiting "activities related to prostitution." The issue before the Court was whether laws prohibiting people from (1) keeping, or being in "a common bawdy house" (any defined location established for the purpose of housing prostitution), (2) "living on the avails of prostitution" (profiting from prostitution), and (3) communicating in a public place "for the purpose of engaging in prostitution or of obtaining the sexual services of a prostitute" violated sex workers' right to life, liberty, and security of the person in section 7 of the Charter of Rights and Freedoms.[2] In a unanimous decision, the Supreme Court ruled in favour of the respondents – all of whom were current or former sex workers – and argued these prohibitions prevented sex workers from implementing safety measures and, as such, risked their safety and lives.[3]

In response to the Supreme Court's ruling in *Bedford*, the Conservative government under Prime Minister Stephen Harper introduced and passed new legislation regulating sex work. In addition to the usual legislative debates, the Harper government engaged in public consultations as it crafted the new legislation. In a survey, and in addition to asking for input on issues related to "living on the avails of prostitution" – which the government reframed as a matter of investigating potential criminal economic gains – and determining whether there ought to be limitations on communication in public places, the government distinguished between people who purchase sexual services and those who sell sexual services, explicitly separating the two in order to enquire about whether or not either activity ought to be a criminal offence.[4] Ultimately the Harper government chose to keep prostitution itself legal, as it has always been throughout Canada's history. However, the new legislation, Bill C-36, the Protection of Communities and Exploited

Persons Act (PCEPA), criminalized the purchase of sexual services and, in doing so, made the act of prostitution (as opposed to particular ways of purchasing it, or regulating where sex work can occur and who may benefit from it) a de facto illegal activity for the first time.[5]

This legislation met with significant opposition from constitutional scholars, human rights organizations, and sex workers who highlighted the ways this legislation recreated dangerous conditions of the kind the court struck down.[6] The Liberal government under Prime Minister Justin Trudeau pledged to revisit the legislation yet has failed to do so (despite a provision in the PCEPA that required a re-examination of the legislation after five years). Several lower court judgments have addressed the constitutionality of specific provisions in Bill C-36, including two Ontario court decisions finding three provisions unconstitutional.[7] Other constitutional challenges are pending.[8]

Background: The *Bedford* Decision

In its unanimous *Bedford* decision, the Supreme Court began its reasoning by noting that the selling of sex was a lawful activity in Canada.[9] The chief justice noted, "These appeals and the cross-appeal are not about whether prostitution should be legal or not. They are about whether the laws Parliament has enacted on how prostitution may be carried out pass constitutional muster."[10] The three contested Criminal Code provisions at the heart of *Bedford* restricted the ability to engage in sex work. The problem, as set out by the appellants, was that they did so at the expense of sex workers' own health and safety. The argument – one ultimately supported by the Court in its decision – was that all three Criminal Code provisions at issue violated sex workers' right to life, liberty, and security of the person in section 7 of the Charter of Rights and Freedoms. The Court noted that the criminal law did not merely impose conditions on the ways sex workers operate: "They go a critical step further, by imposing *dangerous* conditions on prostitution; they prevent people engaged in risky – but legal – activity from taking steps to protect themselves from the risks."[11]

Ultimately the Court overturned each Criminal Code provision on section 7 grounds. All three provisions were found to violate the principles of fundamental justice (the bawdy house and public communications provisions tripped the principle of gross disproportionality in terms of their impact on the safety of sex workers, while the living on the avails provision suffered from overbreadth). The restrictions on sex work, in the Court's determination, "put the safety and lives of prostitutes at risk, by preventing them from implementing certain safety measures – such as hiring security guards or 'screening' potential clients – that could protect them from violence."[12] Comparing these restrictions with (hypothetical) laws prohibiting cyclists from wearing a helmet, the Court emphasized "the causal role of the law in making that activity riskier."[13]

In striking down prohibitions on bawdy houses (section 210) (any defined location established for the purpose of housing sex work), the Court upheld the legislative purpose of "prevent[ing] harms in the nature of nuisance" but found the harmful effects of the law grossly disproportionate to its objective, citing evidence of bawdy houses improving sex workers' safety, and finding that indoor locations are a "'basic safety precaution' for sex workers, one which the bawdy-house provision makes illegal."[14]

Similarly, in their ruling on communicating in a public place "for the purpose of engaging in prostitution or of obtaining the sexual services of a prostitute" (section 213(1)(c)), the Court accepted the legislative purpose – "to prevent the nuisances that street prostitution can cause" – but found similarly that the resulting harms were grossly disproportionate in effect.[15] The Court identified the harm in "the law's effect of displacing prostitutes to more secluded, less secure locations"; harms that include preventing sex workers "from bargaining for conditions that would materially reduce their risk, such as condom use and the use of safe houses."[16] Ultimately the Court ruled "communication is an essential tool that can decrease risk" and, in doing so, noted the severity of the harmful effects of section 213(1)(c), remarking this "assessment is qualitative, not quantitative."[17]

In its analysis of section 212(1)(j), "living on the avails of prostitution," the Court rejected the attorney general's statement that "the true objective of s. 212(1)(j) is to target the commercialization of prostitution, and to promote the values of dignity and equality."[18] Instead, the Court identified a more specific purpose at the core of the prohibition (which states that "everyone who ... lives wholly or in part on the avails of prostitution of another person ... is guilty of an indictable offence and liable to imprisonment for a term not exceeding ten years"[19]). The Court found instead "that the purpose of this provision is to target pimps and the parasitic, exploitative conduct in which they engage."[20] Prohibiting this type of conduct aimed to protect sex workers; importantly – and unlike the overly broad reference to "values of dignity and equality" named by the attorney general – the Court's finding focused on harmful acts perpetuated by individuals on sex workers, rather than identifying the practice of sex work as itself harmful. The latter framing pervaded the broader discussion of sex work in the Canadian discourse and, in its overly broad condemnation of the activity of sex work as responsible for undermining the "dignity and equality" of sex workers, revealed the influence of social and morality politics as it underpinned legislative approaches to sex work. A clear impact of this is, as we detail later in the chapter, contrary to meaningful efforts to treat sex workers with dignity, to uphold their equality, and to craft legislation that aimed for the protections *Bedford* found lacking. Instead, an overly broad understanding of the purpose effectively erased the voices of those in the sex trade in favour of external views – driven by morality politics – of the types of work people ought, and ought not, to engage in.

In rejecting the attorney general's assertion of section 212(1)(*j*)'s purpose, the Court approached protection by examining the harms sex workers experience at the hands of people who exploit them. Identifying pimps as the cause of this harm, the Court held, "The law punishes everyone who lives on the avails of prostitution without distinguishing between those who exploit prostitutes (for example, controlling and abusive pimps) and those who could increase the safety and security of prostitutes (for example, legitimate drivers, managers, or bodyguards). It also includes anyone involved in business with a prostitute, such as accountants or receptionists. In these ways, the law includes some conduct that bears no relation to its purpose of preventing the exploitation of prostitutes. The living on the avails provision is therefore overbroad."[21]

Notably, support for finding 212(1)(*j*) overly broad identified categories of people who fall within the ambit of the prohibition. Here the Court excluded from prosecution people who are not centrally engaged in activities related to sex work (accountants or receptionists) and identified the roles of those who cause harm to sex workers ("controlling and abusive pimps") and those who are ancillary to sex work and whose purpose is to increase sex workers' safety and security (drivers, managers, bodyguards). These distinctions are significant in themselves, but also noteworthy is the way the Court's ruling on the purpose did not rely on social or morality politics to determine whether or not the prohibition on "living on the avails" violates sex workers' section 7 rights to life, liberty, and security of the person. This stands in contrast to the implicit underpinning of the attorney general's claim that the purpose of the prohibition was (in part) "to promote the values of dignity and equality."[22]

As the Court explicitly rejected an overly broad justification for prohibiting people other than sex workers themselves from benefitting financially from sex work, the reasoning highlighted the need to focus on the ways people benefit and, most importantly, whether the type of profit occurs as a result of harm or exploitation. This finding is central to the section 7 analysis, as it requires that any prohibitions be consistent with the life, liberty, and security of sex workers. This clarification is important when evaluating the subsequent legislative responses to the Court's ruling in *Bedford*. As we detail below, legislative responses – and the continual foot-dragging of Trudeau's Liberal government, despite pledges to revisit legislation enacted under the previous Conservative government – are mired in social and morality politics. This is visible in the reluctance to engage in a robust discussion of autonomy and consent – an avoidance that hides diverging and divisive views on a feminist approach to sex work. The influence of social and morality politics shifts the focus of harm away from sex workers, and the power or lack thereof they have to engage in their work under Criminal Code prohibitions, to a conception of social harm imposed upon sex workers. While social harm falls within the purview of legislative response, it underpins much of the shift away from the immediate harms that led to the *Bedford* decision and it moralizes what sex workers ought to do (or rather not do) to preserve their dignity and equality rather than centring the section 7 rights at issue.

Ultimately, the Court found all three Criminal Code prohibitions in violation of sex workers' section 7 rights. The Court suspended its declaration of invalidity, giving Parliament one year to decide how to respond. Noting this deference to Parliament, the Court emphasized, "The regulation of prostitution is a complex and delicate matter," and, as such, "It will be for Parliament, should it choose to do so, to devise a new approach, reflecting different elements of the existing regime."[23] Moreover, as part of its decision the Court explicitly stated that its finding "does not mean that Parliament is precluded from imposing limits on where and how prostitution may be conducted, as long as it does so in a way that does not infringe the constitutional rights of prostitutes."[24] As we discuss below, much of the debate in the wake of *Bedford* and the 2014 implementation of Bill C-36 involved a clash between (1) those who supported criminalization of sex work and sex-work-related activities (and who did so to different degrees, as we discuss below) emphasizing the latitude Parliament has to re-evaluate the legality of sex work as an activity as well as the purpose of new criminal law provisions, and (2) those who supported sex work – and sex workers – and who emphasized the significance of *Bedford*'s analysis of the grossly disproportionate harms sex workers experience as a direct result of Criminal Code provisions that aimed to restrict activities associated with prostitution.

The Conservative Government's Response

The Conservative government responded to the Supreme Court's ruling with Bill C-36, the Protection of Communities and Exploited Persons Act, which made several changes to the Criminal Code. The most
notable was the criminalization – for the first time in Canada's history –
of purchasing sexual services. Bill C-36 expanded the ambit of section
213, formerly "offence in relation to prostitution," to cover "offences in
relation to offering, providing, or obtaining sexual services for consideration."[25] With this change, the government signalled its focus on the
demand for sexual services, targeting purchasers criminally and as a
focus of moral condemnation (we discuss social and morality politics
later on). A focus on demand for sex work also frames provisions dealing with "commodification of sexual activity" as an offence with the
criminal focus on those "obtaining sexual services for consideration" or
communicating for this purpose.[26]

Amendments to the Criminal Code clearly distinguished between
those who can (sex workers[27]) and cannot (people in an exploitative
position relative to sex workers[28]) legally obtain material benefits from
sexual services. This section set out a list of exceptions, enumerating
the legitimate instances in which people may benefit from income generated by sex work: here, exemptions covered people who live in "a
legitimate living arrangement" with sex workers, or with whom sex
workers have "a legal or moral obligation."[29] This section appeared to
be a response to the Supreme Court's distinction between exploitative
and non-exploitative beneficiaries, as set out in *Bedford*,[30] and included
another enumerated list of circumstances in which people were not ex-
empt from legitimate exemptions, noting impermissible actions such
as violence, intimidation, coercion, abuse, illegitimate intoxication, and
anyone who "receive[s] the benefit in the context of a commercial enterprise that offers sexual services for consideration."[31]

Bill C-36 also established two new restrictions on activities related to
sex work: a prohibition on advertising sexual services, with the legal
repercussions targeting those hosting advertisements (section 286.4),
rather than sex workers themselves (section 286.5(1)(b)),[32] and criminalizing "everyone ... who communicates with any person – for the
purpose of offering or providing sexual services for consideration – in
a public place, or in any place open to public view, that is or is next
to a schoolground, playground or daycare centre."[33] Other changes
included updated prohibitions against trafficking (sections 279.02 and
279.03) and the repeal of section 212 (Procuring), which contained "living on the avails of prostitution."[34]

Bill C-36 was met with significant criticism from legal scholars and sex workers. We analyse these criticisms later in this chapter, but first turn our attention to the government's process in creating this legislation. The high-profile nature of the case, as well as the position of sex work in social and moral policy debates, led Justice Minister Peter MacKay to make an official statement in the immediate wake of *Bedford*, noting that in the year before the Supreme Court's invalidation would come into effect the government would "explor[e] all possible options to ensure the criminal law continues to address the significant harms that flow from prostitution to communities, those engaged in prostitution, and vulnerable persons."[35] With this statement, the Conservative government signalled its intent to keep, at minimum, some activities related to sex work as criminal offences. It also emphasized its position on the harms that, in their view, followed from sex work, as well as a broad intent to protect people and communities from those harms. The remaining question was how to do it.

Rather than immediately release a specific position, the Conservative government engaged in a month-long online consultation to "to seek [Canadians'] views and input, to help inform the Government's response to the Supreme Court of Canada decision in *Bedford v. Attorney General of Canada.*"[36] From 17 February to 17 March Canadians were "invited to provide their thoughts and views on the issue."[37] Survey analysis would go on to "identify the proportion of responses in which the respondent expressed a view in favour of or opposed to criminalizing different aspects of prostitution."[38] The online survey contained six questions:

1 Do you think that *purchasing sexual services* from an adult should be a criminal offence? Should there be any exceptions? Please explain.
2 Do you think that *selling sexual services* by an adult should be a criminal offence? Should there be any exceptions? Please explain.
3 If you support allowing the sale or purchase of sexual services, *what limitations should there be*, if any, on where or how this can be conducted? Please explain.
4 Do you think that it should be a *criminal offence for a person to benefit economically* from the prostitution of an adult? Should there be any exceptions? Please explain.
5 Are there *any other comments* you wish to offer to inform the Government's response to the Bedford decision?
6 Are you writing on behalf of an organization? If so, please identify the organization and your title or role.[39]

While the government's news release on the launch of the consultations stated its purpose was to gather "public input to inform government's response to [the] Supreme Court of Canada's decision on prostitution,"[40] the consultations were criticized for their framing and language. As the Pacific AIDS Network noted upon the survey's launch, the wording of both the discussion paper and questions reflected the Conservative government's public support for criminalizing the purchase of sex.[41] This analysis correctly predicted the criminalization of the demand for sex work that we see in Bill C-36 and cast doubt on the genuinely consultative nature of the process. Indeed, Harper had already made the government's position on sex work clear. Following the Ontario Court of Appeal's 2012 *Bedford* ruling, Prime Minister Stephen Harper explicitly declared that the government "view[s] prostitution as bad for society and we view its effects as particularly harmful for our communities and women, and particularly for vulnerable women"; notably, he ended his statement by emphasizing, "We will continue to oppose prostitution in Canada."[42]

Parliamentary Debate: Bill C-36

Justice Minister Peter MacKay introduced Bill C-36 as "a comprehensive and compassionate Canadian response to the Supreme Court Decision in Bedford."[43] As a "direct response" to the Supreme Court ruling, MacKay began by noting the current status of prostitution in Canadian law, where he emphasized that "neither the sale nor purchase of sexual services is illegal," but that would change with Bill C-36.[44] Importantly, he noted this shift in legality "was a key consideration for the government's response."[45]

Taking this departure from Canada's long-standing policy decision not to criminalize prostitution itself, MacKay noted, "For the first time in Canadian criminal law, the bill would criminalize the purchase of sexual services; in other words, it would now make prostitution illegal."[46] MacKay emphasized at the outset of the second reading that the government was free to make this significant departure, drawing on *Bedford* to support his claim: "The Supreme Court was clear. Its decision does not mean that Parliament is precluded from imposing limits on where and how prostitution may be conducted. Significantly, the court recognized not only the complexity of the issue but also the ability of the government to legislate."[47]

After framing the bill in the context of the government's ability to take a new policy approach to prostitution in its response to the *Bedford* ruling, MacKay set out the framework of the new bill, presenting it as an approach "that would signal a significant shift in prostitution-related criminal law policy from treatment of prostitution as a nuisance toward treatment of prostitution for what it is: a form of exploitation."[48] This new framing did two things. First, it changed the context for application and analysis: the government grounded the bill in the Supreme Court's express acknowledgment that "the regulation of prostitution is a complex and delicate matter. It will be for Parliament, should it choose to do so, to devise a new approach, reflecting the different elements of the existing regime."[49] The new approach, as MacKay emphasized, underscored the danger the government saw in prostitution, which it declared "an inherently dangerous pursuit"[50] that required criminalization. Opening parliamentary debate, MacKay underscored the Conservative Party position: "We do not believe that other approaches, such as decriminalization or legalization, could make prostitution a safe activity."[51] Second, the decision to frame prostitution as exploitation rather than a nuisance provided a new way for the government to talk about harm. Under Bill C-36 – with its deliberate characterization of prostitution as *inherently* harmful and, as such, warranting criminalization – the government attributed harm to prostitution itself, and the harm to sex workers a result of their exploitation at the hands of those purchasing sexual services. After setting out the problem in this way, MacKay argued Bill C-36 "is about protecting vulnerable Canadians, as encapsulated in the title" (the Protection of Communities and Exploited Persons Act).

As Bill C-36 made prostitution illegal it did so as a "made-in-Canada" model (as distinct from Nordic and other models).[52] Following from the statement that the bill treated prostitution as a form of exploitation, MacKay noted, "The impact of the new prohibitions would be borne predominantly by those who purchase sex and persons who exploit others through prostitution. The bill is intended to reduce the demands for prostitution, which disproportionately impact on society's most marginalized and vulnerable."[53] Criminalizing the advertisement of sexual services – another major aspect of the bill – works alongside the ban on the purchase of sexual services to form "the legislation's overall objective of reducing the demand for sexual services."[54] This objective was inextricably linked to the government's view on harm in sex work. As he explained the bill's objective and major components, MacKay referred explicitly to the harm- and protection-based arguments that influenced the *Bedford* ruling. The focus of harm in the bill was twofold: assertion that sex work is inherently harmful, and recognition of the particular harm that arises from the exploitation of sex workers. On this second point, MacKay emphasized that Bill C-36 "recognizes the risks associated with allowing persons to benefit from the profits of others' prostitution":[55] a clear call-back to the "living on the avails" section of the Criminal Code that was struck down for violating section 7 in *Bedford*.

On the government's "brand new approach"[56] to prostitution, MacKay emphasized legislative exemptions to aspects of the bill that "criminalize receiving a financial or material benefit, knowing that it was obtained by or derived from the prostitution of others."[57] The criminal focus was on third parties and only those who engaged in exploitation.[58] Indeed, MacKay made particular mention of legislated exemptions for people who were in "legitimate living arrangements" or who offered (non-exploitative) goods or services to those who sell sexual services "such as accountants, taxi drivers, or security companies,"[59] clearly referring to the exploitive/non-exploitative distinction the Court made in *Bedford* and that it used to strike down impugned sections of the (old) law.[60] In making this distinction – and thereby excluding people who may assist or protect sex workers from the law's reach – MacKay stated that the bill "affords some room for sellers of their own sexual services *to take steps to protect themselves in response to the concerns raised by the Supreme Court of Canada in Bedford.*"[61] The inability of sex workers to take steps to protect themselves – an inability created by the laws struck down in *Bedford* – was a key factor in the Court's ruling. In that respect it was unsurprising to see the inclusion of these legislated exemptions – as well as the direct reference to *Bedford* – in Bill C-36.

The government's framing of harm rested upon the view that people working in prostitution are "victims" – a word MacKay used frequently to characterize people selling sexual services – and the claim that harm is done to sex workers by those who purchase sexual services and those who exploit sex workers. With legislated exemptions justified to protect "the specific vulnerability" of those selling sexual services, the bill's focus on preventing harm to sex workers rested on how best to deter and punish the perpetrators of this harm. There were few references to what sex workers can do to protect themselves (we will return to this later).

A second aspect of harm highlighted in MacKay's introduction was "the social harm caused by prostitution's normalization of sexual activity as a commodity to be bought and sold."[62] This characterization of harm was more ambiguous. MacKay made it clear that all people who sell sexual services are harmed by prostitution, yet the inclusion of social harm (rather than a direct reference to harm to sex workers, which led to the finding of unconstitutionality in *Bedford*) went further. After listing offences for separate criminal offences (trafficking and sex offences perpetrated against children), MacKay emphasized that Bill C-36 "recognizes and addresses the harms that prostitution also causes to communities."[63] In calling for increased punishments for those who purchase sexual services if the activity takes place "in public places that are near schools, parks, religious institutions, or places where children can reasonably be expected to be present,"[64] the bill was reminiscent of the overturned prohibitions against communication in a public place in section 213(1)(c), which the Court found to be "a grossly disproportionate response to the possibility of nuisance caused by street prostitution" and in violation of the Charter.[65] The context of Bill C-36 differed insofar as it established – as the Court asserted it was free to do – new criminal prohibitions against prostitution itself. Moreover, the government took the clear position that "the bill is intended to reduce the demands for prostitution,"[66] which it stated was necessary because it "is an inherently dangerous pursuit."[67]

There was much criticism (which we address below) that the communication provisions of the bill were vulnerable to the same section 7 critiques that led the Court to strike down section 213(1)(c). At the same time, the government was clear that the bill intended its efforts to "signal a significant shift in prostitution-related criminal law policy from treatment of prostitution as a nuisance toward treatment of prostitution for what it is: a form of exploitation."[68] Making the stated purpose of the bill to deter prostitution itself enabled the government to establish different grounds for the new prohibitions on public communication. This distinction was significant, as the Court found the old communication prohibitions grossly disproportionate, in part because it ruled "the purpose of the communicating prohibition in s. 213(1)(c) [was] not to eliminate street prostitution for its own sake."[69] The new objective explicitly aimed to deter prostitution itself. The government expressed its confidence in the constitutionality of Bill C-36 through a combination of the legislation's new justification, emphasizing the "entirely new" nature of the offences because they focused on purchase and exploitation, and the Supreme Court's statement that Parliament was free to legislate on the issue.

The issue of Bill C-36's constitutionality, along with the question of its consistency with the Court's decision in *Bedford*, was repeatedly called into question by Liberal and New Democratic Party members. Several people expressed concern that the government "took quite a bit of liberty with the Supreme Court decision,"[70] and there were repeated requests that the government refer the bill to the Supreme Court "to be sure no mistakes have been made."[71] Doubt about the constitutionality of the bill – and the need for legal review – set the tone of the second-reading debates. Scepticism about whether the government fully considered the Court's reasons for overturing the three provisions in

Bedford underpinned doubts about the bill's constitutionality. Members expressed concerns that the proposed legislation was inconsistent with the Court's ruling, with comments that Bill C-36's consistency with the *Bedford* ruling was "debatable"[72] to others who charged that the government had deliberately avoided making the necessary changes, instead observing that the government "twis[ted] itself into a pretzel to push its original idea through and try a second time to get around the court's orders."[73] Central to this critique were concerns that sex workers' safety was at risk because of the new legislation.

Indeed, much of the debate engaged with the government's claim that prohibitions on the purchase and advertisement of sexual services would protect sex workers. Conservative members emphasized "the compassionate side" of the bill,[74] noting the harmful issues connected to sex work targeted in the legislation and drawing from anecdotes to demonstrate support of former sex workers.[75] While a Conservative MP claimed "support [for the bill] does cross party lines,"[76] outside the Conservative Party members targeted their support for aspects of the bill that did not directly address sex work, extending support for the bill's anti-human-trafficking elements.[77] Several members contested, and explicitly refuted, arguments that the bill would protect sex workers. One MP said succinctly, "It is incumbent on the Conservatives to introduce a law that provides a legal framework to make sex work safer. Instead, we have a law that would do the opposite."[78] Pushing the government on this front, several MPs referred directly to the Court's finding in *Bedford* to support their critique. Liberal MP Sean Casey stated his concern that Bill C-36 would not only fail to meet its legislated goal, it would also violate section 7 of the Charter in doing so. He argued,

> Bill C-36 should be about public safety, and I have concerns that the bill falls short of that goal. I am not at all convinced that this bill would protect the women and men who are engaged in sex work. I would also suggest that Bill C-36, in all likelihood, violates the charter with respect to section 7, on life, liberty, and security of the person; with respect to the provisions regarding cruel and unusual punishment; and in respect of the ban on advertising, the charter protection of free speech. One wonders whether the Conservatives and the justice minister know this.[79]

A number of MPs made it clear that, in their view, they could not accomplish the Conservative government's stated purpose with the bill of protecting those who sell sexual services. Liberal and NDP members criticized the insufficiency of the proposed $20 million funding to help sex workers leave prostitution behind.[80] A Conservative member praised this amount as a "wonderful first step" to implement the made-in-Canada model to deter the inherently harmful "prostitution of women."[81] Several members also failed to find the government's justification for the bill – to deter prostitution itself – sufficient to change the context in which the Court found criminal prohibitions on activities related to prostitution unconstitutional. Indeed, members were clear that criminalizing the purchase of sexual services – while itself a new legislative approach to prostitution – would in fact exacerbate the harms that led to the Court's rejection of previous prohibitions on activities relating to prostitution. Casey summed this up, noting, "The Conservatives have a duty to comply with the spirit of the Supreme Court ruling in Bedford. I am not convinced that this is the case, and I doubt that the bill meets the letter or the spirit of the Bedford ruling."[82]

MPs also took issue with the stated punitive focus on purchasers and third-party advertisers and expressed concern that the effects of this new punitive focus would be borne by sex workers themselves, thereby submitting them to the same harms to which the previous legislative scheme exposed them. One main factor in the Bedford ruling was the way the old legislation created dangers for sex workers: the threat of criminal sanction led to rushed and secretive communication, working in spaces that elevated their risk of rape, assault, and death, and created barriers for people who might otherwise be able to help sex workers. In debating the bill, Parliament heard testimony from a sex worker who noted Bill C-36 "will have a catastrophic effect on my safety and my livelihood," elaborating that if the purchasers of sex work were to face criminal sanction, clients "will be unwilling to provide the screening information I require to ensure my safety."[83] As the bill faced criticism for revisiting prohibitions against communicating in public, one Liberal MP had reservations that this would pass a constitutional challenge, noting, "[This] is one of the very components of the existing law that the court had already struck down in Bedford."[84] Returning to the conviction that the government's new express purpose for Bill C-36 would not be sufficient to secure the constitutionality of its specific provisions, critics emphasized that the effects of the proposed legislation would lead to similar findings of unconstitutionality as set out in Bedford and that, rather than protecting the most vulnerable "it would have the opposite effect" and make sex work even less safe.[85] Bluntly, Parliament was told that, ultimately, "Bill C-36 will kill sex workers if it is passed."[86]

Discussion of the bill also addressed social and moral policy, albeit largely indirectly. As much of the debate focused on accepting or rejecting parts of the proposed bill, Liberal and NDP members, as noted earlier, extended support for harms connected to (some) sex work, but largely rejected provisions that explicitly target sex work itself. The reasoning for this was likely due to the deep disagreement between those who adopted different views – ones they anchored in feminist claims – about the values of equality and autonomy embedded in different approaches to the acceptability of sex work. Feminist views ranged from arguments that sex work is fundamentally intertwined with gendered inequality (and as such is inherently harmful)[87] to feminist defences of sex work that centred sex workers' autonomy and argued the problems with sex work lay in a culture of gendered and racialized violence and poverty that were best remedied by offering meaningful structural supports to sex workers: an approach that rested on policies that do not criminalize sex work.[88] Further complicating these divisions was the range of positions that fell between full criminalization and legalization. While there were references to the successes and failures of a range of models throughout the debate, evaluations of these models – as well as of Bill C-36 – most often turned on the perceived harms of the different approaches. These harms were most often rooted in a polarizing divide between policy needed to protect sex workers (from clients and the profession) and what sex workers might need to protect themselves while working. Divisions were evident within and between parties and amongst intervenors and women's groups cited by members during the debate. Despite these disagreements, the Conservative Party maintained a unified position in the debates, with the only sign of its internal division coming from an NDP member's comments.[89]

In the context of casting significant doubt on the bill's ability to meet the standards set out in the *Bedford* ruling, a Liberal MP urged that "Parliament has a duty to protect Canadians, whether or not we personally morally agree with their profession."[90] This was offered in response to the government's broader framing: a view of the inherent danger in, and undesirability of, sex work itself. This sentiment was echoed forcefully by Conservative MPs who spoke in favour of the bill. Conservative MPs condemned sex work with statements such as "Canada's approach must recognize that prostitution itself, not just violence, is a form of violence."[91] This ideological approach towards sex work amplified the preamble to Bill C-36, which acknowledged "the social harm caused by the objectification of the human body and the commodification of sexual activity," and equated engaging in sex work with a loss of dignity and equality ("Whereas it is important to protect human dignity and the equality of all Canadians by discouraging prostitution"). One Conservative MP argued, "A shift toward the legalization or normalization of prostitution ... would be disastrous for women's equality and for our aboriginal populations and other populations. It would turn the clock back years for women's equality."[92] While some feminists do reject sex work, this approach was one that many feminists rejected on equality-based grounds and did so in significant part because of the erasure of agency (as a fundamental component of equality) and the disproportionate effects of punitive approaches to sex work on already marginalized populations – effects that result in the harms underpinning the successful section 7 challenge in *Bedford*.[93]

As MPs noted substantial objections to the bill on the grounds it would be found unconstitutional, they emphasized that a court challenge was inevitable and could be avoided if the government wished. Expressing frustration at the legislative response, a Liberal MP stated, "This bill is also headed, eventually, to the Supreme Court for adjudication on whether it complies with the Charter of Rights and Freedoms."[94] After the House vote on Bill C-36 passed 139 to 117, a member of the NDP echoed this frustration, cautioning, "We saw the Conservatives' prostitution law thrown out by the Supreme Court. The Conservatives have gone right back to the Supreme Court, banging their heads against it with a bill that will also be found unconstitutional, because it ignored the fundamental issues in the Bedford decision."[95]

The Standing Committee on Justice and Human Rights offered only minor technical amendments, after hearing from eighty-one individuals and groups, including the Canadian HIV/AIDS Legal Network, the Canadian Police Association, the BC Civil Liberties Association, Pivot Legal Society, Native Women's Association of Canada, religious organizations, and legal groups like the Criminal Lawyers' Association. Many of these groups submitted briefs reflecting their belief that the proposed law was unconstitutional. One study examining witness testimony before the committee found a significant inequality in the distribution of witnesses, noting that "despite the larger number of potential witnesses articulating serious criticisms of the bill in their written submissions, more witnesses praising the bill were selected to testify. Since the CPC held a majority of seats on the committee, they were able to select more witnesses."[96] The study also found a clear partisan bias in the context, tone, and nature of the questions posed to witnesses based on whether they supported or opposed the bill.[97] Bill C-36 passed the Senate without amendments and received royal assent on 6 November 2014.

Assessing the Bill C-36 Debate

The debate on Bill C-36 raised concerns about whether or not the Conservative government's legislative response would survive Charter scrutiny. Notably, debate engaged questions of Bill C-36's constitutionality without directly addressing the Charter itself. When MPs questioned the likelihood of the legislation surviving future constitutional scrutiny – scrutiny that several MPs viewed as inevitable, given the content of the bill – the discussion focused on the harms sex workers might experience as a direct result of the bill. There were references to the *Bedford* decision but no analysis of the Charter independent of the Court's decision. Instead, MPs disagreed over core questions of whether or not sex workers would experience similar harms that led to the findings of unconstitutionality in *Bedford*.

The focus on the *Bedford* ruling – as opposed to an independent discussion and analysis of the Charter and what might be required under section 7 or any other section of the Charter – was informed by two things: the framing of Parliament as having the legitimacy and authority to legislate on the legality of prostitution itself, as well as to redefine the objective of this legislation, and the specific conception of harm as it relates to sex work. Both framings were instrumental in the justification for the provisions in Bill C-36. The revised scope of the legislation – laws that make prostitution itself illegal for the first time in Canada's history – were grounded in the Court's analysis in *Bedford*. One clear factor in changing the express purpose of the bill was to contextualize, and thus support, prohibitions on prostitution that did not survive Charter analysis in part because the Court rejected the attorney general's presentation of the previous legislative purpose.

Legislative debate raised pronounced concerns that, despite this new legislative purpose, the Bill C-36 provisions were still likely to have the same harmful effects on sex workers. Here disagreeing MPs largely spoke past each other, drawing from substantially different understandings of harm to support their position. Conservative MPs, following the preamble to Bill C-36, took the view that prostitution is inherently harmful and exploitative, and as such is inconsistent with the equality and dignity of people engaged in sex work, as support for their emphasis on the need for the legislation – specifically the criminalization of the purchase and advertisement of prostitution – to protect sex workers. MPs who questioned this approach looked to *Bedford* and used testimony similar to that used in *Bedford* to note the Court's findings emerged from evidence that the impugned Criminal Code sections prevented sex workers from avoiding a number of harms. MPs noted many times that the provisions in Bill C-36, despite focusing criminal sanctions on purchasers and third parties, would continue to subject sex workers to unsafe working conditions that were the direct result of avoiding criminal sanction. In other words, the stated targets of punishing purchasers and third parties would not lessen the harm sex workers experienced, given the impossibility of separating the criminal aspect of purchasing sex work from the practicalities of sex workers negotiating their work environments. The barriers to protecting themselves that sex workers experienced pre-*Bedford*, ones imposed by legislation, do not disappear with the legislative approach in Bill C-36. MPs noted that, if passed, they expected to see the legislation challenged in court.

Another key takeaway is the extent to which debate was mired in social and morality politics. Following from the government's decision to frame prostitution as inherently harmful, support for and criticism of the bill focused on the extent to which the proposed legislation would or would not protect the equality and dignity of sex workers. While Conservative MPs were clear in their conviction that prostitution is in direct opposition to equality and dignity,[98] both Liberal and NDP MPs highlighted concern for the ways criminalizing aspects of sex work would significantly undermine the actions sex workers could take to protect themselves, noting the proposed legislation would create barriers that put section 7 rights at risk yet again. The government's oppositional framing of "the public" versus "prostitutes,"[99] as well as scepticism that the government had a broader and legitimate interest in actively pursuing equality for and protecting women, was cast into doubt by NDP MPs who cited a number of policy actions, inaction, and cuts before offering the rhetorical "It now purports to care about women?"[100] This sentiment was echoed by a Liberal MP.[101]

Division over the extent to which sex workers could be free in their line of work exposed another split on social policy that spoke to another key aspect of section 7. Framing disagreement in terms of the best social policy approach, and shying away from directly addressing Charter requirements, debates exposed a divide over what life, liberty, and security of the person required. The government repeatedly described sex workers as victims in need of saving from their profession and found a solution to the harms of sex work – the perceived inherent harm and the harms that led to the *Bedford* decision – in the necessity of working to eliminate prostitution and of "saving" sex workers from it. The Liberal and NDP MPs who participated in the debates took the opposite approach, focusing on the harms of attempts to reduce and eliminate sex work would have on sex workers, and pushing for the government to separate proposed prohibitions on sex work from punitive measures that target a number of related criminal offences. The government's approach, in characterizing sex workers as victims, denied their agency and sought to reduce (and for some, to eliminate) sex work itself. Opposition MPs, on the other hand, indicated that sex workers themselves ought to be the ones to decide whether or not to engage in sex work. This latter approach acknowledged the harms sex workers experience but did not attribute them to the inherent practice of sex work. Rather, MPs emphasized not only the harms created by prohibitions on sex work and the corresponding need to stop restricting sex workers' access to tactics they could employ to keep *themselves* safe, but also explicitly noted the need to work "to ensure that one day people will choose this line of work solely because of their own personal choices or beliefs"[102] – noting the structural violence and poverty that affects some sex workers and may have undue impact on their decision and the need for other financial and policy support to address the underlying factors themselves[103] – and, in conjunction with that work, to focus on sex workers' safety and security by rejecting a criminal approach to sex work.[104]

The Liberal Government and Bill C-36

Before the Conservative government introduced Bill C-36, Liberal Party Leader Justin Trudeau largely avoided talking about sex work and possible reforms. Trudeau distanced himself from the youth wing of the Liberal Party, which in January 2015 set out a proposal to legalize prostitution, debated at the party convention in February 2014. Trudeau noted that, contrary to the party's position on marijuana, he did not favour legalizing prostitution: "For now, I'm just very, very mindful that the Supreme Court came down very clearly that the current approach is not protecting extremely vulnerable women and sex workers and we need to make sure that we are finding a way to keep vulnerable Canadians protected from violence that surrounds prostitution but also is intrinsic to prostitution."[105] When speaking in French, Trudeau offered a sharper view, noting that violence is intrinsic to sex work and saying that "prostitution itself is a form of violence against women"[106] – a view underpinning the Conservative government's legislative response, which they introduced to Parliament several months later. Trudeau did not speak at, or vote on, the Bill C-36 debates.

The Liberal Party's position on sex work was complicated by a number of factors. After avoiding the issue and echoing the Conservative position in the lead-up to the Liberals' 2015 electoral victory, the newly formed Liberal government announced their intent to review their predecessor's legislation. The directive to do so did not come from Trudeau; rather, Justice Minister Jody Wilson-Raybould communicated it to the public. This followed a pre-election commitment by Hedy Fry, who was the Liberal health critic at the time, that "her party maintained its staunch opposition to Bill C-36 and planned to scrap it."[107]

In making the promise to review the legislation, Wilson-Raybould signalled a shift from the Conservative approach, by emphasizing (1) the government's intent to speak with sex workers (unlike the Conservative government, who were widely criticized for failing to do this in a meaningful way[108]), and (2) an intent to look directly to the Charter as they contemplated changes to the legislation.[109] While they did engage in consultations, the Liberal government did not follow through with legislative action.[110] When a reporter for *Maclean's* approached the Office of the Justice Minister for an interview on this issue, years after the initial promise and after work on legislative reform seemed to stop with the consultations, the request was denied. The succinct response was that this was "not in the mandate letter. Not in the platform."[111] There were no other specifics or timeline, and no commitment to future legislative action.[112] Despite the provision within Bill C-36 to review the laws by the end of 2019, there was no mention of the legislation, or reform to sex work policy, in the Liberal Party's 2019 or 2021 campaign platforms. This omission may have been due to the range of moral and policy positions within the party and a desire to avoid debate on a divisive topic that was unlikely to win the party public support.

When the time frame for Bill C-36 review came and went without governmental attention, a number of organizations sent open letters to Justice Minister David Lametti, urging the government to undertake a review and emphasizing the legal and constitutional imperative to do so. Pivot Legal Society appealed on 6 December – the date, which they underscored, by which review was "legislatively required to be undertaken"[113] – and Action Canada (formerly Planned Parenthood Canada) wrote a week later to emphasize that current "laws and policies ... perpetuate the ongoing violation of sex workers rights under Canadian law."[114] Despite these calls to the Liberal failure to respond to the provision built into Bill C-36 itself, Prime Minister Trudeau's mandate letter to Lametti did not include a review of the law or the need to revisit sex work legislation more broadly.[115] Seven months after the 6 December deadline, Liberal MP Hedy Fry went on record to note her expectation that Lametti would revisit Bill C-36 and "apply a constitutional lens" to do so.[116] Fry – herself an advocate for revisiting the legislation – assured Lametti would "look at it, decide whether or not it is charter-compliant or in compliance with the Supreme Court ruling on Section 7 of the charter – and make amendments and then present the amended bill to the House."[117] Fry also noted the government had intended to do this during its first term, but that Justice Minister Wilson-Raybould "had her plate full with cannabis legalization and medical-assistance-in-dying legislation."[118] Fry based her views on an upcoming review in the mandate letter Lametti received from Prime Minister Trudeau, and specifically the part stating "the government fully defends the Canadian Charter of Rights and Freedoms."[119] Here it is worth restating that any directive to review the legislation was absent from both terms' mandate letters, and so any declaration of (actionable) intent ought to be taken with a grain of salt.

Since this (non) announcement there has been little movement. In a committee meeting on 29 October 2020, NDP MP Randall Garrison addressed Justice Minister Lametti on the government's overdue review of Bill C-36:

> There was supposed to be a review of the legislation that recriminalized sex work after the Bedford decision. That was supposed to start last December. One of the things we've seen happening here is legislative reviews with nobody seeming to be in charge of making sure they actually happen. I wonder if the minister could tell us today when we can expect some initiative on the review of sex work. I believe, and certainly many other advocates for the sex work industry believe, that the current legislation is very damaging and dangerous for those engaged in sex work.[120]

Lametti's brief response noted the *Bedford* decision, highlighting the legality of sex work in that context. He then went on to say, "A bunch of things around it were criminalized by the previous government. That's what we have to review."[121] However, Lametti made no commitments, saying only, "I do hope to be in a position to do that. Again, I can't promise you a date, given current events."[122]

Continuing Constitutional Issues in Sex Work Policy

Critical scholarly appraisals of Bill C-36 tend to question its constitutionality, although scholars also tend to note that the analysis of section 7 will be complicated by the differently framed legislative objectives, or purposes, at stake.[123] It is also important to recognize that discrete provisions, such as the one pertaining to material benefits, could meet constitutional muster, while others, such as the ban on purchasing sex or the provisions concerning advertising, may face more difficult scrutiny if the potential harms at stake become apparent. These constitutional assessments will consider the shifting objectives of the bill and the potential effects on the harms to which sex workers are exposed as a result of the provisions. Scholars have also engaged in the empirical literature on sex work to connect their analysis of Bill C-36's discrete provisions to those harms. For example, the focus of the new legislation on the purchasers or clients of sex workers (broadly referred to as the Nordic model), leads some to conclude that the law "simply transferred the culpability of sex work from the worker to the client; however, the fundamental issues of security, safety, and liberty still remain."[124]

Moreover, the authors of these studies note a significant increase in arrests for offences classified as "commodification of sexual activity" under "violations against the person" as well as slight increases for non-violent prostitution offences, which may indicate that sex workers continue to endure unsafe conditions.[125] Debra Haak cautions that the empirical research on prostitution is incomplete and often focuses on only some groups that Parliament's legislation aimed to protect.[126] The courts thus have an incomplete record before them when adjudicating issues surrounding harm, which has no doubt influenced the disparate outcomes in early litigation surrounding Bill C-36.

There have been several lower court challenges to Bill C-36. One early Ontario Superior Court decision, R. v. Boodhoo, and others, upheld several provisions as constitutional.[127] In two other Ontario-based cases, R. v. Anwar and R. v. NS, trial court judges struck down several provisions of the law on Charter grounds. Shortly after Bill C-36 came into effect, Mr. Anwar and Ms Harvey, the operators of Fantasy World Escorts, were charged under three Criminal Code provisions: section 286.2(1) (receiving a material benefit); section 286.3(1) (procuring); and section 286.4 (advertising an offer to provide sexual services for consideration).[128] In assessing the constitutional challenge, the trial judge found in favour of Anwar and Harvey, declaring that all three provisions violated the Charter: the advertising and procuring provisions were found to violate section 2(b), and the material benefits provisions were found to violate section 7. None of the provisions were justified under section 1.[129]

In R. v. NS the applicant was charged with violating six provisions of the Criminal Code. NS challenged the same three provisions from Bill C-36 as the applicants in Anwar.[130] The Ontario Superior Court judge ruled that section 286.2(1) (receiving a material benefit); section 286.3(1) (procuring); and section 286.4 (advertising an offer to provide sexual services for consideration) infringe section 7 of the Charter and that none of the provisions constitute a justifiable limit under section 1.[131] Section 286.4 was also examined under section 2(b); the applicant argued that the prohibition of advertising violated section 2(b) in addition to section 7. Where the judgment in Anwar concludes that the advertising provision (section 286.4) constituted a section 2(b) violation the court in NS did not.[132] In February 2022 the Ontario Court of Appeal overturned the trial court's finding in NS, upholding the provisions as constitutional.[133] Noting that the trial court dealt with four "reasonable hypotheticals" in its determination that the impugned provisions were overly broad or grossly disproportionate, the Court of Appeal differed in its characterization of the purpose of the new laws. The trial judge found that the purpose of the new legislative scheme was to "immunise from prosecution any individual sex worker who performs sex work, and to allow the assistance of third parties in limited circumstances, while making all other aspects of commercial sex work illegal" and "to protect sex workers from violence, abuse and exploitation to protect the health and safety [of] sex workers, namely women and girls."[134] By contrast, the Court of Appeal identified three purposes:

> first, to reduce the demand for prostitution with a view to discouraging entry into it, deterring participation in it and ultimately abolishing it to the greatest extent possible, in order to protect communities, human dignity and equality; second, to prohibit the promotion of the prostitution of others, the development of economic interests in the exploitation of the prostitution of others, and the institutionalization of prostitution through commercial enterprises in order to protect communities, human dignity and equality; and, third, to mitigate some of the dangers associated with the continued, unlawful provision of sexual services for consideration.[135]

The Court of Appeal adopted a narrower perspective on the health and safety objectives of the new legislative scheme, noting the primary objective was to criminalize demand and reinforce the prohibition on exploitation. It characterized the health and safety objectives as "limited to ensuring that persons who continue to provide their sexual services for consideration, contrary to law, can avail themselves of the safety-enhancing measures identified in *Bedford* and report incidents of violence."[136] This framing of the purposes at stake led the Court of Appeal to analyse where some of the reasonable hypotheticals advanced at trial fell safely as exceptions to the criminalized activities at stake, or a conclusion that the trial judge interpreted certain provisions too broadly.

NS demonstrates the importance of how legislative purposes are characterized and the implications those characterizations can have for section 7 analysis under the Charter. Perhaps more significantly, reliance on reasonable hypotheticals in *NS* may simply mean that the circumstances and facts surrounding that particular case were not conducive to an assessment of all of the relevant harms at stake in Bill C-36's provisions. At the time of writing, one of *Anwar*'s applicants is pursuing change in a separate legal challenge. In March 2021 Tiffany Anwar (formerly Tiffany Harvey), the Canadian Alliance for Sex

Work Law Reform, and five other sex workers applied to the Superior Court of Justice in Toronto to strike down the three provisions found unconstitutional in *R. v. Anwar*, along with three other provisions from the PCEPA – laws that prohibit impeding traffic, public communication, and purchasing.[137] This application challenges fundamental premises of the PCEPA, arguing that sex work "is not inherently violent, but criminalization produces conditions that create vulnerabilities to targeted and gendered violence and other abuses."[138] There is no date for this hearing. As of this writing, there are at least eight ongoing constitutional challenges against Bill C-36 provisions across Ontario alone.[139]

Conclusion

Our analysis of parliamentary debate notes a clear focus on whether or not Bill C-36 adheres to *Bedford*, discussion that very much divided legislators between its supporters and those who repeatedly emphasized the legislation would, if passed, make its way to the Supreme Court for failure to avoid the same unconstitutional harms. The focus on *Bedford* took the place of any robust independent parliamentary assessment of rights considerations under the Charter. MPs focused on whether or not they thought the legislative scheme complied with the Court's section 7 findings. Missing from this assessment was an expansive discussion of the ways Bill C-36 might violate a number of other Charter provisions. A clear omission here is analysis – or even basic discussion – of the Charter's equality provisions. Despite repeated references to the equality and dignity of sex workers (references that denied this equality on both sides of the debate) there was no discussion of the section 15 principles that legislation might take into account in the stated aim to better protect sex workers. There were many references to "protecting women," but they took place alongside the view enshrined in Bill C-36 that sex work was not like other work, which the government communicated with its oppositional framing of "the public" versus "prostitutes."[140] There were also references to "the most marginalized and victimized of our citizens," specifically Indigenous peoples and "new Canadians," yet this acknowledgment of systemic harms (made without using that language) did not prompt any meaningful discussion of equality rights. While the constitutionality of Bill C-36 is itself in serious question, even if it were to survive on section 7 grounds (which some think is unlikely), the narrow focus of the debate is a missed opportunity to craft legislation that does more than the bare minimum of complying with a past Supreme Court decision, but actively and more meaningfully works to protect the freedom and equality of sex workers.

Future determinations of the constitutionality of Bill C-36 are complicated by the shift in legislative objectives. As the Conservative government presented the legislation to Parliament it made much of its prerogative – explicitly noted in the *Bedford* decision – to craft its own approach to sex work policy. The government took a historic approach to sex work legislation: choosing to make the purchase of sex a criminal offence it made prostitution de facto illegal for the first time. In taking this legislative stance, the government changed the purpose of the legislation. The new move to criminalizing the purchase of sex work and framing of sex workers' *exemptions* to criminal prosecution (as a way to "save" them from an "inherently violent" profession), the government made it clear that an express purpose of Bill C-36 was to deter prostitution itself. The Crown, in its factum to the trial court in *NS*, emphasized that "because there has been a paradigm shift, the framework for constitutional analysis has also changed,"[141] and the Court in *NS* noted, "The objective and purpose of the impugned sections is fundamentally different than the sections scrutinized in *Bedford*."[142] On the most obvious level, this has implications for the analysis of arbitrariness. Indeed, we see the trial court in *R. v. NS* find that impugned sections do not violate the principle of arbitrariness (as the old ones did in *Bedford*).[143] With the Court of Appeal adopting a different characterization of the legislative scheme's purposes, how future jurisprudence might settle the questions on constitutionality and address other principles at stake remains to be seen.

As constitutional challenges unfold, sex workers are subject to an uneven and uncertain environment in enforcement of legislation governing sex work. Questions of enforcement have been complicated in Ontario by the recent lower court rulings, leaving sex workers subject to individual police departments' directives on enforcement and prosecution. The most notable outlier in enforcement is the Vancouver Police Department, which in 2012 (pre-*Bedford*) and in response to the serial murders of sex workers, "drafted a new policing strategy that completely overhauled how they deal with sex workers, and the sex trade more broadly."[144] Key to its approach are guidelines that "outline how police should 'use discretion' in dealing with complaints regarding prostitution [and] has meant that in Vancouver, sex work is effectively decriminalized."[145] There are now few arrests of sex workers in the city.[146] In the rest of Canada, sex workers continue to experience unwanted police action and state inaction, both of which result in harm. Action Canada notes that since the implementation of Bill C-36 "sex workers have reported increased antagonism with law enforcement, targeted violence and fear of reporting, unwanted and unsolicited law enforcement of Indigenous, Black, trans, migrant, drug using sex workers, and detainment and deportations of Asian and migrant sex workers."[147] A study by researchers at the University of British Columbia also found that since Bill C-36 there have been increasing numbers of sex workers in BC unable to access health services.[148] These data support what sex workers and activists have been reporting long before *Bedford*: criminalizing sex work, and elements of sex work, increases harm to sex workers and so disproportionally affects the most marginalized of sex workers.[149] With no sign of genuine commitment to revisit – let alone change – the legislative scheme, sex workers continue to face a work environment that is made uncertain and unsafe as a direct result of this legislation and the hands-off responses to lower court rulings.

6 Legislative Responses under the Charter: Medical Assistance in Dying Policy

In its 2015 decision in *Carter v. Canada (Attorney General)*[1] the Supreme Court determined that the Criminal Code provisions prohibiting assisted suicide were an unconstitutional violation of the right to life, liberty, and security of the person under section 7 of the Charter of Rights and Freedoms. This chapter examines the reactions of government and Parliament's legislative response to the decision. Subsequent litigation and another round of legislation that resulted are also explored. The erection of a medical assistance in dying regime immediately following *Carter* straddles two governments. Where the Conservatives appeared to engage in issue avoidance, the Liberals, forming government after the 2015 election, crafted legislation to balance access to medical aid in dying with protections for vulnerable persons. In doing so, however, serious constitutional questions emerged about the disparities between the legislation and the apparent threshold for access articulated by the Court. As a result, this case study offers insights into how the government viewed the institutional relationships between the courts and Parliament vis-à-vis policy design and the Charter.

As with the other policy issues examined in this book, partisan divides emerged in legislative debate. The Conservatives expressed concerns about the protection of vulnerable people, while NDP members pushed the government on access and consistency with the Court's ruling. The Liberals justified their approach as a balance of the two concerns. However, somewhat unlike the policy issues explored in the other chapters, there is striking evidence of intra-party disagreement in both the Liberal and Conservative caucuses. For the governing Liberals especially, these internal tensions may have contributed to a willingness to depart from the explicit threshold articulated by the Court.

The legislation passed by Parliament in 2016 in response to *Carter* raised significant constitutional questions, many of which were subject to parliamentary scrutiny. The timing also coincided with the introduction of Charter compatibility statements from the ministry of justice, which played a role in legislative debate and were key to the government's framing of the distinctive role Parliament plays in relation to the Charter and the Court. We find that the government was willing to claim an independent role for Parliament in interpreting the Charter's requirements and deviate from the Court's policy prescription. Moreover, the opposition parties focused on the divergence between the legislation and the Court's reasons. This brought explicit focus in parliamentary debate to a key distinction animating the analysis in this book: whether constitutionality rests on Parliament's or the government's assessment of its requirements under the Charter or whether it rests on consistency with the Court's decision.

This issue ultimately came to a head in the context of medical assistance in dying after a lower court ruling invalidating one of the new legislative provisions. We conclude the chapter with an exploration of that decision and the subsequent introduction of a new bill with further amendments to the medical assistance in dying regime, legislation that more closely matches the access requirements articulated by the Court in *Carter* but that also leaves a number of issues unsettled.

Background

The unanimous Court in *Carter* portrayed its decision in stark terms, noting that "people who are grievously and irremediably ill cannot seek a physician's assistance in dying and may be condemned to a life of severe and intolerable suffering. A person facing this prospect has two options: she can take her own life prematurely, often by violent or dangerous means, or she can suffer until she dies from natural causes. The choice is cruel."[2]

The Court effectively overturned its 1993 decision in *Rodriguez v. British Columbia*,[3] in which it upheld the law. In that case, a forty-two-year-old woman, Sue Rodriguez, suffering from amyotrophic lateral sclerosis challenged the law on the basis that the rapidly deteriorating and terminal condition would leave her unable to eat or breathe on her own. She wished to control the circumstances, timing, and manner of her death and to live so long as she still had the capacity to enjoy her life but to allow a qualified medical practitioner to aid her in ending her life at a time of her choosing. The Court split 5–4, with the majority upholding the law on the basis that its purpose was to protect vulnerable people, that striking down the law would establish a constitutional right to legally assisted suicide beyond that of any country in the Western world, and that insufficient safeguards would result (effectively a slippery slope argument).

The *Carter* Court, by contrast, upheld the trial judge's findings that the prohibition engaged the right to life because it "had the effect of forcing some individuals to take their own lives prematurely, for fear that they would be incapable of doing so when they reached the point where suffering was intolerable."[4] Similarly, the Court upheld the trial judge's finding that the right to liberty and security of the person was interfered with by depriving patients of fundamental autonomy over medical decision-making, control over bodily integrity, and imposing pain and psychological stress.[5]

In affirming the way the *Carter* trial court distinguished *Rodriguez* from *Carter*, the Supreme Court identified two key developments. First, jurisprudentially, the legal framework applying to section 7 rights had evolved considerably since 1993. While the *Rodriguez* Court examined whether the criminal prohibition was "over-inclusive" it did so by analysing whether the law was "arbitrary" – one of the key principles of fundamental justice developed at the time. In the period since, "overbreadth" and "gross disproportionality" are now explicitly recognized as principles of fundamental justice, meaning that laws infringing the right to life, liberty, and security of the person must not interfere with conduct that has no connection to the law's objectives or cause harm that is much more severe than the ameliorative objective the law seeks to address.[6] The trial judge found that the prohibition on assisted suicide breached both principles. Second, the Court noted that new legislative and social facts provided a different evidentiary "matrix" for the trial judge to consider compared to the *Rodriguez* Court.[7] Thus, the trial judge was able to consider evidence from other countries that have legalized medical assistance in dying and effectively dispute the notion that an absolute prohibition was necessary to guard against a slippery slope.

Having upheld the trial judge's finding that the criminal law provisions prohibiting assisted suicide were unconstitutional, the Court declared them "void insofar as they prohibit physician-assisted death for a competent adult person who (1) clearly consents to the termination of life; and (2) has a grievous and irremediable medical condition (including an illness, disease or disability) that causes enduring suffering that is intolerable to the individual in the circumstances of his or her condition."[8] The Court suspended its declaration of invalidity for one year to allow Parliament to develop response legislation.

The Court thus appeared to set a constitutional threshold for access, one that did not explicitly address mental illness (although might be read to include it) or minors. Notably, the Court's threshold does not require those seeking medical aid in dying to have a terminal disease, only a grievous and irremediable one that causes intolerable suffering. This would become a key issue in subsequent legislative debates and litigation.

The Conservative Government's (Non-)Response

The initial response by the Conservative government to *Carter* was less openly critical of the Court than its reaction to the Insite or prostitution decisions. Prime Minister Stephen Harper simply informed the House that "this is obviously a sensitive topic for many Canadians, and there are strong opinions on both sides. We will examine this decision and hold broad consultations on all aspects of this difficult issue."[9] The promise of broad consultations was a repeated talking point in the weeks following the decision.

Yet it was months before the government took formal action to initiate a policy response, waiting until July 2015, five months after the Court's decision, to establish the External Panel on Options for a Legislative Response to *Carter v. Canada*. The panel's mandate was to consult with groups that had participated in the *Carter* case as third-party interveners, medical authorities, and Canadians writ large in order to develop policy options for parliamentary consideration.[10] Two-thirds of the government's appointed members were known critics of medical aid in dying.[11] Five months earlier, the government opposed a motion put forward by Liberal Leader Justin Trudeau to expedite a parliamentary response to *Carter*. As one Conservative MP stated, "The government opposes the motion to appoint a parliamentary committee to consult on a legislative framework and response to the Carter decision and instead plans to engage with Canadians, the provinces and territories, the medical profession, and the many affected groups in a national conversation on these very important issues."[12]

The government's delay in initiating consultations, coupled with the federal election campaign that commenced in early August and ended on 19 October 2015 with Canadians electing a Liberal majority to Parliament, meant virtually no progress was made on developing a legislative regime on medical aid in dying policy. The new Liberal government found itself with only four months of the Court's twelve-month suspended declaration of invalidity remaining before medical aid in dying would be legalized. It therefore sought an extension from the Court.

Carter II, the Liberal Government's Response, and Bill C-14

After winning the October 2015 election, the Liberals were compelled to act quickly on the assisted dying file. The new government retained the External Panel established by the previous government, but removed from its mandate any prescription of legislative options.[13] In December 2015 Parliament formed the Special Joint Committee on Physician-Assisted Dying to investigate policy options and make recommendations. While the work of these bodies progressed, the government submitted a motion to the Supreme Court requesting a six-month extension of the suspended declaration of invalidity in order to have time to develop new legislation.

In a decision issued in January 2016 the Court granted a four-month extension (instead of the requested six) on the basis of "the length of the interruption of work on a legislative response" that resulted from dissolution for the election until Parliament resumed sitting.[14] In granting the extension, there appears to have been no consideration of whether the previous government had dragged its feet or whether the initial twelve-month period for the suspended declaration was appropriate. The Court acknowledged that suspended declarations of invalidity are "an extraordinary step" but critics have pointed out their increasing frequency and, more significantly, the obvious detrimental impact of leaving in place laws that have been found to infringe individual rights.[15] Robert Leckey suggests that a reliance on twelve-month periods for suspended declarations in contexts implicating complex social policy needs to be reconsidered because, in his analysis of the legislative examination after *Carter*, one year simply is not enough time for meaningful deliberation.[16] The Court's decision to suspend the declaration in this particular case was also criticized on the basis that no federal response legislation was necessarily required.[17] The Court's reasons in the first *Carter* decision even suggested that Parliament had the option of not choosing to enact replacement legislation (nor is it clear that the language the Court used did not in fact *read down* the impugned provisions rather than invalidate them entirely).[18] Despite these critiques, the Court's decision to extend the suspended declaration was not surprising, given that the logic of providing such remedies in the first place is usually to prevent a legislative vacuum.[19]

In June 2016 Parliament passed Bill C-14, which adopted a threshold for access to medical aid in dying that was considerably more narrow than the one articulated by the Court. Consistent with the Court's ruling, access to medical assistance in dying was granted only to those eligible for health services funded by a government in Canada, who were at least eighteen years of age, and who had a grievous and irremediable medical condition. However, the legislation defined a grievous and irremediable medical condition as involving several criteria, including a serious and incurable illness, disease, or disability in "an advanced state of irreversible decline in capability" and requiring that the person's "natural death has become reasonably foreseeable." Without using the word "terminal," the guidelines effectively required a patient to have a terminal illness or be near death, which was a state not contemplated by the Court's prescribed threshold for access. Only a month prior, the Alberta Court of Appeal determined that the *Carter* decision did not limit access to the terminally ill.[20]

Further, while other language in the legislation suggested that those suffering from mental illness might have access (the requirement that physical or *psychological* pain that is intolerable to the person is one of the factors specified in the law), necessitating a reasonably foreseeable "natural death" would seem to preclude patients suffering from many mental illnesses from obtaining access.[21] The minister of justice clarified that this was not the legislative intent, so confusion reigned, leading to disparate levels of access across the country in the aftermath of the bill's enactment into law.[22]

The government's approach under Bill C-14 also avoided considering other barriers to access left unexamined by the Court. While the Court's *minimum* requirements for access specified an adult capable of consent, the decision did not preclude Parliament from crafting a law that would permit mature minors from having access. Similarly, advance requests or directives were not permissible under the law, meaning that patients who wanted to receive medical aid in dying in the event they may develop dementia or become incapacitated could not do so. Instead, the government pledged that these matters would receive future study.

What is notable about the exclusion of all of these factors from the legislative framework – non-terminal illness, mental illness, mature minors, and advance directives – is that federal and provincial advisory bodies recommended their consideration. The Joint Committee's report recommended access for both terminal and non-terminal patients, noting that limiting medical aid in dying to terminal patients "would result in Canadians with grievous and irremediable conditions faced with enduring and intolerable suffering having to continue suffering against their will."[23] The report also recommended that individuals not be excluded on the basis of having a psychiatric condition.[24] The Joint Committee also concluded that "it is difficult to justify an outright ban on access to [medical aid in dying] for minors," and recommended that provisions to allow access to mature minors who can demonstrate capacity for consent be implemented no more than three years after the first stage of legislation.[25] Finally, the Joint Committee also recommended that advance requests be permitted, as it was "deeply concerned that by excluding individuals who want access to [medical aid in dying] but have lost competence, such individuals will be left to suffer or end their lives prematurely."[26] A dissenting report by the Conservative members of the Joint Committee disagreed with the main report's recommendations on mature minors and advanced directives. It also argued that the main report fails to provide adequate protections for people suffering from mental illness.[27]

A Provincial-Territorial Expert Advisory Group on Physician-Assisted Dying, created by all provinces and territories except for Quebec (with British Columbia as an observer), recommended an even more liberal approach. In addition to recommending access for non-terminal patients, patients with mental illness, mature minors, and allowing for advance directives, its report recommended that patients not be subject to a prescribed waiting period between the initial request and declaration.[28] Finally, while the amendment to the federal External Panel's mandate prohibited it from providing specific policy recommendations, its report[29] explicitly and repeatedly noted that the Court's decision did not limit access to those with terminal illnesses (although it did point to experts who argued the threshold for access should be narrowed to those with terminal illnesses, or adopting language from Quebec's legislation that mandates an "advanced state of irreversible decline in capability").[30]

That the Liberal government would advance a law through Parliament that deviated so substantially from the policy prescription of the Supreme Court and recommendations derived from expert consultations might be surprising. Many view the Liberal Party as the party of the Charter,[31] and in the context of legislative responses to Supreme Court rulings under the Charter, the most comprehensive study of the topic demonstrates that governments rarely fail to comply with judicial policy prescriptions.[32] The Trudeau government also branded itself as a government devoted to "evidence-based policy," with the explicit message that evidence should guide decisions.[33]

Elements of Bill C-14 appear to ignore the relative consensus about factors that should be considered in ensuring access for medical aid in dying, as reflected in the recommendations advanced by the advisory bodies. This does not mean the issues at stake were not complex or contested. Questions about how to achieve safe access that included protections for vulnerable populations were important and had been raised by scholars in relevant fields, including among those who advocated for greater medical aid in dying access but also noted that improving broader end-of-life and palliative care was crucial to the policy discussion.[34]

Access for patients with psychiatric disorders is particularly fraught, given the need to assess an individual's capacity to give consent. Although much discussion of mental health often refers to patients suffering from severe depression, in Belgium and the Netherlands access to medical aid in dying has been granted for "people with chronic schizophrenia, posttraumatic stress disorder, severe eating disorders, autism, personality disorders and even prolonged grief."[35] As a result, some scholars are critical of the "idealized" recommendations of the Special Joint Committee, noting that the "key eligibility criterion of 'irremediable' condition is inherently vague and unreliable," particularly in the context of certain psychiatric conditions that might be prolonged but where remission is possible if subject to high-quality treatment.[36] If it is not necessarily clear how the Court will deal with a case specifically focused on access as the result of an irremediable medical condition, then it is not necessarily clear whether the law was unconstitutional on the specific factor of mental illness.

By contrast, access for mature minors settles on arguably clearer equality rights arguments, particularly given jurisprudence on imposing life-saving medical treatment, such as consent to blood transfusions.[37] Even here, however, it is not necessarily certain how the courts would deal with the distinction between compelling life-saving treatment for a mature minor and refusing access to medical aid in dying for a mature minor.[38] Scholars have also noted that Bill C-14 might run "contrary to existing provincial and territorial health law" on medical consent for mature minors[39] (although this was unlikely to make C-14 ultra vires, given the restriction would likely be read as a valid exercise of the federal criminal law power).

Certain provisions of the legislation might also have been unconstitutionally vague or, at a minimum, required clarification by courts in order to ensure access in certain contexts. For example, the provision requiring that "natural death has become reasonably foreseeable" was subject to scathing criticism. The legislative goal was to leave it to medical professionals to determine "reasonably foreseeable" on a case-by-case basis, but as Jocelyn Downie and Jennifer Chandler have noted, it could be interpreted as referring to temporal proximity to death or the presence of a terminal illness.[40] The authors argue that it should not be necessary for both conditions to exist for the patient to meet that eligibility criterion (as supported by an Ontario Superior Court judgment on the matter).[41]

It should be noted that some scholars viewed Bill C-14 as constitutional and expected deference from courts pending any Charter challenges.[42] Our own analysis suggests that if the Court's articulation of a threshold for access is regarded as providing a bare minimum standard, then it is difficult to view the more restrictive access set out in Bill C-14 as consistent. Yet as Carissima Mathen notes, a constitutional challenge to Bill C-14 would focus on the new law's objective, which "might well impact the section 7 analysis and, in particular, the degree to which further limits could found to be overbroad."[43] Without predicting how courts might assess all issues that remain subject to contestation, the fact that the government would craft the law in a way that departed from the Court's dictates is nonetheless noteworthy. In the next section we examine how the government defended its choice to do so.

Parliamentary Debate and Bill C-14

In her statement introducing Bill C-14, Minister of Justice Jody Wilson-Raybould directly addressed the question of constitutionality and the government's assessment of what the Court's *Carter* decision requires: "A question that many have about the bill is whether it is consistent with the Carter ruling. There will always be a diversity of opinions about what is required to respond to a particular judgment, but it falls to Parliament not only to respect the court's decision, but also to listen to diverse voices and decide what the public interest demands. *It is never as simple as simply cutting and pasting words from a court's judgment into a new law.*"[44] She continued that the "bill before the House today respects Carter and complies with the Charter of Rights.... The court did not define the term 'grievous and irremediable condition.' It left the task of definition, as well as the elaboration of public policy and safeguards, to Parliament."[45] Most directly, Wilson-Raybould argued that the Court's decision "did not require Parliament to enact a specific medical assistance in dying regime"[46] and cited the Court's reasons, which stated that "Parliament faces a difficult task in addressing this issue; it must weigh and balance the perspective of those who might be at risk in a permissive regime against that of those who seek assistance in dying."[47]

The minister's argument at once claimed that Bill C-14 was consistent with the Court's reasons while simultaneously noting that Parliament enjoyed the discretion to deviate from a judicially derived threshold for access. The minister's comments on the eligibility requirements, specifically that a person's natural death has become "reasonably foreseeable," reflects this dual (arguably conflicting) justification. She argued,

"The bill does not require that people dying from a fatal illness or disease be terminally ill. Rather it uses more flexible wording; namely, that 'their natural death has become reasonably foreseeable, taking into account all of their medical circumstances.' This language was deliberately chosen to ensure that people who are on a trajectory toward death in a wide range of circumstances can choose a peaceful death instead of having to ensure a long or painful one."[48] In making this argument, Wilson-Raybould emphasized that Kay Carter, one of the *Carter* claimants, would have been eligible for medical aid in dying under Bill C-14's criteria, despite the protestations of critics of the bill to the contrary. Carter, the minister explained, "was 89 and according to the court suffered from spinal stenosis, which itself does not cause death but can become life-threatening in conjunction with other circumstances such as age or frailty."[49] The minister noted that "this approach to eligibility responds directly to the Supreme Court's ruling, as it noted in paragraph 127: 'The scope of this declaration is intended to respond to the factual circumstances in this case. We make no pronouncement on other situations where physician-assisted dying may be sought.'"[50]

Despite the minister's assertion, it is unclear whether an eligibility requirement like "reasonably foreseeable" death was consistent with what the Court intended as a threshold for access. The Court made no mention of the reasonable foreseeability of Kay Carter's death. Neither her age nor her frailty was part of the analysis. It is therefore difficult to reconcile the reality of Kay's non-terminal condition and the Court's lack of reference to her reasonably foreseeable death with the inclusion of the latter as an eligibility factor in the new law. Defining "reasonably foreseeable" in such a way that it hypothetically would have rendered Carter herself eligible, while rendering many conditions – or even *the same* painful, irremediable condition, but in younger patients – ineligible may be superficially consistent with the Court's threshold of access but arguably violates its spirit.

The issue of Bill C-14's constitutionality or its consistency with the Court's decision in *Carter* was emphasized repeatedly by New Democratic Party members in parliamentary debate, who asked whether the bill ought to be submitted to the Court as part of a reference to ensure it met the constitutional standard,[51] noted that the reasonably foreseeable natural death criterion was vague,[52] and expressed concerns about whether it was too limited in scope and did not fully comply with the Court's decision.[53] In virtually all of the questions and comments posed by NDP MPs from the floor of the House regarding access, consistency with the Supreme Court decision was directly referenced (many of the other interventions by NDP MPs involved questions about expanding palliative care). For example, Anne Minh-Thu Quach noted that the Court "referred to the cruel choice faced by patients with degenerative disease" when questioning why the government's bill did not provide options for patients to provide advance directives.[54] Don Davies referred to conformity with the Court's decision when pressing the government on why it narrowed access to medical aid in dying by including the reasonably foreseeable death requirement.[55] Davies also expressed disagreement, based on his reading of expert commentary on the bill, with the minister of justice's conclusion that Kay Carter would have been eligible for medical aid in dying under C-14.[56]

Where the NDP expressed concerns about overly restrictive access under C-14's eligibility requirements, the Conservatives generally posed questions indicating they felt the law would be too permissive. Conservative MPs raised questions about the way the government understood "reasonably foreseeable death," how it could possibly not mean "terminally ill" while not also promoting premature death,[57] whether it provided safeguards to protect vulnerable persons, especially people with mental health issues,[58] and the lack of provisions to protect the conscience rights of physicians and health professionals who do not wish to participate in providing medical aid in dying.[59] Each of these interjections specifically referred to the Supreme Court's reasoning that Parliament was expected to find the balance of a permissive regime with properly designed safeguards.[60] In House debate, some Conservative MPs were more critical than others. Garnett Genuis, for example, criticized the bill as follows: "This legislation contains no meaningful safeguards. Even its exceptions are full of holes. The written consent provision excludes those who cannot sign. The waiting period can be routinely waived. Mental illness is not excluded. The requirement that death be reasonably foreseeable would exclude no one, and the requirement that two doctors sign off merely encourages doctor shopping. Even if the already ambiguous criteria are not followed, someone who kills an unwilling patient can be let off the hook if he or she claims a reasonable but mistaken belief that the criteria applied."[61]

In response, Liberal MP Rob Oliphant asked, "Does the member support the unanimous decision of the Supreme Court judges in honouring the request of Ms. Taylor and Ms. Carter to have assistance in dying?"[62] Genuis replied, "The task that the court gave the government was to develop a system that would make this happen while also protecting the vulnerable. The government replaced some criteria in the court decision with equally, if not more, ambiguous criteria in its response."[63]

Throughout the debate, members on the government side and of both major opposition parties, despite holding divergent views, continually referred back to the Court's decision to justify their position. While this may reflect ambiguity in the Court's reasons, it largely reflects competing points of emphasis the different parties placed on different aspects of the decision. The NDP's concerns about access pointed to the basic threshold for access identified by the Court, while the Conservative criticisms emphasized the Court's acknowledgment of the need for protections for vulnerable persons. In defending the legislation, the Liberal government pointed out that the Court restricted its reasoning to the case before it, rather than providing a more robust policy prescription.[64] The government also repeatedly indicated that it was committed to further study on access in relation to mature minors, advance requests, or requests in cases where the sole underlying medical condition was mental illness.[65]

It is noteworthy, however, that three Liberal MPs voted against the bill at third reading, two under a belief "that it was neither Charter- nor *Carter*-compliant."[66] This included then Liberal backbencher David Lametti, who would eventually become justice minister. Lametti noted his "worry about passing legislation that is at serious risk of being found to be unconstitutional. On these grounds, I was not able to give it my vote in good conscience."[67] By contrast, Liberal MP Robert-Falcon Ouellette voted against the bill out of a belief that if there were mistakes in crafting the law, the negative effects would disproportionately affect marginalized peoples. Ouellette felt the law "sends a troubling message to Indigenous communities who are already fighting a battle against suicide."[68] While Ouellette was apparently the only Liberal to vote no, on the basis of this rationale, he was not the only one to struggle with the way the bill balanced concerns. For example, Liberal MP Arif Virani described feeling torn between his own education and faith – that if someone is thinking of ending their life, society should help prevent it – and the "small 'l' liberal ideas about empowering individuals to make choices and autonomy."[69] The votes on the bill at third reading thus do not reflect the fact that the intra-caucus debates likely presented a challenge for the government and partially explain why the bill was crafted in a way that did not simply follow the Court's policy prescription.

Wilson-Raybould, the justice minister, and Jane Philpott, the minister of health, were the two key cabinet point-persons on the file. In her book *Indian in the Cabinet*, Wilson-Raybould describes cabinet as generally having a strong consensus throughout deliberations about the approach to take with medical aid in dying policy.[70] However, even cabinet consensus did not apparently prevent the Prime Minister's Office from attempting to dictate serious changes to the policy. Wilson-Raybould describes a meeting:

Jane and I were in my office in Centre Block on the phone with the PMO. We were being told – at basically the eleventh hour, after we had been working around the clock – that we had to change our approach and proceed in a way that did not make sense to us for any substantive reason. Jane was crying out of sheer frustration. I started getting angry and, uncharacteristically, raised my voice and stormed out of the room. We wanted none of what they were saying; we thought it was ill-informed, superficial, political, and mostly just a series of ideas disengaged from the very serious and real issues at hand.[71]

Wilson-Raybould does not provide specifics on what changes the PMO was pushing, and it does not appear the centre was able to alter the approach from what cabinet's consensus established, but the anecdote is further evidence of intra-party divisions on the policy.

The Liberals were not the only caucus divided on the issue. While the NDP voted unanimously against the bill out of access and constitutional concerns, fourteen Conservative MPs ultimately voted in favour.

The divergent nature of the parliamentary debate over Bill C-14 also allowed the government to justify its choices as reflecting a reasonable balance. In responding to NDP demands that the government refer Bill C-14 to the Supreme Court for review, the prime minister noted that "the NDP has put forward amendments to enlarge the scope of the allowances. The Conservatives are putting forward amendments to further restrict it. We are listening to all proposals. We are working hard to ensure that Canadians have the right legal framework to help them with these incredibly personal and sensitive decisions."[72] The disagreement within the prime minister's own caucus added to the difficulty of this balancing act.

Charter Statement on Bill C-14

As explored in chapter 2, in 2016 the federal government began to issue Charter statements in relation to certain pieces of legislation. Legislation introduced in Parliament in June 2017 made the release of Charter statements for all legislation a statutory requirement for the minister of justice.

Bill C-14 was the first piece of legislation for which the government issued a Charter statement.[73] What is significant about this statement was the resulting pressure on the government to clarify and substantiate its claims about Charter consistency in the face of criticism about compliance with the *Carter* decision. We think this is worth discussing because it suggests that the government may have to revisit how it conceives Charter statements, particularly if Parliament places emphasis on Charter consistency when evaluating a bill and considering whether amendments are warranted. In this case, although the government was willing and able to defeat Senate amendments (specifically, the Senate amended the bill to remove the requirement of a reasonably foreseeable natural death), pressure from the Senate about why the legislation departed from the Supreme Court's position on certain issues nevertheless resulted in the Department of Justice adding an addendum to its original Charter statement. The addendum more clearly outlined the government's assumptions about why it felt justified to pursue a position different from the one suggested by the Court.

The minister of justice's initial discussion of Charter implications formed part of a lengthy background document that included a detailed description of the legislative objectives, eligibility criteria, safeguards, and other aspects of the bill, and a separate section titled "Potential Charter Impacts." The document explained the government's policy rationale for how it responded to the Court's ruling. It was less effective in justifying the government's substantive decisions about the scope of the legislation in light of their Charter implications.

The government's Charter statement acknowledges that by restricting access only to persons whose natural deaths are reasonably foreseeable, the law has the potential to infringe sections 7 (the right to life, liberty, and security of the person) and 15 (equality rights). It explains the policy rationale for this decision, including respect for human life and advancing the objective of suicide prevention and the protection of the vulnerable. The statement also asserts that in recognition of "the complexity of the legal and social issues associated with medical assistance in dying," the approach taken "strikes an appropriate balance between the competing rights, interests and values."[74]

What is missing from the initial statement is an explanation for why denying medically assisted suicide for those who incur pain, distress, or lack of dignity from conditions that do not lead to foreseeable death is justified under section 1 of the Charter. In other words, the legislation advances the policy justifications for why the government's approach could be considered reasonable, but fails to address the reasonableness of its choices in light of rights that are infringed. Yet it is precisely this issue that would be front and centre of any potential challenge to the legislation (see below) and is thus essential for Parliament to address if it were to satisfy itself that the legislation is consistent with judicial Charter norms or is nevertheless justified despite this inconsistency with the Court.

Thus, while the statement provides Parliament ample information to assess the justification of the government's objectives, as a matter of policy, it is not as effective in providing the context for assessing whether these objectives are being carried out in a manner that will likely satisfy the courts' assessment of reasonableness under section 1. The government's disclaimer that Charter statements are not legal opinions or comprehensive justificatory statements is not sufficient, in our view, to excuse this concern. In fact, this critique goes to the very purpose of having Charter statements in the first place, which presumably is to provide context for legislative choices and to help inform the decision-making process.

Instead, the government's position relied heavily on the expectation of judicial deference, in the likely event the legislation would be subject to a Charter challenge. However, judicial deference is not open-ended and could be heavily constrained if the Court does not accept that the legislation has been sufficiently attentive in mitigating the adverse effects for those rights that are infringed. To that extent, the bill prohibits rather than restricts the ability to seek medically assisted death where death is not reasonably foreseeable.

What is also missing from the initial statement, which would have helped Parliament assess the significance of this departure from the Court's remedy in *Carter*, is a more substantive explanation for why the minister of justice believes it is acceptable for Parliament to deviate from the Court's remedies. This is a more difficult issue to present, as it represents institutional and philosophical arguments about the relationship between Parliament and courts when legislating on morally contentious issues. To simply assert the possibility of judicial deference, even as reinforced by the Court's indication it would exercise deference if called upon to review Parliament's legislative response, or draw attention to the complex nature of an issue, may not be sufficient to satisfy the Court. As these arguments could be made for almost any legislative objective Parliament addresses, it is essential Parliament have a better understanding of whether deference is appropriate, how far it is likely to extend, and why.

Impact on Parliamentary Debate

There is little indication that MPs engaged specifically with the Charter statement, particularly in assessing the competing claims made by witnesses who argued that the more restrictive criteria in the bill were unconstitutional and conflicted with the minister of justice's arguments, and those of Department of Justice lawyers, that the legislation complies with the Charter. Yet the Commons Standing Committee on Justice and Human Rights heard from several witnesses who argued that the more restrictive criteria for eligibility for medically assisted death were inconsistent with the Charter and, as some argued, could lead to prolonged litigation or invalidation of the legislation.[75] Downie was extremely critical of the quality of the government's explanation of Charter issues, suggesting that the information provided in the background note was inaccurate and misleading, had relied on "a staggeringly unbalanced set of experts," and used an "ethical distinction" explicitly rejected by the judiciary. She also characterized the discussion of relevant Charter considerations as "grossly inadequate" as justifications for limiting rights.[76] The committee ultimately heard from eighty-eight witnesses and received 228 briefs in its comprehensive examination of the bill, but offered only relatively minor amendments, including amendments to the bill's preamble to recognize and affirm freedom of conscience and religion under section 2 of the Charter, and to recognize the diverse situations and needs of different groups in end-of-life care.

The situation was considerably different in the Senate. The Senate was in the midst of a sweeping institutional and cultural change as the prime minister had recently altered the appointments process to focus on the selection of independent (non-partisan) senators.[77] Public and media attention on how the Senate was dealing with government bills, particularly high-profile ones like C-14, was considerable. Senators questioned whether the legislation was consistent with the Charter because the bill differed from key elements of the Court's ruling in *Carter*. Senate Liberal Leader James Cowan asked for an opinion to confirm that the bill would likely survive a Charter challenge. The minister responded that the background paper (with its Charter statement) provided the explanation. The senator rejected it, saying, "That's not an opinion. That's a background paper."[78] Senator Serge Joyal also raised Charter concerns, indicating he did not think that limiting the scope to "foreseeable death" would satisfy the Court's interpretation of section 1 in the event of a challenge.[79] Senator Joyal would eventually make a motion, approved by a vote of 41–30, that the eligibility for assistance be broadened to enable all Canadians with "a grievous and irremediable medical condition" causing "enduring suffering" the right to access assisted death. This change effectively replaced the language in the bill with the language of the Court in *Carter*.[80]

In response to concerns raised in the Senate, the Department of Justice added the addendum to the Charter statement. The addendum includes two significant elements that were earlier lacking. First, it presented the government's view about the legitimacy of Parliament's role to enact an appropriate legislative scheme to regulate medically assisted death, and second, it explained the context for assessing when a legislative response that differs from the courts' can be considered to comply with the Charter.

The addendum made a much stronger and more compelling argument for judicial deference. It stated explicitly the government's view that it was Parliament's responsibility to decide on an appropriate regulatory regime for medically assisted death, and that Parliament's judgment was a valid constitutional response that need not mirror or echo the Court's ruling in Charter jurisprudence. Thus, the addendum asserted that although the Court's *Carter* ruling was the impetus for Bill C-14, the key constitutional question "is not whether the Bill 'complies with *Carter*' but rather, whether it 'complies with the *Charter*.'" In justifying a position that differed from that suggested by the Court in *Carter*, the addendum asserted that the government's position was that the Supreme Court "did not intend, in declaring the total prohibition invalid, to constitutionalize any particular legislative model – let alone the broadest possible model, which exists in only three jurisdictions in the world."

The government relied on the idea of dialogue to support its position that it was legitimate to disagree with the Court (in a way that does not require section 33).[81] Reliance on the concept of dialogue was not in the metaphoric sense frequently used in the academic literature, which assumed a reasonably strict adherence to judicial prescriptions under section 1, but in a more fundamental sense of recognizing Parliament's legitimate judgment on how protected rights should guide or constrain legislation deemed in the public interest. Thus, the addendum stated, "*Carter* was a case about whether the total criminal prohibition on assistance in dying was consistent with the *Charter*. It was not a case about the relative merits, risks and benefits of one type of legislative regime as opposed to another."

In staking out this role to define a legislative regime that differed from that of the Court's, the addendum not only justified this position in institutional responsibility, but also institutional competence. To that end, the addendum addressed the complexity of regulating medical assistance in dying, not only because of the need to balance competing interests, but also because of "complicated questions of social science that elude scientific proof, including predictions about human behaviour" and the need for a "prudent" approach to an issue that was subject to considerable contestation – an approach that in the government's view was "the best and most responsible model for Canada unless and until robust and reliable data, gathered in the Canadian context, can offer sufficient assurance that expansion beyond this approach would not put vulnerable Canadians at risk."[82]

Assessing the Impact of Judicial Norms

Scholars examining the fallout of the *Carter* decision and Parliament's response have analysed the resulting debate from the perspective of dialogue theory. As noted in chapter 1, the empirical identification of legislative-judicial dialogue over the Charter has been subject to considerable contestation in academic debate.[83] The initial theory was described as an inter-institutional phenomenon demonstrating that courts do not always get the "final say" about policies implicated by the Charter and has been defined as occurring when legislatures pass a new law in response to a judicial decision that reverses, modifies, or avoids its policy effects. Despite proffering this definition, proponents of dialogue consider instances where legislatures merely enact judicially prescribed policies as counting as dialogue (and dialogue's original proponents even count instances where legislatures repeal laws subject to judicial invalidation). As they have argued, "It is always possible that the outcome of a dialogue will be an agreement between the participants!"[84] Critics of this view argue that in order for legislatures to have a meaningful final say on implicated policies, the legislative response should not reflect mere compliance with the dictates of courts.

In relation to Bill C-14, Emmett Macfarlane contends that Parliament's response legislation appears to fit both proponents' and critics' understanding of dialogue, because the legislation is more restrictive than the threshold for access articulated by the Court, thus modifying it.[85] Importantly, it does not necessarily constitute an "in your face reply" – an attempt to effectively reverse a judicial decision without recourse to the notwithstanding clause, as has happened on rare occasion in the past[86] – because it narrows or modifies the scope of the decision instead of reversing or avoiding it entirely. Notably, Peter Hogg, one of dialogue's original proponents, initially argued that Bill C-14 is unconstitutional. Macfarlane asserts that it is difficult to see how unconstitutional legislation could be viewed as a legitimate form of dialogue, but as Thomas McMorrow notes, Hogg had elsewhere "come to embrace the post-*Carter* legislative reply as an illustration of dialogue."[87] McMorrow explains that Hogg and Ravi Amarnath "acknowledge that Parliament did not heed the Court's guidance on how to legislate in relation to access to [medical aid in dying] but that is okay because on this point, the Court was only offering advice. One may infer, then, that listening to the Court is all it takes for dialogue to work."[88]

If McMorrow's inference is correct, it exposes the weakness of dialogue as a concept for empirically assessing inter-institutional relationships under the Charter. In its original formulation, dialogue was not about whether a legislature appeared to listen to a court, but about whether a legislature had the ability to "reverse, modify, or avoid" the policy implications of a judicial invalidation. Indeed, as Hogg and colleagues have noted, the purpose of their original article on dialogue "was to challenge the anti-majoritarian objection to the legitimacy of judicial review."[89] Moreover, many dialogue proponents maintain that courts retain interpretative supremacy over the Charter.[90] It remains difficult to see how a legislative reply that does not conform to the Court's interpretation – indeed, one that Hogg has called unconstitutional – would be consistent with any of these views.

Other commentators have noted that efforts to apply the "dialogue" label in the context of Bill C-14 is misleading. Eleni Nicolaides and Matthew Hennigar contend that the government's arguments amount not to dialogue but "coordinate construction" or coordinate interpretation of the constitution (precisely what dialogue theorists deny legislatures should be permitted to do). In their view, the government's defence amounts to an assertion "that Parliament could legitimately engage in constitutional interpretation."[91] They note that as debate progressed on the bill, the minister of justice "reneged on her earlier reassurance that the bill complied with *Carter*, stating on 31 May that the law must 'comply with the charter, but that *does not require replicating the Carter decision.*'"[92] The minister's comment at report stage that "nobody has a monopoly on interpreting the Charter" is more consistent with a model of coordinate construction than the oft-cited dialogue metaphor.[93]

Our analysis eschews a focus on inter-institutional dialogue in favour of examining the government's approach to its *Carter* response. The government only sporadically referenced the concept of dialogue in advancing Bill C-14 – the minister of justice referred to it just once in her response to Senate amendments to the legislation, for example[94] – preferring to make more substantive arguments about the complexity of the legislation vis-à-vis debate over its constitutionality, and highlighting the balancing act that the Court recognized as belonging to Parliament in crafting a regulatory regime for access to medical aid in dying.

Yet, as emerged in a 2019 trial court decision, Parliament's discretion to balance competing values has limits. In a decision implicating one of the controversial elements of Bill C-14 – the reliance on reasonably foreseeable death as a criterion for access – a Quebec Superior Court judge found that it violates the right to life, liberty, and security of the person under section 7 and equality rights under section 15.

The Courts Strike Again: Reasonably Foreseeably Death and Bill C-7

One of the first constitutional challenges against Bill C-14 came in *Truchon c. Procureur general du Canada*.[95] The applicants, Jean Truchon and Nicole Gladu, were deemed ineligible for medical assistance in dying on the basis that, under Bill C-14, their natural death was not foreseeable (the litigants also challenged a similar provision in Quebec's provincial law requiring that they be at the end of life). In 2019 a Quebec Superior Court judge found that the law violated both sections 7 and 15 of the Charter and issued a suspended declaration of invalidity to give Parliament six months to develop Charter-compatible legislation (while granting a constitutional exemption to the applicants so that they could obtain medical aid in dying if they met the other eligibility conditions in the federal and provincial legislative schemes). The Quebec law was found unconstitutional on the same grounds. It is noteworthy that the trial judge, while dealing only with the question of the reasonably foreseeable natural death requirement in the federal legislation, noted that the law "still prompts concern in many and continues to raise questions that remain unanswered, such as, should minors or persons who are incapable be allowed access to medical assistance in dying and should such assistance be permitted on the basis of medical instructions given ahead of time?"[96] It remains to be seen how courts might deal with these and other issues.

One of the federal government's core arguments in defence of the law as crafted was that it struck a balance between access to medical aid in dying and protecting vulnerable people. In the court's view, however, the government's conception of vulnerable people was effectively to categorize them on the basis of the very health issues that put them in the position of desiring access to medical aid in dying in the first place. The judge wrote that the court "cannot accept the concept of collective vulnerability suggested by the Attorney General because the broad protection that results therefrom is too general an application of precautionary principles. Vulnerability should not be understood or assessed on the basis of a person's belonging to a defined group, but rather on a case-by-case basis, at least for the purposes of an analysis under section 7."[97] The key factor, in the court's view, was that a "person's individual capacity to understand and consent in a free and informed manner to such a procedure, based on his or her specific characteristics."[98] As a result, the court concluded that "for a doctor working in the area of medical assistance in dying, a vulnerable person should be defined as a person who is incapable of consent, who depends on others to make decisions regarding his or her care, or who may be the victim of pressure or abuse. These conditions are already included in the legislation."[99]

Several implications emerge from this part of the court's analysis. The first is that this framing of vulnerability signals a death knell for the government's justification of the reasonably foreseeable death provision. In the context of the Supreme Court's *Carter* ruling especially, where the focus was on the presence of an irremediable medical condition imposing severe pain or psychological suffering, it becomes difficult for the government to justify blocking access to medical aid in dying when a patient is capable of consenting, for reasons described below. Second, the particular conception of vulnerable persons espoused by the court might have implications for other issues of access, especially mature minors or advanced directives (and may especially impair justifications for limits on the former). Finally, the trial court went on to assess the impact that the presence of a psychological condition might have on physician assessment of the capacity of consent, and concluded that the existing safeguards ensure the process is sufficiently rigorous.[100]

On the interpretation of the Supreme Court's judgment in *Carter*, the trial court was unequivocal: "Had the Supreme Court wanted to establish or impose a temporal relationship between the administration of medical assistance in dying and the imminence of death, it would certainly have stated it explicitly in its reasons for judgment, whereas it actually took great care to set out the conditions giving rise to access."[101] Citing "the cruel choice" elaborated on by the Supreme Court, the trial judge noted that a core part of the basis for the section 7 infringement in the original prohibition on assisted suicide was the imposition of taking one's life prematurely or suffering until one's natural death occurs. Thus, the trial judge concluded, "the more distant in time the [natural] death appears, the more cruel the situation."[102] The Supreme Court's conclusion can be summed up, the trial judge noted, by a focus on "the respect of the person's wishes, the preservation of the person's dignity and, above all, the alleviation of the person's intolerable suffering associated with a grievous and irremediable illness."[103]

The trial judge also noted that although the provision at issue was inconsistent with the *Carter* parameters, that does not, in fact, make it de facto unconstitutional.[104] This goes to the heart of the institutional relationships surrounding public policy that has been implicated by the Charter of Rights. In other contexts, the trial judge noted, the "Supreme Court has already confirmed the constitutionality of provisions enacted by the legislature in response to some of its judgments, even though they differed from its teachings."[105] Parliamentary sovereignty and the exercise of legislative authority, the court noted, "is essential for our democracy to function."[106]

Having determined the necessity of engaging in an independent section 7 analysis of the reasonably foreseeable nature death requirement, the trial judge found that it violates the right to life for the very same reason the prohibition did in the Supreme Court's *Carter* analysis: it compels those suffering intolerably to end their life prematurely.[107] The provision also directly interferes with the physical integrity of the applicants, imposing physical and psychological pain and depriving them of the autonomy to make a fundamental decision respecting their personal dignity and integrity. It thus clearly infringes their rights to liberty and security of the person. The court concluded that although the provision is not arbitrary, it is both overly broad and its effects are grossly disproportionate. The nature of these infringements could not be saved under section 1.

In these respects, the reasonably foreseeable natural death requirement was found to infringe the Charter in much the same manner as its critics predicted. Moreover, the trial court also found that the provision "perpetuates prejudice and disadvantage for the applicants and the physically disabled precisely because of this personal characteristic."[108] It thus engages the applicants' section 15 rights, violating them while betraying "a paternalistic view of people like the applicants" and could not be saved by section 1.[109] Similar findings were made regarding the provincial legislation.

Both the federal government and the province of Quebec decided not to appeal the Superior Court's decision. This followed the urging of experts to avoid needless appeals.[110] The court suspended the effects of its declaration of invalidity for six months. The relatively short time was based on the fact that "a complete legislative debate took place at both the federal and provincial levels, so any possible responses should be easy to identify."[111]

Parliamentary Debate and Bill C-7

Following the 2019 federal election, which reduced it to minority status, the Liberal government introduced new legislation. Bill C-7 repealed a reasonably foreseeable natural death as an eligibility requirement, thus complying with the outcome in *Truchon*. However, the legislation went well beyond this simple change, bringing in a host of modifications to the broader medical aid in dying scheme. Most controversially, the bill amended the eligibility criteria to establish that mental illness is not an illness, disease, or disability for access to medical aid in dying. This change appeared despite the fact that *Truchon* did not involve the issue of whether mental illness as a sole condition satisfies the definition of illness in the existing legislation. Prohibiting access to those with mental illnesses – which may lead to intolerable suffering and stand as irremediable conditions – raises a host of constitutional issues, and may constitute discrimination under section 15 of the Charter.

Bill C-7 also proposed two separate regimes for access – one for those whose natural death is reasonably foreseeable and another for those where it is not. The bill eliminated a ten-day waiting period for the former group but imposed a ninety-day waiting period on the latter between the time the first assessment was made and the provision of medical aid in dying, unless a loss of capacity was imminent. This too raised constitutionality questions, as the imposition of a ninety-day waiting period may be deemed arbitrary or grossly disproportionate under section 7 of the Charter for inflicting further and unnecessary suffering by making people wait.

Finally, Bill C-7 included provisions for a waiver for the final consent requirement. Under the previous legislative scheme, a person needed the capacity to consent immediately prior to the provision of medical assistance in dying. Bill C-7 outlined a stringent set of conditions that might allow some individuals to have this final consent requirement waived. These conditions included that a natural death was reasonably foreseeable, that the arrangement was put into writing with the relevant physician or nurse practitioner for a specified day, that they had lost capacity to consent and that they were informed of the risk of losing that capacity prior to the day, and that the person did not refuse, through actions or words, the administration of a substance to cause their death on the day it was to be administered. In simplistic terms, the new provisions provides a partial option for advance directives. However, even this section of the bill raised questions, including why persons whose death was not reasonably foreseeable but who met the other requirements (especially the loss of capacity to consent) did not have access to this option.

Legislative statements help to explain the rationale for some of these changes. Minister of Justice David Lametti, in first introducing the bill, stated that the government "decided not to appeal the decision because we want to reduce the suffering of people waiting for medical assistance in dying."[112] Lametti described a two-week consultation process on eligibility requirements and safeguards that resulted in 300,000 responses, including round tables in several cities. Lametti noted that "a majority of respondents also thought it would be important to require additional safeguards," with the idea of two separate sets of safeguards in an expanded regime being suggested by many of those who took part in the round tables. In explaining the decision to explicitly prohibit access for persons whose sole underlying condition was a mental illness, Lametti noted, "We are subject to a court-imposed deadline and this matter requires more in-depth review and debate. We have learned that the trajectory of a mental illness is more difficult to predict than that of most physical illnesses. This means that there is a greater risk of providing medical assistance in dying to people whose condition could improve."[113]

In the legislative debate that followed, NDP MP Alistair MacGregor, noting the New Democrats' support for the bill in principle, raised the issue of the ninety-day waiting period for those not facing a reasonably foreseeable natural death. MacGregor stated, "We have already heard from some physicians who have concerns with the fact that they have to tell patients to bear their illness and suffer for another 90 days."[114] Lametti's response was that the waiting period "is the assessment period; it is not a reflection period. We have eliminated all reflection periods. This is the period of time in which the doctor or the nurse practitioner is assessing the condition of the patient."[115] He further noted that other jurisdictions have waiting periods of up to six months. However, he did not address the potential constitutional infringement at stake.

The Conservatives, for their part, criticized the government for refusing to ensure clarity on the issues addressed in *Truchon* via an appeal up to the Supreme Court. CPC MP Rob Moore stated that "rather than defending the will of elected representatives in court, the Liberals immediately backed down."[116] He also accused the government of committing an affront against Parliament by introducing legislative measures beyond those at stake in *Truchon* even though there was an upcoming parliamentary review of the existing legislative scheme.[117] Nonetheless, Lametti also noted that the upcoming parliamentary review would re-examine the issue of mental illness as the sole underlying condition, as well as advance requests and mature minors. That review began in May 2021 (although it was interrupted by the summer recess and federal election).

Upon reintroducing the bill after a prorogation in the summer of 2020, debate at second reading focused on numerous policy and rights issues. The Conservatives again criticized the government for failing to defend the balance struck by Bill C-14, for failing to protect freedom of conscience rights of physicians (criticizing requirements for physician referral), and for insufficiently failing to protect human life generally.[118] By contrast, the NDP spoke in support of Bill C-7 but also criticized the government for not moving swiftly enough to remove remaining barriers to advance requests.[119] As with Bill C-14, House debate over Bill C-7 did not feature a robust rights debate. The Charter was invoked largely in reference to the original *Carter* decision or the *Truchon* decision, and often in response to criticisms from the opposition. For example, the minister responded to the complaint from the Conservatives about insufficient respect for conscientious objection protections for doctors by referring to the Charter rights at stake of patients seeking access to medical aid in dying services.[120] Indeed, most invocations of the Charter were made simply to defend Bill C-7 in light of the requirements of the *Truchon* decision. Rarely were rights invoked independent of Charter considerations, although one example was Conservative criticism of *Truchon* as insufficiently protective of the substantive equality rights of people with disabilities.[121]

A Charter statement on Bill C-7 was tabled by the minister of justice in October 2020. It noted that the expanded eligibility requirements were consistent with sections 7 and 15 of the Charter, indicating, for example, that eligibility "under the expanded law would not be based on negative stereotypes equating disability with loss of dignity of quality of life, but on the respect for the autonomy of all persons with a serious and incurable illness, disease or disability to choose [medical assistance in dying] as a response to intolerable suffering that cannot be alleviated by means acceptable to them."[122] On the exclusion of individuals whose sole condition was a mental illness, the statement acknowledged the potential to engage liberty and security of the person, as well as section 15. According to the statement, several considerations supported the consistency of the exclusion with the Charter. First, it noted that the *Carter* Court stated that persons with psychiatric disorders did not fall within the parameters of its reasons (presumably referring to a brief reference at paragraph 111 of the decision in reference to an expert affidavit on the Belgium experience). Second, the statement asserted that Bill C-7 drew the exception narrowly, as individuals with mental illnesses were still eligible if they had another medical condition meeting the threshold requirements for access. Instead, the statement justified the exclusion "based on the inherent risks and complexity that the availability of [medical assistance in dying] would present for individuals who suffer solely from mental illness."[123] The statement did not downplay the inherent harms or suffering imposed on those who suffered from mental illness or the obvious discriminatory impact of the exclusion, but nor did it provide further analysis of how the complexity of assessing individual suffering or capacity justified a flat exclusion. As such, the statement provides little in justification for reasonable limits.

Similarly, the statement acknowledged that the two-track process for those whose natural death was reasonably foreseeable and those that did not risked implicating sections 7 and 15, but this was essentially reduced to a balancing act. The statement noted that sufficient safeguards were needed to protect vulnerable persons against abuse or error on the one hand, while noting that overly burdensome safeguards risked unnecessary barriers to access on the other. With respect to the ninety-day assessment period for those whose death was not reasonably foreseeable, the statement simply asserted that this minimum period "would help to ensure that there is adequate time to explore all the relevant aspects of the person's situation." The statement did not provide evidence for why the ninety-day period was the appropriate length or address the fact that there were likely considerable asymmetries to individuals' unique circumstances. On this point, the ninety-day period risks appearing arbitrary in any potential section 7 analysis.

The Standing Committee on Justice and Human Rights received 108 briefs and heard testimony from sixty-eight witnesses. These were sharply divided, with some disability groups, academics, legal experts, physicians, and religious groups opposed to the repeal of the reasonably foreseeable death requirement. A primary concern for some witnesses was the vulnerability of people with disabilities who could not be protected without significant improvements to palliative care, and social and income supports. The lack of sufficient supports, and the failure to guarantee that individuals would not have exhausted alternative care options or have quality of life concerns met, were factors these critics characterized as coercive and as vitiating genuine agency and capacity for consent. By contrast, other expert witnesses emphasized the protection of decision-making autonomy and the agency of people with disabilities. As Nicolaides notes, these witnesses characterized the mental illness exclusion as unconstitutional, including many of the physicians, academics, and legal experts who appeared before the committee.[124]

Similar patterns of opinion were expressed by the eighty-three witnesses who appeared before the Senate's Standing Committee on Legal and Constitutional Affairs. Debate in the Senate was considerably more grounded in rights considerations. Consider, for example, Conservative Senator Claude Carignan's assessment of the mental illness exclusion:

> The mental illness exclusion provided for in Bill C-7 explicitly establishes a distinction based on the fact that an individual has a mental illness. If this exclusion comes into force, a person whose sole condition is a serious and incurable mental illness that causes enduring and intolerable suffering and results in an irreversible decline in capability will be deprived of any right

to medical assistance in dying, even if two independent medical practitioners or nurse practitioners decide that the individual has the capacity to provide informed consent. By contrast, a person suffering from a physical illness of the same severity, who is not affected by the exclusion provided for in Bill C-7, could have the right to medical assistance in dying.

The exclusion set out in Bill C-7 explicitly creates a distinction that puts people suffering from mental illness at a disadvantage by depriving them of an advantage, that of obtaining medical assistance in dying. Furthermore, this exclusion perpetuates the prejudice that, generally speaking, people with a mental disability are not capable of giving informed consent to make crucial decisions about their lives, such as deciding to use medical assistance in dying to put an end to intolerable and irremediable suffering.[125]

This reflects the sort of equality rights analysis undertaken by courts (perhaps not surprising, given Senator Carignan's legal background). Other senators also commented on the fact that Senate amendments to Bill C-14 would have removed the reasonably foreseeable death requirement, but that this was rejected by the House.[126]

The Senate passed an amendment inserting an eighteen-month sunset clause on the mental health exclusion, which the House accepted but extended to twenty-four months. The government also "accepted a Senate proposal to collect race-based data on those who access medical assistance in dying, and expanded the monitoring regime to include persons with disabilities. Additionally, the Government added the words 'Indigenous identity' to the data collection in order to capture as many groups as possible."[127] Bill C-7 received royal assent on 17 March 2021.

Implications and Conclusion

The government's defence of Bill C-14, and the parliamentary debate over the bill more broadly evinced a more comprehensive and substantive assessment of the Court's decision, if not the Charter, than is apparent in the cases involving criminal justice matters, supervised consumption sites, or sex work. There was certainly a broader range of rights issues invoked. Yet many of the factors influencing the legislative response mirror what we have described in relation to those other cases. The government oscillated on the question of whether the new law was consistent with the Court's decision, ultimately arguing that, however it departed from the specific dictates outlined by the Court, it was consistent with the Charter. This was despite the myriad expert commentators who warned that Bill C-14's threshold for access was likely unconstitutional. As with all of the other cases, no section 4.1

report under the Department of Justice Act was forthcoming from the minister of justice.

On one hand, the government provided a relatively serious assessment, at least in terms of the eventual addendum to its Charter statement, on possible section 1 justifications for the bill. On the other hand, the government avoided crucial subsidiary issues (including access for mature minors, advance directives, and a lack of clarity on access for those suffering from mental health issues) that the Joint Committee and other bodies had already seriously considered, in favour of putting them off for "future study."

The influence of judicial norms in parliamentary debate around Bill C-14 make a clear distinction between the requirements of the Court's *Carter* decision and what is required by the Charter itself. The tension in the government's ultimate justification – initially, at least, it argued compatibility with the Court's ruling and then later made arguments that sounded very much like an assertion of Parliament's coordinate or independent ability to interpret the Charter – was stark. As with other cases examined in this book, the opposition parties were able to grab onto key aspects of the Court's decision in order to criticize the government's approach. In this case, the NDP were critical of the government for departing from the apparent threshold articulated by the Court, resulting in a bill that arguably restricted access more than the Charter permits, while the Conservatives complained that the legislation lacked sufficient safeguards and was thus too liberal in granting access.

Yet the ability of the government to advance its preferred policy was clear in the context of its majority. It controlled the House committee, which advanced only minor clarifying amendments but faced more substantive amendments from the increasingly independent Senate.

If there was a major constraining factor, it may have been the presence of intra-party disagreement within the Liberal caucus, or even between the cabinet and the PMO. As a result of cabinet confidence, it is impossible to know to what extent those around the cabinet table agreed on the final version of the bill that was ultimately introduced to Parliament, but we have already presented evidence regarding at least a handful of Liberal MPs who voted against or expressed concerns about the legislation. Caucus disagreement in the context of a morally laden social policy issue would be far from unprecedented, nor would disagreement within cabinet (although we have noted Wilson-Raybould's claims in her book that there was consensus). Declassified documents from the Progressive Conservative government under Brian Mulroney reveal a deeply divided cabinet over abortion in the aftermath of the Supreme Court's 1988 decision in *Morgentaler*, which invalidated the existing criminal law. Various proposals were discussed, including criminal penalties for women who self-aborted. Cabinet was divided between anti-abortion ministers who advanced the view that life starts at conception and those who argued for more free choice for women.[128]

There is little evidence that the Trudeau cabinet faced quite so stark divisions on medical assistance in dying, but in addition to public-facing statements from some Liberal MPs already detailed in this chapter, some MPs also expressed concern about the non-responsiveness of cabinet members to Bill C-14 in interviews with Alex Marland for his book on party discipline. These include complaints that Wilson-Raybould was not receptive to concerns about the bill as expressed by backbenchers, and the feeling that Philpott similarly did not value their concerns when she promoted Bill C-14's passage.[129] These comments should be taken in their full context: Wilson-Raybould and Philpott would later be removed from caucus in the midst of the Trudeau government's SNC-Lavalin ethics scandal, a break-up that may have weighed on the minds of Marland's interviewees. Nonetheless, the comments add further support to the idea that the legislation was developed at the very least amidst disagreement within Liberal ranks.

A final pattern emerges that offers a distinction between the nature of the legislative response as it pertains to compliance with the Court's decision and the question of judicial finality. Bill C-14 demonstrated that even a Liberal government is willing to "push back" against a relatively clear judicial policy prescription to pass legislation that is, at best, constitutionally questionable. Yet as we have seen with respect to the other cases in this book, the new legislation is rarely the end of the story. The government has capitulated to a lower court ruling striking down the most glaring restriction on access by passing Bill C-7, removing the reasonably foreseeable natural death requirement, and establishing a threshold that basically matches the one articulated by the Court. In the end, the judiciary retains the final say on the policies implicated by the Charter. This distinction – whether legislatures can respond to judicial decisions in an independent fashion, without merely enacting the dictates of the courts, versus whether those policies will stand – is an important one, often lost in the expansive literature on inter-institutional "dialogue." Our analysis thus confirms the findings of Emmett Macfarlane on "second look" cases: where courts evaluate legislative responses to Supreme Court rulings, if those responses depart from the judicial policy prescriptions at stake, they are almost always found unconstitutional.[130] Judicial finality seems to win out irrespective of how assertive the government or Parliament might be with respect to legislative responses to court rulings on rights.

7 Transparency, Accountability, and Robust Legislative Scrutiny on Rights: Possibilities for Reform?

The Supreme Court of Canada is a powerful and popular institution, and debates about its policymaking role and relationship with the other branches of government tend to centre on whether judicial review transforms Canada into a system of judicial supremacy. Despite a general deference to the courts evinced by governments throughout the Charter's history, the executive-dominated legislative process in Parliament means that in the context of highly salient areas of public policy relating to criminal justice or controversial social issues, governments are willing to advance their ideological preferences even when legislative initiatives are likely to implicate Charter rights. The well-established centralization of power in the executive, coupled with a relatively weak Parliament and opposition, has hamstrung parliamentary scrutiny of legislation on the Charter. The processes around legislative review within the executive are opaque. While court decisions may determine policy outcomes on subsequent rounds of judicial review, the fact that government and parliamentary processes do not adequately scrutinize policies for consistency with Charter rights is a considerable problem.

In this chapter we advance reform proposals that we argue would shed light on the rights implications of legislation and executive processes under the Charter, and improve parliamentary scrutiny of governmental bills. These include separating the functions of the attorney general and minister of justice into distinct portfolios, waiving solicitor-client privilege in the context of the constitutional advice that governmental lawyers provide to the executive, enhancing ministerial Charter statements, and establishing a joint committee of Parliament for Charter rights. We conclude with a discussion of the changes in political and legislative culture that we hope such reforms will bring into effect, including compelling governments to do a better job of justifying legislative choices, strengthening the role of Parliament in holding governments accountable, improving the protection of rights, and even influencing Charter jurisprudence. We then briefly analyse contemporary uses of the Charter's notwithstanding clause, finding that until governments and Parliament take more seriously the rights issues at stake in the legislative process, normatively justifiable use of section 33 is a dubious proposition.

Reforming or Enhancing Executive and Legislative Processes

Our conclusion that Parliament has not performed well as a principled venue for deliberation over rights would not be surprising to even casual observers of the institution. Yet it should also be put into context. It does neither scholarship nor political practice (and practitioners) any good to hold Parliament to the standards of some naive ideal theory. Parliament is there to hold the government to account. That is not the same thing as replicating a debate club or a graduate philosophy seminar. There are no plausible or realistic circumstances under which we should expect – or even desire – a Parliament *devoid of politics* or political contestation. In practice, the government-opposition dynamic and the existence of political parties means that ideological world views, innate policy preferences, regional and sectoral interests, and electoral considerations all matter, and rightly so. It is also important to remember that the rights issues themselves are hardly reducible to easy questions of right and wrong. Reasonable people will reasonably disagree over whether specific limits on rights are justified. Governments and Parliament will not always be wrong to disagree with or push back on contested judicial decisions.

Even with this realism in mind, the gap between where Parliament is and where it could be when it comes to ensuring rights considerations play a meaningful and robust role in legislative development is more chasm than mere crack. Even in the context of executive dominance, the system as a whole can accommodate better debate and Charter scrutiny by both government and Parliament. As Dennis Baker writes, "While it is obviously foolish to believe that legislatures have as much influence over public policy as the executive, as a purely formal understanding of the constitution might suggest, behavioural models of fusion, which dismiss constitutional forms to conclude that the executive can always have its way over the legislature, are equally misleading."[1] The question of institutional relationships between courts and legislatures, Baker notes, is not the one-dimensional "which institution is superior" that too often preoccupies the scholarly literature but about the multidimensional institutional relationships that account for the sometimes subtle checks and balances in existing institutional design. Given how Parliament and governments perform in practice, the question is whether there are meaningful reforms that might enhance the relationship between the executive and legislative branches and make those subtleties more apparent, and more readily exercised, in reality.

Reforms that strengthen Parliament vis-à-vis the executive, or that make it more difficult for the government of the day to advance its policy agenda, face an obvious uphill battle. What government would willingly handcuff its agenda by making the legislative process more challenging? Some might think that such reform proposals are therefore fanciful. While we agree that institutional reform in the Canadian system presents a challenge, and that the incentives for governments once in power are to retain a status quo that entrenches their dominance over the legislature, reform is far from impossible. The 2016 changes to the Senate appointments process, establishing a merit-based, non-partisan system for senatorial selection, inevitably created legislative difficulties for the Liberal government. As explored in Emmett Macfarlane's book *Constitutional Pariah*, the more independent upper house has advanced a sharp increase in proposed amendments to government bills.[2] This reform was neither inevitable nor necessary. The government could have retained the old patronage system and avoided a lot of headaches.[3] Meaningful reform, then, should not be discarded as an impossibility. We believe that encouraging political parties – especially when not in government – to adopt policy proposals as part of their campaign platforms and the concomitant pressure to enact them after they form government is a reasonable proposition, and the policy options we lay out here should be read in that light.

Separate the Attorney General and Minister of Justice Roles

The Canadian practice of fusing the roles of attorney general and minister of justice by having both held by a single cabinet minister is detrimental to the practice of executive review of legislation for compatibility with the Charter. The minister of justice role is a conventional political position, responsible for developing justice policy and for the administration of the justice system. The attorney general is charged with providing legal advice to the government, representing the government in legal proceedings, and upholding the rule of law. As a full-fledged cabinet minister who holds both portfolios, the attorney general lacks the independence needed to separate government scrutiny of rights with the political objectives of the government.

Notably, the attorney general is not a formal member of the cabinet in England and Wales, and was not at the time of Confederation. Thus, despite being modelled explicitly on a "Constitution similar in principle to that of the United Kingdom," Canada adopted a different tradition when it chose to fuse the two roles. England and Wales flirted with having the attorney general as a sitting member of cabinet in 1912, a practice that ended in 1928 after a scandal involving political interference in a prosecution.[4] Since then, the attorney general attends cabinet deliberations by invitation. Although New Zealand's attorney general is a sitting cabinet minister, the position is held only rarely by the person serving as the minister of justice. In the regular ministerial briefing to the incoming attorney general in New Zealand, it is emphasized that the "Attorney-General has a different role to that of all other Ministers of the Crown. The fundamental responsibility of the Attorney-General, when acting as Law Officer, is to act in the public interest. In exercising the powers, functions and duties of a Law Officer, the Attorney-General disregards any political interest or partisan considerations."[5] This contrasts with the mandate letter received by the minister of justice and attorney general of Canada, which is situated within the political promises of the government as a whole and, while noting the rule of law focus of the role, generally treats the function as akin to other cabinet ministers.[6]

This is not to say that the New Zealand and United Kingdom experiences leave their respective attorneys general free from political pressures or even cabinet solidarity. As James Kelly and Matthew Hennigar write, the "New Zealand and United Kingdom examples demonstrate that, even when the attorney general has a unique relationship with the cabinet, the tension between law and politics remains and can undermine the credibility of this parliamentarian in relation to the provision of legal advice."[7] Yet in arguing for the separation of the portfolios, they note that the issue is "more acute" in Canada as a result of having the attorney general role fused with the justice portfolio.[8] In the context of legal advice on the Charter, they write that this is especially "problematic because of the combination of legal tests and political tests within the Charter, such as section 1, for determining the constitutionality of the government's legislative agenda."[9]

The question of separating the attorney general and minister of justice portfolios arose most recently in the aftermath of the SNC Lavalin scandal. SNC Lavalin, a large Montreal-based engineering and construction firm, faced fraud and corruption charges for activities in Libya. In 2019 it was revealed that the Prime Minister's Office under Justin Trudeau improperly sought to influence then attorney general Jody Wilson-Raybould to intervene in the director of public prosecution's decision not to negotiate a deferred prosecution agreement for the company, in an action they thought would save thousands of jobs.[10] Trudeau appointed Anne McLellan, a former minister of justice and attorney general under the Liberal government of Jean Chrétien, to serve as special advisor on the roles and to examine whether structural reform was necessary. Her report dismissed the need for any major changes, noting that while "there is no system for managing prosecutorial decisions that absolutely protects against the possibility of partisan interference, while providing for public accountability," Canada's current system was suitable and "provides strong structural protections against political interference."[11] This conclusion is somewhat dubious in light of the SNC Lavalin scandal itself. The only thing that prevented political interference was Wilson-Raybould's adherence to principle, and the pressure she faced became public only after she was shuffled out of the portfolio. This does not illustrate particularly robust protections for the attorney general.

McLellan's report focused narrowly on prosecutions, but she makes other questionable claims in arriving at her conclusion. She argues, for example, that removing the attorney general from cabinet "would also affect the credibility and quality of legal advice they provide" because, as a member of cabinet who understands the full political context in which cabinet operates, cabinet colleagues will be more likely to heed the attorney general's advice.[12] She premises this conclusion on the notion that the fused role was deliberately chosen at Confederation because it "creates important synergies," giving one person "perspective over the entire system which could not be achieved if the roles were divided."[13]

Yet it is just as arguable that a degree of independence afforded to an attorney general who had a distinct relationship with, or sat outside of, cabinet would allow for more objective and forthright legal advice. As Adam Dodek argues, the combination of responsibilities "does not accord with modern concerns about duties of loyalty and conflicts of interest. And it certainly does not mesh with what we know about how the brain operates and how certain types of cognitive biases affect how we make decisions."[14] As we explored in chapter 2, the government's low standards for exercising the Department of Justice Act's section 4.1 reporting obligation – which requires the minister to report a bill's inconsistency with the Charter to the House of Commons – has meant that no such report has ever been issued, despite many instances of legislation that raises obvious constitutionality concerns. Dodek specifically cites this fact in underlying the impossible contradiction someone fulfilling both roles finds themselves in. The minister of justice as a "decidedly partisan" actor and the attorney general, tasked with providing "the best independent legal advice to their own department," results in little more than "a clash of loyalties and a conflict of interest."[15]

In our view, the current arrangement and approach to section 4.1 allows governments to discourage or confuse Parliament's assessment of whether legislation is consistent with the Charter. The lack of a meaningful section 4.1 process allows governments to exploit the absence of a report, both by leveraging the lack of a report to give the misleading impression to the House that legislation is constitutionally sound, and to dismiss opposition arguments about the Charter and the need for rights-protecting amendments. Hiebert and Kelly note that in New Zealand, where the attorney general is usually a separate portfolio, a similar reporting obligation resulted in sixty-give reports under the Bill of Rights Act. A former attorney general explained the frequency of reports as "the professional responsibility of the Attorney General who, as 'the Government's lawyer,' must act independently and 'must not be swayed by party political considerations but must objectively come to certain conclusions.'"[16] A willingness to issue reports, then, might be tied to the relative independence of the attorney general (in the United Kingdom a handful of reports have been issued, but the Human Rights Act assigns the reporting obligations to any minister introducing a bill rather than to the attorney general specifically). Hiebert and Kelly note, however, that another factor that may liberalize reporting in New Zealand is that such reports rarely interfere with the government's legislative agenda. Of the sixty-five reports, only twenty-eight involved government bills, and of those, only two were subject to amendments on the rights concerns expressed in a report.[17]

It would thus be unwise to overstate the effect such a reform might have. Nonetheless, there are good reasons to believe that greater independence for the attorney general – which at a minimum should include separation from the minister of justice portfolio, but ideally would include sitting outside of cabinet – would prompt more robust and effective scrutiny of legislation on Charter grounds and under the section 4.1 obligation.

Short of such reform, the section 4.1 reporting requirement should be repealed. Under the current process and culture, the obligation is perhaps worse than useless: it arguably misleads Parliament and undermines its legislative scrutiny function as it regards the Charter.

Waive Solicitor-Client Privilege and Secrecy as It Pertains to Bureaucratic Advice about the Constitutionality of Legislation

The advice governments receive from Department of Justice lawyers is protected by solicitor-client privilege. The courts have recognized that the Crown is not in a different position from a private individual or other organization when it comes to solicitor-client privilege.[18] Deborah MacNair analogizes privilege in the government context to the role of in-house counsel in other large organizations, and thus privilege extends to traditional lines of protection encompassing lawyers' files and communications for the purposes of providing legal advice, which include notes, legal research, and related documents.[19] Government lawyers, the Supreme Court acknowledges, wear different hats, such that not all of their work is protected by solicitor-client privilege, including policy advice that might not be rooted in their legal expertise.[20] MacNair notes that the constitutional context presents complications, such as when Department of Justice lawyers are called before parliamentary committees to provide factual context around legislative drafting and must tread carefully to balance what they can say, something reflecting their "dual roles as lawyers and policy advisors."[21]

While solicitor-client privilege between government lawyers and the Crown may be fundamentally important in certain contexts, there are few good reasons for not opening up the constitutional advice the government receives from the civil service to public scrutiny. Dodek even argues that an overly broad, absolutist conception of solicitor-client privilege had developed when it is best properly conceived as an individual right.[22] The consequence of this reconceptualization would be that organizations – including governments – would be largely unable to claim privilege. While privilege might be helpful to governments, Dodek argues, the abolition of privilege would not leave all communications open to disclosure, as litigation privilege and rules of discovery would continue to provide protections.

We do not propose the abolition or reconceptualization of solicitor-client privilege in the government context. Instead, our argument narrowly concerns constitutional advice on the legislative development process. The advice received by governments from government lawyers should be public, both to better inform Parliament of the constitutional questions and issues surrounding government bills and in the broader interests of transparency and accountability. A government that pursues constitutionally questionable legislation should be prepared to defend it rather than attempt to conceal the fact that there may be legitimate concerns with its proposed policies.

A standing policy of waiving privilege vis-à-vis constitutional advice, at least in the Charter context, would prompt greater scrutiny to potential rights issues at stake in legislation. Some critics may object to this proposal for fear of the implications on the quality of the advice itself. Patrick Monahan writes that solicitor-client privilege is key to ensuring "candid, thorough and objective legal advice": "The fact that privilege attaches to the opinions provided by their legal advisors encourages and facilitates the seeking of such advice by government decision-makers in a timely way. It also enables such advice to be developed in a consistent and principled fashion, in accordance with strict standards for review and approval, thus enabling a single, authoritative source of legal advice within government. In short, solicitor-client privilege within government reinforces and advances respect for the rule of law in the administration of public affairs."[23] In Monahan's view, the elimination or qualification of solicitor-client privilege would undermine rule of law principles, making governments reluctant to seek timely legal advice or "request such advice be provided orally rather than in writing."[24] Similarly, legal advisors may become less candid and objective for fear of political repercussions of their advice being subject to public scrutiny.[25]

In our view, such concerns reflect precisely the sort of political considerations that contribute to the executive dominance, centralization of power, and lack of transparency that infects Canadian politics more broadly and that has hampered principled deliberations and honesty about the constitutional implications of public policy. Moreover, some of these concerns can be mitigated by creating legal obligations for departmental staff, such as inserting provisions into the Department of Justice Act to mandate that legal advice be provided in writing and that compels staff lawyers to provide objective and candid advice to the best of their ability on the perceived constitutionality of every government bill. The government would then, by law, receive constitutional advice by departmental lawyers rather than being left to exercise discretion to avoid having it exposed to public scrutiny. It is worth noting that since 2003 New Zealand has effectively waived secrecy on legal advice the attorney general receives from its Ministry of Justice and the Crown Law Office on the consistency of bills with the Bill of Rights Act. Legal advice is publicly posted online for all bills (with the exception of appropriation bills, which are not scrutinized).[26] There is no evidence that New Zealand's transparency has harmed the quality of legal advice received or the government's willingness to receive it.

Enhanced Charter Statements

In chapter 2 we described the 2016 introduction of Charter statements for government bills. As noted, Charter statements are intended to inform parliamentary and public debate and increase awareness and understanding of the Charter. Our analysis found that Charter statements provide no explicit explanation of whether the government anticipates serious difficulty convincing a court about its legislative justifications. The statements do not discuss alternative legislative options in terms of their practicalities or implications for protected rights, or explain why the government has chosen the option it has and rejected other, perhaps less restrictive, measures. We also found that Charter statements do not explain the reasons or assumptions for the minister of justice's judgment that legislation complies with the Charter, and thus seem divorced from the section 4.1 process. Nor do Charter statements outline the criteria used for concluding that legislation is more likely than not to be upheld as a reasonable limit under section 1, if subject to a Charter challenge.

Making Charter statements more robust would help to ensure they better inform parliamentary debates about rights in relation to specific bills and increase public awareness of rights issues implicated by the government's legislative agenda. Improved attention to the justifications for potential limits on rights need not be carried out in a legalistic manner or one designed to try to predict how courts will scrutinize the bills at stake. In considering section 1 issues, for example, we do not consider it necessary or desirable for a Charter statement to mechanically apply an Oakes-style test as courts do in the course of their own reasonable limits analysis. Instead, Charter statements should do a better job engaging in a more comprehensive proportionality analysis from a policy analytical perspective to justify potential limits on rights. It would be reasonable for Department of Justice staff to consult with relevant ministries when developing Charter statements to canvass policy alternatives at stake and to more fully explore design and implementation challenges associated with the rights issues at stake.

The Charter statement on Bill C-7, the Liberal government's recent amendments to its regime for access to medical assistance in dying, would have benefitted enormously from a more robust approach. As we note in chapter 6, the statement fails to make a vigorous proportionality analysis of the sort we suggest here, refusing to justify its absolute exclusion of mental illness as a sole condition for access with regard for the individual suffering and capacity issues at stake, or providing any evidence to support a ninety-day assessment period for individuals whose natural death is not reasonably foreseeable. Without attention to such policy justifications and proportionality considerations, any Charter statement will be insufficient or incomplete. In their current formulation, Charter statements seem more designed to pre-empt or anticipate debate than to contribute to or foster it.

Establish a Joint Committee on Rights

Executive dominance of the committee process in the House of Commons generally ensures that government bills are passed with relatively limited scrutiny. Substantive amendments (as opposed to technical or procedural amendments) from House committees are rare. The Senate, especially in the years following the 2016 reform to the senatorial appointments process, is generally more robust in assessing bills with respect to constitutionality. Yet as the Senate is an appointed body, governments have not been shy about rejecting or ignoring the Senate's concerns. A joint committee of Parliament, modelled on the United Kingdom's Joint Committee on Human Rights (JCHR) and given the mandate of scrutinizing legislation for consistency with the Charter, would amplify and improve parliamentary rights debate.

In the UK context, the JCHR's criticism of the lack of ministerial justifications in support of claims that bills are compatible with the Human Rights Act led to changes in the Cabinet Office guidelines to provide more detailed information on human rights considerations in government bills.[27] There is a belief among relevant actors that the JCHR's scrutiny leads to more careful consideration of legislation in the United Kingdom. The JCHR quickly developed a reputation for persistent questioning of departments and ministers and for following up on unanswered questions, which Hiebert and Kelly suggest had the effect of pushing public servants and ministers to provide more substantive explanations on rights compatibility and legislative objectives. Hiebert and Kelly also note that the JCHR's evidence-based approach to assessing bills has enhanced its influence over policy development, particularly where new coercive powers for the state depart from judicial norms or the Human Rights Act.[28] In their view, "Robust, frequent and critical reports serve as constant reminders to public officials, ministers and cabinet that unresolved compatibility queries will be questioned. JCHR reports encourage them to anticipate critical reviews and be prepared to respond to JCHR queries."[29]

This scrutiny does not prevent governments from dismissing or avoiding JCHR recommendations and pursuing their policy objectives. No parliamentary committee can eliminate or even fully counterbalance executive power or the political factors influencing a government's pursuit of its legislative agenda. Yet, as Hiebert and Kelly conclude, the "JCHR's robust approach to its scrutiny function and its impressive work ethic ensure that parliament has access to critical analysis of how bills implicate rights at a stage in which the bill is being debated before at least one house of parliament, and thus parliament can demand amendments if it is convinced that legislation imposes an unwarranted or unjustified restriction on rights."[30]

The Parliament of Canada does not rely heavily on joint committees. There are only two standing joint committees: the Standing Joint Committee for the Scrutiny of Regulations and the Standing Joint Committee on the Library of Parliament. Both are composed of five senators and eleven or twelve MPs. A similar structure for a Joint Committee on Rights would ensure that even governments enjoying strong majorities in the House would not normally be in a position to dominate. Indeed, the Scrutiny of Regulations Committee is co-chaired by a senator and a member of the official opposition. The presence of non-partisan senators would help to mitigate the usual inter-party competitive dynamics that normally encompass committees in the House, without fully diluting the important role opposition party members play in parliamentary debate. If such a committee committed to serious and robust scrutiny of rights issues implicated by bills, it could prove as useful as its counterpart in the United Kingdom has been in elevating attention to rights, and increasing transparency around government justifications for potential limits on rights to improve parliamentary debate and accountability. To do so, it would need the resources to ensure parliamentarians can develop their own assessments, including that the joint committee have its own counsel.[31]

A Change in Culture

The reforms we propose are designed to increase transparency surrounding the legislative process under the Charter and to strengthen accountability. Governments need to do a better job of justifying proposed limitations on rights and considering Charter obligations in the course of developing new policies. The role of Parliament in facilitating debate on rights and holding the government to account over its choices under the Charter is crucial. The opacity of the executive's Charter vetting process hinders this practice and is unjustified. The reforms proposed in the preceding section would make it substantially more difficult for governments to hide, or mislead Parliament about, the extent to which certain policies unreasonably infringe Charter rights.

The analysis in this book also suggests that when attention is paid to Charter rights, far too much of the government's justifications, the opposition's criticisms, and the parliamentary debate as a whole is preoccupied with whether legislation matches the dictates of existing jurisprudence and not enough reflects any attempt by elected decision-makers to articulate an independent perspective on what the constitution requires. Strengthening the culture around the Charter in the executive and legislative branches might begin to remedy this, and to encourage proactive thinking about rights that encourage governments and legislators to go beyond merely meeting the minimum requirements of recent court decisions. We discuss this further in the concluding chapter.

Perhaps more fundamentally, a strengthened rights culture within the executive and legislative branches might inform and influence subsequent Charter jurisprudence. If governments and Parliament give robust attention to the requirements of the constitution, engage in transparent and vigorous proportionality analysis, as well as debates over policy alternatives – including taking proposed amendments seriously – then governments will be in a much better position to defend laws before courts when they are subject to Charter challenge. In short, governments will have spent more time carefully framing their policy objectives, canvassing policy alternatives, and defending policy proposals in light of Charter concerns by considering proportionality and minimal impairment arguments. Greater transparency about how governments assess the Charter's requirements on specific laws may also prompt courts to be more deferential, at least in section 1 considerations. This would not necessarily flow from judicial forays into parliamentary debates. Léonid Sirota, writing on recent UK jurisprudence about the "inappropriate" use by courts of parliamentary debates or material to assess compatibility of legislation under the Human Right Act, argues that the "quality of reasons given by individual Members of Parliament, or even by Ministers, is not what is at issue when courts assess the effect of statutory provisions on rights or their justification and proportionality in a democratic society."[32]

The UK Supreme Court has recently stated that reliance on parliamentary debates on compatibility assessments should generally be rare, citing concerns about separation of powers and respect for parliamentary privilege.[33] Nonetheless, the justices did acknowledge that deference may be owed where "Parliament can be taken to have made its own judgment of the issues which are relevant to the court's assessment."[34] The Court also noted that the absence of such parliamentary debate does not "count against"[35] the compatibility of the legislation. Moreover, the courts' analysis does not extend to an evaluation of the cogency or quality of parliamentary debate.[36] Sirota critiques instances where Canadian courts have engaged in precisely this sort of assessment,[37] and we do not advocate judicial appraisal of parliamentary debate per se. Individual MP's statements on constitutionality are unlikely to play a significant role in judicial determination of a law's

Charter consistency. Nor do we propose fostering parliamentary debate that specifically mimics judicial reasoning. Instead, the procedural and transparency reforms we advocate would further force governments to confront and justify rights infringements, especially in a way conducive to section 1 justifications, that would likely inform how they advance such justifications in Charter litigation. Moreover, to the extent that executive and legislative processes shed light on these considerations and martial evidence or arguments that demonstrate the rationality of a law's connection to its objectives or the proportionality between its effects and the limits it places on a particular right, they should be regarded as useful for that purpose and courts might heed them.

Finally, a strengthened rights culture will better protect Charter rights. First, because a lot of legislation may never be subject to judicial review, in these cases legislatures are the only bodies that can ensure bills are rights compliant. Robust legislative scrutiny under the Charter provides protections independent of judicial review. Second, as just noted, taking the Charter seriously requires governments and legislatures to go beyond merely meeting the minimum standards articulated by courts. A strong rights culture would see elected decision-makers enhancing the rights themselves.

More controversially, a vigorous rights culture in the executive and legislative branches can even help remedy judicial mistakes and failures to balance competing rights appropriately. As noted in chapter 1, rights considerations have influenced legislative responses to judicial rulings on the law surrounding sexual assault.[38] The government and Parliament responded to concerns of women's groups following common law decisions implicating the disclosure of private records and concerning the use of the extreme intoxication defence. In the former case, the Supreme Court upheld Parliament's legislation, even though it differed significantly from the common law regime articulated by a majority of the Court.[39] In the latter, Parliament prohibited the use of the extreme intoxication defence in response to a common law decision by the Court to uphold it, although the Court struck down the prohibition over two decades later.[40] Both these contexts involved balancing the rights of the criminally accused with the privacy or security interests of sexual assault complainants. Legislative responses that "push back" against judicial reasons are justifiable only to the extent they rest on coherent and robust considerations of the relevant section 1 issues at stake.

Section 1 is not the only mechanism in the Charter designed to facilitate executive and legislative assertions of appropriate outcomes under the Charter. The notwithstanding clause, which has recently seen a minor resurgence at the provincial level, allows legislatures to temporarily immunize legislation from the effects of judicial review. It has never been used at the federal level but remains a viable and (constitutionally) legitimate instrument for correcting judicial missteps or for asserting a vision of Charter rights and their scope or application that is different from that of the courts. Under what conditions might use of the notwithstanding clause be considered? We briefly turn to tackling this difficult question.

A Robust Legislative Rights Culture and the Notwithstanding Clause

The notwithstanding clause under section 33 of the Charter allows legislatures to expressly declare in legislation that a law or a provision thereof shall operate notwithstanding section 2 or sections 7 to 15 of the Charter. The clause thus applies only to certain rights provisions, and it must be renewed every five years via legislative enactment in order to remain in force. It is thus a temporary instrument to immunize specific laws, or aspects of laws, from the effects of judicial review. Section 33 has never been invoked federally, and through 2017 had been used only three times by jurisdictions (Yukon, Alberta, and Saskatchewan) other than Quebec, which had employed it fourteen times, including in omnibus fashion.[41] Almost all of these uses occurred within the first two decades of the Charter's existence. While Quebec's use of section 33 in response to the Supreme Court's decision in *Ford v. Quebec*[42] to shield its French-only signs law provoked extreme controversy in the rest of the country (it came during efforts to ratify the Meech Lake Accord, which ultimately failed), Tsvi Kahana points out that many uses of the notwithstanding clause involved matters that were not high on the public agenda and ignored by the media, in part because they were more complicated matters than the uses involving broader social issues like language rights.[43]

The notwithstanding clause was so rarely invoked in the first decade and a half of the twenty-first century that some have speculated about whether there exists a convention of disuse, especially at the federal level,[44] although a recent resurgence in provincial use arguably puts that to rest. Several recent provincial cases have provoked controversy for the manner in which the clause was used and especially for the issues involved. In 2018, Saskatchewan employed section 33 in response to a lower court decision finding that government funding for non-Catholic students to attend Catholic schools violated the Charter's freedom of religion and equality rights provisions.[45] Although the decision was also appealed (and overturned by the Saskatchewan Court of Appeal),[46] the government did not exhaust legal appeals before passing the bill.

In 2019 Quebec employed the clause when passing Bill 21 – An Act respecting the laicity of the State – legislation that so plainly and unreasonably violates religious freedom by preventing visibly religious people from being hired in public sector positions, like teachers or public servants, that pre-emptive use of section 33 was the only chance to prevent courts from striking it down on first challenge (although litigation concerning other sections of the Charter commenced almost immediately). The Bill 21 case represents such an egregious example of legislative disregard for rights that it has led Robert Leckey to conclude that "our assumption that political actors operate within a framework based on the importance of human rights no longer applies. Deciding that fundamental rights and freedoms don't need to be taken into account at all is a radical shift, so radical it's disorienting."[47] Quebec similarly employed the notwithstanding clause in 2022 with the passage of Bill 96, a blatantly unconstitutional update to its language laws.

Ontario employed the notwithstanding clause for the first time in 2021 to restore new third-party election-spending restrictions that were struck down in a lower court decision.[48] A key issue in the case concerned amendments to increase the pre-election restricted spending period from six to twelve months. As with the Saskatchewan schools case, the government did not wait for an appeal of the decision before introducing Bill 307 to use section 33 (it had similarly introduced a bill invoking section 33 to cut the size of the City of Toronto's municipal council after previous legislation had been struck down by a trial judge,[49] but that decision was overturned on appeal prior to its passage[50]). The quick turnaround – the original law was struck down on 8 June 2021 and Bill 307 received royal assent a mere six days later – illustrates how little contemplation the government and the legislature gave to the lower court's decision or to the consequences of using section 33. The controversy was compounded by the fact that the policy involves electoral regulation and Bill 307 was pushed through over the objection of the opposition parties.

These recent cases threaten to further delegitimize the notwithstanding clause. The reactionary and virtually instantaneous nature of Ontario's use reflects a complete disregard for any moral or political obligation to properly justify employing a power like section 33. Quebec's Bill 21 is even more nefarious, given it so plainly violates rights in the name of a law that targets vulnerable minorities on the basis of religion, with little to no societal benefit. It feeds the perception that the notwithstanding clause is a device for "overriding" Charter rights, rather than reflecting the actual political bargain at play when the Charter was enacted, which was to ensure that legislatures would "preserve some ability to disagree with judicial rulings where claims of rights arise."[51] For some of the provincial participants in the 1981 constitutional negotiations, this compromise was not premised on the idea that legislatures merely wanted to retain the capacity to violate rights, but that courts might make imprudent or incorrect decisions (harkening back to the American Lochner-era Court that prevented the expansion of welfare policies to respond to the Great Depression).[52] As Dwight Newman notes, section 33 "was not a rights override, but was adopted as a clause permitting legislatures to protect unenumerated rights and to engage in reasonable disagreements with courts about rights."[53]

While it would be too much to suggest that the political compromise leading to section 33 resulted in a comprehensive or sophisticated theory of how and when legislatures ought to use it,[54] an important rationale underpins its existence. Governments and legislatures should invoke section 33 only when they are willing to provide robust justifications for doing so. This has not happened with recent uses. Yet on the basis of the key purposes of section 33 noted by Newman, the government should be able to explain why it introduced a bill invoking the notwithstanding clause that either involves protecting some right (whether another Charter right or an unenumerated one) or explains why it believes a judicial decision erred. Quebec's Bill 21 represents the antithesis of this context. In its blatant disregard for religious freedom, the province operates as the "singular antagonist of the individual"[55] to advance a policy agenda of dubious and entirely symbolic quality. Of the recent cases, the Saskatchewan schools case provides the best example where potentially competing rights are at stake, and the government made a justifiable decision to invoke section 33 in order to protect school choice. Yet moving so quickly after the initial trial decision, without first exhausting judicial appeals, was imprudent at best and did not result in extensive deliberation or justification for invoking the power. The Ontario case was even worse in this specific regard.

Given the analysis in this book, how confident should we be about the capacity of legislatures and executives to properly justify use of the notwithstanding clause? The answer, unfortunately, is not confident at all. The conception of section 33 as an "override" of rights is so dominant that no federal party has seriously considered using the clause for fear of the political controversy that would inevitably follow. Even if the recent provincial activity may have loosened those constraints (although it is perhaps more likely that these largely populist invocations of section 33 have only cemented its negative reputation), until there is a significant change in culture around rights within the executive and Parliament, the risks associated with use of section 33 are too great.

This is not to say there may not be occasions where it would be valid for Parliament to employ the notwithstanding clause. But we are sceptical that a federal government would be well equipped to properly justify the clause's use and that Parliament is in a good position to deliberate and scrutinize legislation invoking it absent the reforms we advance above and a resultant improvement in the general political culture around rights discourse that would hopefully follow.

Conclusion

Legislating under the Charter occurs under an executive-dominated legislature, within a culture of judicialization, and in a system with effective strong form judicial review. Governments have incentives to minimize scrutiny of rights issues, and the executive process of Charter scrutiny is almost entirely opaque. Parliament and the opposition parties are relatively weak and disadvantaged by the lack of transparency surrounding bureaucratic assessments and the section 4.1 process. The introduction of Charter statements by the Ministry of Justice have not had a significant ameliorative effect on these problems.

As a result, we believe reforms to shed light on the executive review process and to strengthen Parliament's accountability function under the Charter are necessary, not only to push governments to better justify policies that risk violating rights and to minimize judicial invalidation of legislation, but also to better protect rights generally, including laws that might not come under judicial scrutiny.

No legislature featuring an entrenched party system and electoral incentives will meet high-minded deliberative ideals, and in a democracy attempts to shield legislative decision-making from politics is fundamentally undesirable. Law-making is political. Rights are political. There is no objective or scientific basis on which to resolve disputes over reasonable limits on rights in a free and democratic society. Yet the relatively paltry attention to the rights issues implicated by bills analysed in this book is unacceptable. Governments do not sufficiently justify their choices, and parliamentary debate that adopts a substantive or robust approach to the constitution's requirements is lacking. The status quo cries out for improvement, and while the reforms we propose will not eliminate rights concerns outright, they will compel more careful consideration of the Charter in legislating and strengthen the role of Parliament in holding the government to account over policies implicating rights.

Conclusion

We opened this book with a brief account of the flurry of federal and provincial legislative activity following the Supreme Court's ruling in *M. v. H*,[1] which concerned the constitutionality of the definition of "spouse" in Ontario legislation concerning spousal benefits. Although the Court limited its decision under the Charter to the specific legislative scheme at hand (indeed, the definition of spouse at issue only applied to one part of the law at stake), Parliament and the provincial legislatures proactively amended a host of legislation in response. Some did so grudgingly, making explicit that their legislative activity was the result of the Court's decision, and some jurisdictions did not go as far as others, but the generally robust legislative response was notable. While legislative action to enhance the scope of rights protection absent judicial decisions under the Charter is far from unprecedented – governments at all levels moved to add protections for gender identity and gender expression to statutory human rights codes without a host of judicial decisions, let alone a Supreme Court decision, requiring it, for example[2] – a proactive approach to rights is not necessarily the norm. When it comes to the Charter, governments and legislatures have tended to be reactive rather than proactive.

The problems with legislating under the Charter will sound familiar to observers or students of Canadian politics. Regardless of party, the opaque nature of government assessments of the rights compatibility of legislation allows ministers to assert the constitutionality of bills without providing substantive justification. Executive dominance over Parliament limits the opposition's capacity to meaningfully hold the government to account or to effect changes to legislation. Party discipline enables party leadership to quell intra-caucus dissent and the government to exert control over committees, hindering the chances of amendments that might meaningfully improve bills or reduce the risk that laws will infringe the Charter. Parliamentary debate that explicitly considers rights is far from robust, often reduced to talking points and rarely evincing independent judgement about what the Charter requires. Instead, when rights are invoked by elected representatives, it is usually in the context of some claim about whether a bill is consistent with a given court decision, sometimes even a single passage of that decision.

These issues generally hold even in the context of the highly salient, morally controversial policy issues examined in this book. As the scholarly literatures on party politics and morality policy suggest, such policy issues are where we would be most likely to see party discipline loosen. While there was some evidence for this in our case studies, the context was not enough to fully overcome the broader institutional challenges our analysis identifies. It is true that the judicially mandated policy outcome tends to win in subsequent rounds of litigation. Governments may be willing to "push back" against court decisions in rare instances, but ultimately unconstitutional legislation will be invalidated if litigated. For some observers this might mitigate concerns about the quality of executive and parliamentary scrutiny, at least to some extent. Yet this ignores the fact that not all legislation will be subject to judicial review, and even where litigation does occur, the final determination on constitutionality usually takes years. After briefly summarizing our findings, grounded in a discussion of judicialization and the institutional relationships that implicate legislating under the Charter, we conclude with a discussion of how a more robust rights culture might act to achieve rigorous rights protection that goes beyond judicially imposed norms.

Judicialization, Politics, and the Executive-Legislative Approach to the Charter

Canada is a leading exemplar of the "judicialization of politics," understood as the willingness of, and reliance on, courts to exercise judicial review to settle social and policy disputes.[3] Studies of legislative responses to court decisions under the Charter find that there is a tendency to adhere to judicial policy prescriptions,[4] providing strong evidence for the point that, despite inhabiting the so-called Commonwealth[5] or weak-form[6] model of judicial review (said to be a middle ground between judicial supremacy and traditional parliamentary sovereignty), Canada stands as a strong-form system in practice.[7] The strategic use of the reference procedure allows governments to shift contentious policy issues to the courts, as part of an effort to avoid blame, as was arguably the case with the same-sex marriage reference.[8] The relative public popularity of courts compared to legislatures only encourages this behaviour.[9] In short, although courts cannot control their overall policy agenda, in that they are constrained by having to deal with whatever matters come before them, the breadth of moral, social, and public policy issues ultimately settled by the judiciary under the Charter is considerable.[10]

In some ways, then, readers might be of two minds in considering the results of the analysis in this book. On the one hand, it may be surprising to find that governments and Parliament, typically deferential to courts, might exhibit a strong willingness to propose and defend the passing of constitutionally risky legislation, even when the likelihood of judicial invalidation is high. On the other hand, in the context of the highly salient, morally laden policy issues explored in this book, the inclination of governments to pursue policy objectives despite likely rights implications is consistent with broader understandings of executive power in the Canadian system, which encourages a preoccupation with short-term electoral thinking and issues management, whether to manage intra-party compromise or leverage inter-party competition.[11]

Although our findings might seem counter-intuitive on one level, they are consistent with judicialization, where blame avoidance becomes a key driver for governments dealing with controversial issues on which they might prefer not to expend political capital. Our analysis of the medical aid in dying regime, for example, emphasizes the extent to which the Liberal government cited its efforts to balance access to the service with protections for vulnerable persons when it crafted Bill C-14. There is at least some evidence that this was an attempt to navigate intra-caucus divisions over the legislation, and from the broader perspective of the competing positions taken by the parties in the House, the legislation certainly was a compromise. Yet in passing legislation that departed in specific ways from the Supreme Court's decision in *Carter*,[12] the government also knew the new law would be subject to subsequent judicial review. When a trial court in *Truchon*[13] found that the threshold for access established by Bill C-14 was unconstitutional, the government immediately introduced legislative amendments in the form of Bill C-7. That the government did not appeal the trial court decision, and instead dove straight into new amendments, lends some credence to the notion that, rather than having an ideological or evidence-based policy commitment to a particular regime for determining access, the government was happy to lean on the judicial decision to provide cover for implementing changes to bring the legislative scheme closer to the Supreme Court's established requirements. Complicating this understanding, however, is that the previous justice minister, Jody Wilson-Raybould, had been replaced by David Lametti, who was one of the few Liberals who refused to vote in favour of Bill C-14. Nonetheless, much of the justification for the new changes were premised on the judicial decisions in *Carter* and *Truchon*. Had the cabinet as a whole had strong objections to the *Truchon* court's decision, an appeal would seem to be a more likely avenue than immediate legislative changes to conform to it.

In contrast to its reactive approach to *Truchon*, the Liberal government's inaction on trial decisions implicating the Bill C-36 provisions on prostitution signify a reluctance to address constitutional issues head-on. The government inherited a legislative regime passed under the previous Conservative government and is unlikely to have a strong ideological commitment to that particular scheme. From a policy perspective, one of the only ways to eliminate some of the rights questions addressed in *Bedford* is arguably to legalize and regulate sex work from a health and safety perspective. Yet doing so was not an explicit policy prescription of the Court's, unlike its decision requiring access to medically assisted dying in *Carter*. Moreover, the lower court cases scrutinizing the Bill C-36 provisions have not fully addressed many of the issues presented by them, and the government has political incentives to wait until their status under the Charter is confirmed by further litigation. This unwillingness to proactively address the obvious constitutional issues with the Conservative government's post-*Bedford* legislation is consistent with judicialization.

However, not all governmental and legislative behaviour under the Charter that we have analysed is a product of judicialization or blame avoidance. The Conservative government under Stephen Harper explicitly advanced a "tough on crime" agenda and aggressively pursued criminal justice policy, even in the face of experts who warned about the constitutional riskiness of punitive policies on issues like sentencing.[14] The government was willing to incur criticism over Charter-vulnerable legislation. More significantly, the Conservatives were noted for an occasionally critical and rocky relationship with the courts, which boiled over with an unprecedented public relations spat between the Prime Minister's Office (PMO) and the Supreme Court over the failed appointment of Marc Nadon.[15] In *Reference Re Supreme Court Act*,[16] the Court determined that Nadon, Harper's nominee and a member of the Federal Court of Appeal, was not eligible for appointment to one of the "Quebec seats" on the Supreme Court. In the aftermath of the decision, the PMO issued a press release that strongly implied that then chief justice Beverley McLachlin had acted inappropriately by phoning the minister of justice and prime minister during the appointments process to warn them about the potential legal issue at stake.[17]

This combative approach to the judiciary, and a willingness to pass legislation that many experts warned would likely be struck down, was the product of a complex mix of ideology and political strategy.[18] Part of the Conservative Party's antipathy to the Charter arises from socially progressive outcomes in cases ranging from abortion to same-sex marriage,[19] and another part from the Charter's association as a "Liberal" document and, indeed, the courts as "Liberal" institutions.[20] Yet judicial losses also provided a strategic opportunity to further sell the government's particular policy agenda, especially in the criminal justice realm,[21] and its rhetoric around courts, including its occasionally hostile relationship with the judiciary, should be viewed in the context of partisan contestation and playing to its political base.

These governmental motivations are consistent with Emmett Macfarlane's analysis of the regime politics thesis, which states that the Supreme Court largely operates in a way that advances and protects the policy agenda of the existing dominant governing coalition. Macfarlane posits that "until 2006, a bipartisan pro-Charter regime in favour of the Court's role and supportive of judicial power held government."[22] The formation of the Conservative government under Harper signalled a shift to a government hostile to the broader Charter project and judicial review generally. Thus, while the Court rarely invalidates laws passed by the sitting government, in the context of highly salient policy issues, including those relating to criminal justice as explored in chapters 3 and 4, and a government that sits outside the long-standing regime, which includes the Court itself, an important shift occurs in the inter-institutional dynamics at stake. The Harper government is the only government of the Charter period to have policies from its election platforms blocked by judicial review, including invalidation of some of those criminal justice policies examined in chapter 3. The regime politics framework thus offers important insights into the *government*–courts relationship, as distinct from a traditional focus of other theories on the *legislature*–court relationship. Given the central role the executive plays in the development of legislation, understanding the distinct approaches of different governments to the Charter and to the courts is crucial.

Our analysis here suggests that issue salience is a fundamental variable, even for governments that support the Charter project. The Liberal government's willingness to pursue legislation that diverged from the Court's policy prescriptions on medical aid in dying is significant. Intra-party and inter-party dynamics play a key role within the context of morality policy, as noted in the Introduction, and open the door to much stronger influence for political factors to overwhelm a traditional deference to judicial decisions. The Liberal government remains broadly aligned with judicial consensus on some issues of morality policy. Thus the Trudeau government's decision to proactively adopt legislative reform to the ministerial approval process for exemptions under the Controlled Drugs and Substances Act is explained by not only a desire to adhere to the Court's policy prescription in *PHS Community Services*[23] but also by an ideological perspective consistent with liberalizing access to harm-reduction services. The Liberals also had a perspective on access to safe consumption services broadly consistent with the NDP's, and thus its political left flank was protected.

The political and inter-party dynamics around medical aid in dying were more fractured and complex, and the Liberals found themselves operating on a middle ground between the NDP pushing for more liberalized access and the Conservatives' strong opposition to further legislative changes. Consistent with the morality policy literature described in the Introduction, highly salient and controversial policies can weaken the factors associated with executive dominance, especially party discipline (as we saw on votes on Bill C-14). Yet even in the context of morality policy, executive power remains relevant. While the Liberal Party promised to revisit sex work legislation (and was in fact required to do so after five years, as per Bill C-36 itself), we have seen no progress or timelines on this after eight years. Several Liberal MPs and party members have called for it, as well as former justice minister Wilson-Raybould. Resistance appears to come from the Prime Minister's Office and is likely due to a political calculus about the potential controversies surrounding sex work and being seen as the party that supports prostitution.

If various factors explain some of the different outcomes in the cases explored here, what might our analysis say more broadly about the institutional dynamics at stake? First, despite a willingness to pass constitutionally dubious legislation and even to push back against, or alter, judicial policy prescriptions under the Charter, the outcomes in these cases demonstrate Canada's status as a system of strong-form judicial review. Many of the Harper government's criminal justice policies were invalidated by the courts. Legislative responses, whether regarded as consistent with either dialogue or coordinate interpretative approaches, have reverted to the judicially asserted policy outcome. In the case of new safe consumption sites, the Liberal government replaced the onerous regime established by the Conservatives after *PHS Community Services* by implementing guidelines that almost perfectly match the criteria outlined by the Court. In the case of medical aid in dying, Bill C-7 now establishes rules for access that more closely match the threshold required in *Carter*, although it leaves open a number of rights issues left unaddressed by the Court. Finally, lower court decisions on Bill C-36's provisions on sex work suggest a similar trend is possible in that policy area.

In short, even in these highly salient policy areas where governments evince a willingness to depart from judicial dictates, the courts retain the final word on constitutionality and, indeed, on the policies at stake. These outcomes generally comport with earlier findings by Macfarlane that legislative responses to court rulings under the Charter "will not pass muster unless they toe the judicial line in full."[24]

Yet Canada's status as a strong-form system in practice does not mean that governments and legislatures blindly defer to courts in all instances. Analysis of the institutional dynamics around legislating under the Charter must not only recognize that the inter-institutional tennis match that produces policy outcomes is iterative and ongoing, but it must also move past that simple exchange to examine the ways policymaking occurs within a broader, complex environment. In both legislative design and in implementation, many features of particular policies necessarily go unaddressed in judicial decisions.

Moreover, this book demonstrates that in highly salient policy issues, the normal political factors consistent with Westminster-style parliamentary government – including executive control of the legislative agenda, party discipline, inter-party contestation, and relatively weak opposition forces – play a significant role in ensuring legislation is passed, largely on the basis of ideological and electoral considerations rather than principled considerations of a government's rights obligations. In certain policy areas, this may result in legislative foot-dragging or non-compliance. One area where scholars, including James Kelly and Stéphanie Chouinard, suggest this occurs is with respect to minority language education rights.[25]

In the realm of criminal justice policy and the social policies examined in this book, parliamentary scrutiny of legislation on rights is relatively thin. The opposition largely focuses on compliance with judicial decisions rather than robust engagement with the demands of the Charter. To the extent governments are compelled to address the rights implications of their legislative initiatives, they can easily cherry pick elements – sometimes even a single line – of a judicial decision to claim the compatibility of their policies. Governments evince little independent thinking about the Charter. Perhaps the most pertinent development in recent years was the advent of Charter statements by the Department of Justice. These sometimes acknowledge potential implications for specific Charter provisions but do not engage in robust limitations or proportionality analysis. As we noted in preceding chapters, we do not think it useful for, nor do we expect, governments to mechanically import Oakes-test-style reasoning to justify policies. But proportionality considerations are central to good policy analysis, and engaging in such analysis of potential rights violations would help facilitate better parliamentary debate and more carefully crafted legislation, and ensure improved protection for rights overall.

If we take rights seriously, the current process for ensuring Charter compatibility of legislation should concern us, and the unwillingness or inability of Parliament to hold the government to account or to compel it to offer more robust justifications for legislative choices that implicate rights is unacceptable.

The reform proposals advanced in chapter 7 will not usher in an idealized deliberative body that focuses solely on principle as inoculated against politics. Yet increasing transparency on executive scrutiny of the Charter, and implementing processes that encourage more substantive consideration of rights in Parliament, should seriously improve the current state of affairs. Politics will inevitably play a role in how governments and legislatures balance the rights issues at stake with their policy objectives. Encouraging a more proactive stance on how governments and Parliament account for the Charter and its requirements does not detract from the role of courts, where, it should be noted, politics also plays a significant role in decision making.[26] A more proactive role for governments and legislatures in considering the Charter would not just improve rights protection in the sense of strengthening legislation against potential litigation, but would also encourage thinking that extends the protection of rights beyond the minimal requirements of the constitution. We conclude here with a brief account of what that renewed rights culture might look like.

Taking the Charter Seriously

In Vanessa MacDonnell's view, the Charter mandates a "framework for governance" where government is properly viewed not merely as the key actor that might infringe Charter rights but as a key body responsible for constitutional implementation.[27] Our analysis is fundamentally about key roles of the executive and legislature as implementers of the constitution, and our reform proposals call for a more robust and proactive approach to this role. As we also suggest in chapter 7, the "courts might be more likely to defer to the government's approach to constitutional implementation if the government were to demonstrate heightened awareness of its status as a constitutional player."[28] Where the government fails to do so, "the courts will retain their dominance."[29]

In this regard, our study has much more to say about the medium- and long-term implications of a more serious effort of the executive and legislative branches to account for rights. Like MacDonnell, we would emphasize that this is not just about the short-term dynamics between institutions as embedded in descriptions of dialogue or coordinate construction, but in the longer-term institutional relationships at stake. In her view, "Parliament's authority is constrained and legitimated by its respect for constitutional rights. If Parliament and the executive show a commitment to rights, there is good reason to expect that courts will grant them wider berth to interpret and implement constitutional rights. The opposite is also true. If Parliament were to internalize this reality, it might experience an expansion in sovereign authority relative to courts."[30] If Parliament and governments were to take the Charter more seriously, such that they approached legislative initiatives with more robust attention to rights than fleetingly considering whether legislation may survive judicial review, then the legislation examined in this book, and the process and debates surrounding it, might have been quite different. Consider, for example, the fundamental deficiencies with how governments and Parliament assessed the rights infringements at stake and the justifications for the limits imposed.

In chapter 4 we analysed the onerous requirements the Conservative government imposed via amendments to the Controlled Drugs and Substances Act, which some critics suggested were unconstitutional to the extent the scheme was an attempt to limit or preclude the creation of new sites in the aftermath of *PHS Community Services*.[31] There was no resolution to this question by judicial review because, upon forming government, the Liberals introduced amendments to establish an approval process that expressly followed the smaller list of factors mandated by the Supreme Court, as an attempt to balance public health and public safety. These include "evidence, if any, on the impact of such a facility on crime rates, the local conditions indicating a need for such a supervised injection site, the regulatory structure in place to support the facility, the resources available to support its maintenance, and expressions of community support or opposition."[32] The Supreme Court expended no energy to explain why these were the factors that "must" be considered by the minister in making a decision on exemptions. More importantly, there was no deliberation in Parliament that seemed to suggest anyone in government or in the House of Commons raised objections to the idea that community support (i.e., public opinion) should have any weight in a context where the rights of those suffering from addiction were implicated. A more robust rights culture would have engaged in more explicit consideration of whether certain factors are relevant.

A vigorous rights culture would also lead decision-makers to consider whether concerns about "safety" or security in relation to safe consumption sites are substantial enough to require balancing with the health-care rights of those suffering from addiction. The Court did not declare a positive right to safe consumption services, but the underlying logic of *PHS Community Services* strongly implicates a right of access *to* the service for those who need it.[33] More to the point, nothing prevents laws that *exceed* the constitution's minimum standards. A rights-enhancing approach to public policy arguably lends itself to policy measures that boost access to services in some contexts. Rather than 'pushing back' against the Court's policy prescription in a way that might limit rights, Parliament might have considered amendments to the CDSA approval process that rejected factors like public opinion entirely, despite the Court having included them in its policy prescription, in order to more robustly protect the rights of those suffering from addiction.

Another context that would benefit from a proactive rights approach would be to consider addressing issues that are related to, but not directly addressed by, judicial decisions under the Charter. For example, in the medical assistance in dying context a strong rights culture would offer incentives to governments and Parliament to consider access for mature minors. We noted in chapter 6 that parliamentary review of this issue began in May 2021 – more than six years after the initial *Carter* decision.[34] Such delay in examining an issue of access like this one is antithetical to a robust approach to rights. Mature minors, by definition, are capable of consenting to medical decisions and making decisions affecting bodily autonomy.[35] The Court's decision did not address the issue because mature minors were not implicated in the facts of the case before it, but that does not mean those under eighteen lack Charter rights. Governments and legislatures that refuse to tackle relevant issues because they have not been litigated are not exercising their responsibility to protect rights.

A fundamental issue with the parliamentary focus on judicial decisions is that it means legislators are inattentive to sections of the Charter that did not play a determinative role in the outcome of litigation. Yet all of the major policy areas examined in this book implicate more than a single Charter right. When the Supreme Court issues a judgment on appeal, once it has determined that a legislative provision violates a particular section of the Charter, such as section 7, it will often refrain from analysing the same law in relation to other rights, such as the right to equality under section 15. Yet many of the cases examined in this book implicate equality rights and, as Macfarlane has argued, might have been considered "first and foremost" equality right cases.[36] David Lepofsky writes that *Carter* was fundamentally a case about a "glaring Charter disability equality violation," and the Court's decision to focus on section 7 instead of section 15 arguably resulted in a narrowly tailored examination of the rights issues at stake.[37] Had Parliament given sustained attention to Bills C-14 or C-7 from an equality rights perspective, it might have compelled legislators to consider some of the conspicuous rights issues that remain live – including access for mature minors or people suffering from mental health issues.

Policy debates over sex work are also deeply implicated by equality rights considerations, even though *Bedford* was ultimately resolved under section 7. Yet parliamentary debate over Bill C-36 neglected a deeper analysis of the freedom and equality-based arguments implicated in the legislation in favour of a focus on whether the new provisions replicated section 7 violations. There was no Charter-grounded analysis of equality rights, despite much rhetoric surrounding "equality and dignity" of sex workers. Brenda Cossman writes that the governance of sex work also frames sex workers as both tragic victims and sexual deviants, and this prevents legislators from addressing more fundamental questions of whether "sex worker specific criminal laws perpetuate the stigmatization of sex workers."[38] In our view, this is principally an equality rights question, and mandates consideration of policy alternatives that do not rely on the criminal law. Parliament engaged in no meaningful consideration of potential section 15 challenges, and section 2 rights were noted only briefly. A proactive analysis of the broader Charter issues implicated in the legislation would not only guard against risks of Charter challenges beyond section 7, but would also arguably lead to the crafting of much more careful, and ultimately better, public policy.

A more robust rights culture would encourage greater parliamentary, executive, and bureaucratic attention to policy analysis dedicated to considering the full gamut of rights enjoyed by Canadians, rather than adopting a posture largely predicated on existing jurisprudence, which is inherently limited by the nature of cases that come before courts. The analysis in this book suggests that Parliament is ill-prepared for that task. Parliamentary debate is, in a limited fashion, influenced by judicial norms about Charter rights, and rather than sharpening and enlivening debate over rights consideration, judicial norms stimulate a narrow focus on often singular provisions of the Charter rather than broad engagement with all the rights implicated by particular policies and bills. Coupled with the short-term ideological, partisan, and electoral thinking that dominates the executive-led legislative process, the rights of Canadians receive inadequate protection when Parliament passes laws. Reforms to increase transparency in executive Charter-vetting processes and to better enable accountability on rights are crucial to remedying these serious problems.

Notes

Introduction

1 *M. v. H.*, [1999] 2 S.C.R. 3.
2 Brenda Cossman, "Canadian Same-Sex Relationship Recognition Struggles and the Contradictory Nature of Legal Victories," *Cleveland State Law Review* 48 (2000): 49–59, 56.
3 Ibid., 57.
4 Erin Melrose and Rais Khan, "Bill 41 Ignores M. v. H.'s Broader Implications as Well as the Government's Responsibility to Respect the Charter of Rights and Freedoms," *Policy Options*, 1 November 2001. https://policyoptions.irpp.org/magazines/the-911-attack/missing-the -big-picture-manitobas-bill-41-and-m-v-h/.
5 Emmett Macfarlane, "Dialogue or Compliance? Measuring Legislatures' Policy Responses to Court Rulings on Rights," *International Political Science Review* 34 (2013): 39–56.
6 Janet Hiebert conducted research interviews with several lawyers in the Human Rights Centre at the Department of Justice in 1999 and 2000, on the basis of anonymity. She also had the opportunity for repeated and candid conversations (with attribution granted) with former deputy ministers of justice, John Tait (1994–5) and George Thomson (1998–9), with Edgar Schmidt (2014–15), and former minister of justice Irwin Cotler (2015), as well as interviews conducted on the basis of anonymity with former officials in the department in 2014 and 2015.
7 Stephen Gardbaum, *The New Commonwealth Model of Constitutionalism: Theory and Practice* (Cambridge: Cambridge University Press, 2013), 1. See also Mark Harding's recent comparative analysis of legal and political constitutionalism: *Judicializing Everything? The Clash of Constitutionalism in Canada, New Zealand, and the United Kingdom* (Toronto: University of Toronto Press, 2022).

8   Mark Tushnet, *Weak Courts, Strong Rights: Judicial Review and Social Welfare Rights in Comparative Constitutional Law* (Princeton, NJ: Princeton University Press, 2008).

9   Ibid., 23.

10   Peter W. Hogg and Allison A. Bushell, "The Charter Dialogue between Courts and Legislatures (or Perhaps the Charter of Rights Isn't Such a Bad Thing after All)," *Osgoode Hall Law Journal* 35, no. 1 (1997): 75–124.

11   Legislative responses to judicial decisions are, as widely noted, possible in the US system as well, as a significant "dialogic" or "interbranch" literature demonstrates. See Mark C. Miller and Jeb Barnes, eds., *Making Policy, Making Law* (Washington, DC: Georgetown University Press, 2004); Martin J. Sweet, *Merely Judgment: Ignoring, Evading, and Trumping the Supreme Court* (Charlottesville: University of Virginia Press, 2010); Mark C. Miller, *The View of the Courts from the Hill: Interactions between Congress and the Federal Judiciary* (Charlottesville: University of Virginia Press, 2009); Louis Fisher, *Constitutional Dialogues: Interpretation as Political Process* (Princeton, NJ: Princeton University Press, 1988); Louis Fisher, *Reconsidering Judicial Finality: Why the Supreme Court Is Not the Last Word on the Constitution* (Lawrence: University Press of Kansas, 2019).

12   Macfarlane, "Dialogue or Compliance?"

13   For two leading examples, see Janet Hiebert, *Charter Conflicts: What Is Parliament's Role?* (Montreal and Kingston: McGill-Queen's University Press, 2002); James B. Kelly, *Governing with the Charter: Legislative and Judicial Activism and Framers' Intent* (Vancouver: UBC Press, 2005).

14   Lee Epstein and Jeffrey A. Segal, "Measuring Issue Salience," *American Journal of Political Science* 44, no. 1 (2000): 66–83.

15   For a good discussion of this, see James B. Kelly, "Legislative Capacity and Human Rights in the Age of Populism – Two Challenges for Legislated Rights: Discussion of *Legislated Rights – Securing Human Rights through Legislation*," *Jerusalem Review of Legal Studies* 21, no. 1 (2020): 94–111.

16   Jean-François Godbout, *Lost on Division: Party Unity in the Canadian Parliament* (Toronto: University of Toronto Press, 2020); Alex Marland, *Whipped: Party Discipline in Canada* (Vancouver: UBC Press, 2020).

17   For more analysis of the causes and efffects of party discipline and a comparative analysis of Westminster-based jurisdcitions, see C.J. Kam, *Party Dicispline and Parliamentary Politics* (Cambridge: Cambridge University Press, 2009); R.A. Rhodes, J. Wanna, and P. Weller, *Comparing Westminster* (Oxford: Oxford University Press, 2009).

18   In February 2013 NDP Justice Critic Francoise Boivin put forth a motion to the Justice and Human Rights Committee that a "thorough study" into how section 4.1 was being interpreted be conducted. Justice and Human Rights Committee, 13 February 2013, Evidence.

19 Statement provided by the parliamentary secretary to the minister of justice, read into the proceedings of the Justice and Human Rights Committee, Meeting 59, 13 February 2013, Evidence.

20 Aaron Wherry, "The Independent MP for Edmonton–St. Albert and His Bill," *Maclean's*, 10 June 2013. https://www.macleans.ca/politics/ottawa/the-independent-mp-for-edmonton-st-albert-and-his-bill/.

21 Hiebert, *Charter Conflicts*; Kelly, *Governing with the Charter*.

22 Janet L. Hiebert and James B. Kelly, *Parliamentary Bills of Rights: The Experiences of New Zealand and the United Kingdom* (Cambridge: Cambridge University Press, 2015), 10.

23 Jeremy Waldron, "The Core of the Case against Judicial Review," *Yale Law Journal* 115 (2006): 1346–1406.

24 Macfarlane, "Dialogue or Complaince?"

25 *R. v. Morgentaler*, [1988] 1 S.C.R. 30.

26 For a more in-depth read on the case and its aftermath, see Rachael Johnstone, *After Morgentaler: The Politics of Abortion in Canada* (Vancouver: UBC Press, 2017).

27 Rachael Johnstone and Emmett Macfarlane, "Public Policy, Rights, and Abortion Access in Canada," *International Journal of Canadian Studies* 51 (2015): 97–120; Emmett Macfarlane and Rachael Johnstone, "Equality Rights, Abortion Access, and New Brunswick's Regulation 84–20," *University of New Brunswick Law Journal* 72 (2021): 302–24.

28 For a discussion of punctuated equilibrium theory – which purports to explain large or sweeping policy change – and courts, see Marc Zanoni, "The Supreme Court of Canada, Judicial Remedies, and Punctuated Equilibrium," *Policy Change, Courts, and the Canadian Constitution*, ed. Emmett Macfarlane (Toronto: University of Toronto Press, 2018), 61–78.

29 Emmett Macfarlane, "Judicial Policy Impact in Canada," in *Policy Change, Courts, and the Canadian Constitution*, ed. Macfarlane (Toronto: University of Toronto Press, 2018), 4.

30 Gerald N. Rosenberg, *The Hollow Hope: Can Courts Bring About Social Change?* 2nd ed. (Chicago: University of Chicago Press, 2008); Rosenberg, "Positivism, Interpretivism, and the Study of Law," *Law and Social Inquiry* 21 (1996): 435–55; Michael McCann, "Causal versus Constitutive Explanations (or, On the Difficulty of Being So Positive...)," *Law and Social Inquiry* 21 (1996): 457–82; McCann, "Reform Litigation on Trial," *Law and Social Inquiry* 17, no. 4 (1992): 715–43; McCann, *Rights at Work: Pay Equity Reform and the Politics of Legal Mobilization* (Chicago: Chicago University Press, 1994).

31 Troy Q. Riddell, "The Impact of Legal Mobilization and Judicial Decisions: The Case of Official Minority-Language Education Policy in Canada for Francophones outside Quebec," *Law and Society Review* 38 (2004): 583–609.

32 Christopher P. Manfredi, *Feminist Activism in the Supreme Court: Legal Mobilization and the Women's Legal Education and Action Fund* (Vancouver: UBC Press, 2004).

33 Stéphanie Chouinard, "Section 23 of the Charter and Official-Language Minority Instruction in Canada: The Judiciary's Impact and Limits in Education Policymaking," in *Policy Change, Courts, and the Canadian Constitution*, ed. Emmett Macfarlane (Toronto: University of Toronto Press, 2018), 230–49; James B. Kelly, "The Charter of the French Language and the Supreme Court of Canada: Assessing Whether Constitutional Design Can Influence Policy Outcomes," in Macfarlane *Policy Change*, 250–68; Rachael Johnstone, "Canadian Abortion Policy and the Limitations of Litigation," in Macfarlane, *Policy Change*, 336–55.

34 Christopher Z. Mooney, "The Politics of Morality Policy," *Policy Studies Journal* 27, no. 4 (1999): 675.

35 Ibid.

36 Julia Mourão Permoser, "What Are Morality Policies? The Politics of Values in a Post-Secular World," *Political Studies Review* 17, no. 3 (2019): 311.

37 Mooney, "Politics of Morality Policy," 676.

38 Christoph Knill, "The Study of Morality Policy: Analytical Implications from a Public Policy Perspective," *Journal of European Public Policy* 20, no. 3 (2013): 312.

39 Stephan Heichel, Christoph Knill, and Sophie Schmitt, "Public Policy Meets Morality: Conceptual and Theoretical Challenges in the Analysis of Morality Policy Change," *Journal of European Public Policy* 20, no. 3 (2013): 319.

40 Ibid., 327, citing L. Marvin Overby, Raymond Tatalovich, and Donley T. Studlar, "Party and Free Votes in Canada: Abortion in the House of Commons," *Party Politics* 4, no. 3 (1998): 381–92.

41 Ibid., 323.

42 Recent Canadian studies examining court decisions on agenda-setting theories like punctuated equilibrium or the multiple streams approach help to characterize how this happens. See Dave Snow and Kate Puddister, "Closing a Door but Opening a Policy Window: Legislating Assisted Dying in Canada," in *Policy Change, Courts, and the Canadian Constitution*, ed. Emmett Macfarlane (Toronto: University of Toronto Press, 2018), 40–60; Zanoni, "Supreme Court of Canada."

43 Gary Mucciaroni, "Are Debates about 'Morality Policy' Really about Morality? Framing Opposition to Gay and Lesbian Rights," *Policy Studies Journal* 39, no. 2 (2011): 187–216.

44 *Canada (Attorney General) v. PHS Community Services Society*, 2011 SCC 44, [2011] 3 S.C.R. 134.

45 *Canada (Attorney General) v. Bedford*, 2013 SCC 72, [2013] 3 S.C.R. 1101.
46 Macfarlane, "Dialogue or Compliance?"

Chapter 1

1 Michael Mandel, *The Charter of Rights and the Legalization of Politics in Canada* (Toronto: Thompson Education Publishing, 1994); Allan C. Hutchinson, *Waiting for Coraf: A Critique of Law and Rights* (Toronto: University of Toronto Press, 1995); Ian Greene, Carl Baar, Peter McCormick, George Szablowski, and Martin Thomas, *Final Appeal: Decision-Making in Canadian Courts of Appeal* (Toronto: Lorimer, 1998); Peter McCormick, *Supreme at Last: The Evolution of the Supreme Court of Canada* (Toronto: Lorimer, 2000); F.L. Morton and Rainer Knopff, *The Charter Revolution and the Court Party* (Toronto: University of Toronto Press, 2000); Christopher P. Manfredi, *Judicial Power and the Charter: Canada and the Paradox of Liberal Constitutionalism*, 2nd ed. (Oxford: Oxford University Press, 2000); Patrick James, Donald E. Abelson, and Michael Lusztig, eds., *The Myth of the Sacred: The Charter, the Courts, and the Politics of the Constitution in Canada* (Montreal and Kingston: McGill-Queen's University Press, 2002); Paul Howe and Peter H. Russell, eds., *Judicial Power and Canadian Democracy* (Montreal and Kingston: McGill-Queen's University Press, 2001); Emmett Macfarlane, *Governing from the Bench: The Supreme Court of Canada and the Judicial Role* (Vancouver: UBC Press, 2013).
2 Peter W. Hogg and Allison A. Bushell, "The Charter Dialogue between Courts and Legislatures (or Perhaps the Charter of Rights Isn't Such a Bad Thing after All)," *Osgoode Hall Law Journal* 35, no. 1 (1997): 75–124.
3 Ibid., 81.
4 See discussion of "dialogue as prescription" in Emmett Macfarlane, "Conceptual Precision and Parliamentary Systems of Rights: Disambiguating 'Dialogue,'" *Review of Constitutional Studies* 17, no. 2 (2012): 73–100.
5 Tsvi Kahana, "The Notwithstanding Mechanism and Public Discussion: Lessons from the Ignored Practice of Section 33 of the Charter," *Canadian Public Administration* 44, no. 3 (2001): 255–91. The notwithstanding clause has been used only a handful of times since Kahana's 2001 study, including in Quebec, Saskatchewan, and, for the first time in its history, in Ontario in 2021.
6 Richard Albert, "The Desuetude of the Notwithstanding Clause – and How to Revive It," in *Policy Change, Courts, and the Canadian Constitution*, ed. Emmett Macfarlane (Toronto: University of Toronto Press, 2018), 146–55.

7 Christopher P. Manfredi and James B. Kelly, "Six Degrees of Dialogue: A Response to Hogg and Bushell," *Osgoode Hall Law Journal* 37, no. 3 (1999): 521.
8 Hogg and Bushell, "Charter Dialogue between Courts and Legislatures," 80.
9 Emmett Macfarlane, "Dialogue or Compliance? Measuring Legislatures' Policy Responses to Court Rulings on Rights," *International Political Science Review* 34, no. 1 (2012): 39–56.
10 Rosalind Dixon, "The Supreme Court of Canada, Charter Dialogue, and Deference," *Osgoode Hall Law Journal* 47, no. 2 (2009): 235–86.
11 Matthew A. Hennigar, "Expanding the 'Dialogue' Debate: Canadian Federal Government Responses to Lower Court Charter Decisions," *Canadian Journal of Political Science* 37, no. 1 (2004): 3–21; Mark V. Tushnet, *Weak Courts, Strong Rights: Judicial Review and Social Welfare Rights in Comparative Constitutional Law* (Princeton, NJ: Princeton University Press, 2008), 44; Macfarlane, "Dialogue or Compliance?"
12 Kent Roach, *The Supreme Court on Trial: Judicial Activism or Democratic Dialogue*. Rev. ed. (Toronto: Irwin Law, 2016), 336.
13 Hennigar, "Expanding the 'Dialogue' Debate," 8.
14 Ibid., 8.
15 Grant Huscroft, "Constitutionalism from the Top Down," *Osgoode Hall Law Journal* 45, no. 1 (2007): 91–104.
16 Roach, *Supreme Court on Trial*, 337.
17 Ibid., 336, pointing out that following the *Schachter* case Parliament lowered the benefits it extended, or that following *Chaoulli* "Quebec expanded the debate by improving its mechanisms for managing wait times, thus dampening the demand for private insurance." Citing *Schachter v. Canada*, [1992] 2 S.C.R. 679; *Chaoulli v. Quebec (Attorney General)*, 2005 SCC 35.
18 For example, consider restrictions on prisoner voting rights. Christopher P. Manfredi, "The Day the Dialogue Died: A Comment on *Sauvé v. Canada*," *Osgoode Hall Law Journal* 45, no. 1 (2007): 105–23.
19 Macfarlane, "Conceptual Precision and Parliamentary Systems of Rights."
20 Peter W. Hogg, Allison A. Bushell Thornton, and Wade K. Wright, "Charter Dialogue Revisited – or 'Much Ado about Metaphors,'" *Osgoode Hall Law Journal* 45, no. 1 (2007): 26.
21 Robert Leckey, *Bills of Rights in the Common Law* (Cambridge: Cambridge University Press, 2015), 167.
22 Aileen Kavanagh, "The Lure and the Limits of Dialogue," *University of Toronto Law Journal* 66, no. 1 (2015): 95.
23 Carissima Mathen, "Dialogue Theory, Judicial Review, and Judicial Supremacy: A Comment on Charter Dialogue Revisited," *Osgoode Hall Law Journal* 45, no. 1 (2007): 125–46.

24   Kavanagh, "The Lure and the Limits of Dialogue"; Matthew A. Hennigar, "Unreasonable Disagreement? Judicial-Executive Exchanges about Charter Reasonableness in the Harper Era," *Osgoode Hall Law Journal* 54 (2017): 1248.
25   Roach, *Supreme Court on Trial*, 311.
26   Dennis Baker, *Not Quite Supreme: The Courts and Coordinate Constitutional Interpretation* (Montreal and Kingston: McGill-Queen's University Press, 2010), 4.
27   Ibid., 5.
28   Included in Baker's discussion are legislative responses at issue in *R. v. Mills*, [1999] 3 S.C.R. 668; and *R. v. Hall*, [2002] 3 S.C.R. 309.
29   Rainer Knopff, Rhonda Evans, Dennis Baker, and Dave Snow, "Dialogue: Clarified and Reconsidered," *Osgoode Hall Law Journal* 54 (2017): 609–44.
30   Ibid., 622–3.
31   *R. v. Daviault*, [1994] 3 S.C.R. 63; *R. v. O'Connor*, [1995] 4 S.C.R. 411.
32   *R. v. Mills*, [1999] 3 S.C.R. 668.
33   Dennis Baker and Rainer Knopff, "*Daviault* Dialogue: The Strange Journey of Canada's Intoxication Defence," *Review of Constitutional Studies* 19, no. 1 (2014): 35–58.
34   *R. v. Brown*, 2022 SCC 18.
35   *R. v. Morales*, [1992] 3 S.C.R. 711.
36   Knopff et al., "Dialogue," 639.
37   *R. v. Hall*, [2002] 3 S.C.R. 309, 2002 SCC 64, at para. 127.
38   Knopff et al., "Dialogue," 641, citing Hogg, Thornton, and Wright, "Charter Dialogue Revisited," 31.
39   Roach, *Supreme Court on Trial*, 308.
40   James B. Kelly and Matthew A. Hennigar, "The Canadian Charter of Rights and the Minister of Justice: Weak-Form Review within a Constitutional Charter of Rights," *International Journal of Constitutional Law* 10, no. 1 (2012): 35–68.
41   *Sauvé v. Canada (Attorney General)*, [1993] 2 S.C.R. 438.
42   *Sauvé v. Canada (Chief Electoral Officer)*, [2002] 3 S.C.R. 519, 2002 SCC 68.
43   Manfredi, "The Day the Dialogue Died."
44   Janet L. Hiebert, *Charter Conflicts: What Is Parliament's Role?* (Montreal and Kingston: McGill-Queen's University Press, 2002).
45   Ibid., xv.
46   Ibid., 224.
47   James B. Kelly, *Governing with the Charter: Legislative and Judicial Activism and Framers' Intent* (Vancouver: UBC Press, 2005).
48   Ibid., 263.
49   Ibid., 262.
50   Janet L. Hiebert, "The Charter, Policy, and Political Judgment," in *Policy Change, Courts, and the Canadian Constitution*, ed. Emmett Macfarlane (Toronto: University of Toronto Press, 2018), 83. See also Janet L. Hiebert,

"The Charter's Influence on Legislation: Political Strategizing about Risk," *Canadian Journal of Polticial Science* 51, no. 4 (2018): 727–47.

51 Hiebert, "Charter, Policy, and Political Judgment," 96.

52 Janet L. Hiebert and James B. Kelly, *Parliamentary Bills of Rights: The Experiences of New Zealand and the United Kingdom* (Cambridge: Cambridge University Press, 2015), 407.

53 Jeffrey Simpson, *The Friendly Dictatorship* (Toronto: McClelland & Stewart, 2001).

54 Donald J. Savoie, *Governing from the Centre: The Concentration of Power in Canadian Politics* (Toronto: University of Toronto Press, 1999).

55 Paul G. Thomas, "The Influence of Standing Committees of Parliament on Government Legislation," *Legislative Studies Quarterly* 3, no. 4 (1978): 683–704.

56 Emmett Macfarlane, *Constitutional Pariah: Reference re Senate Reform and the Future of Parliament* (Vancouver: UBC Press, 2021).

57 Royce Koop and Amanda Bittner, "Parachuted into Parliament: Candidate Nomination, Appointed Candidates, and Legislative Roles in Canada," *Journal of Elections, Public Opinion and Parties* 21, no. 4 (2011): 431–52.

58 Paul E.J. Thomas and J.P. Lewis, "Executive Creep in Canadian Provincial Legislatures," *Canadian Journal of Political Science* 52 (2019): 363–83.

59 Herman Bakvis, "Prime Minister and Cabinet in Canada: An Autocracy in Need of Reform?" *Journal of Canadian Studies* 35, no. 4 (2001): 60–79.

60 J.P. Lewis, "Elite Attitudes on the Centralization of Power in Canadian Political Executives: A Survey of Former Canadian Provincial and Federal Cabinet Ministers," *Canadian Journal of Political Science* 46, no. 4 (2013): 799–819.

61 David E. Smith, *The People's House of Commons: Theories of Democracy in Contention* (Toronto: University of Toronto Press, 2007), 86.

62 Ibid., 87.

63 Jean-François Godbout, *Lost on Division: Party Unity in the Canadian Parliament* (Toronto: University of Toronto Press, 2020), 57–60.

64 David E. Smith, *Across the Aisle: Opposition in Canadian Politics* (Toronto: University of Toronto Press, 2013).

65 Ibid., 161–6.

66 Gwyneth Bergman and Emmett Macfarlane, "The Impact and Role of Officers of Parliament: Canada's Conflict of Interest and Ethics Commissioner," *Canadian Public Administration* 61, no. 1 (2018): 5–25. The influence of the privacy commissioner is similarly conditional on the government's willingness to listen: Gwyneth Bergman and Emmett Macfarlane, "Protecting Privacy? Government and Parliamentary Responsiveness to the Privacy Commissioner of Canada," *Canadian Public Administration* 64, no. 3 (2021): 437–57.

67 Ian Brodie, *At the Centre of Government: The Prime Minister and the Limits on Political Power* (Montreal and Kingston: McGill-Queen's University Press, 2018), 135.

68 Ibid.

69 Ibid., 137.

70 Ibid., 137–8.

71 Samara Centre for Democracy, *"It's My Party": Parliamentary Dysfunction Reconsidered* (Toronto: Samara Centre for Democracy, 2011); Samara Centre for Democracy, *The Real House Lives: Strengthening the Role of MPs in an Age of Partisanship* (Toronto: Samara Centre for Democracy, 2018).

72 Kelly Blidook, *Constituency Influence in Parliament: Countering the Centre* (Vancouver: UBC Press, 2012), 9.

73 Ibid., 10.

74 James B. Kelly and Kate Puddister, "Criminal Justice Policy during the Harper Era: Private Member's Bills, Penal Populism, and the Criminal Code of Canada," *Canadian Journal of Law and Society* 32, no. 2 (2017): 391–415.

75 David C. Docherty, *Mr. Smith Goes to Ottawa: Life in the House of Commons* (Vancouver: UBC Press, 1997), 137.

76 Godbout, , *Lost on Division*, 80.

77 Neil Longley, "Legislative Systems with Absolute Party Discipline: Implications for the Agency Theory Approach to the Constituent-Legislator Link," *Public Choice* 97 (1998): 136.

78 L. Marvin Overby, Raymond Tatalovich, and Donley T. Studlar, "Party and Free Votes in Canada: Abortion in the House of Commons," *Party Politics* 4, no. 3 (1998): 389.

79 L. Marvin Overby, Christopher Raymond, and Zeynep Taydas, "Free Votes, MPs, and Constituents: The Case of Same-Sex Marriage in Canada," *American Review of Canadian Studies* 41, no. 4 (2011): 465–478.

80 Docherty, *Mr. Smith Goes to Ottawa*, 140.

81 Alex Marland, *Whipped: Party Discipline in Canada* (Vancouver: UBC Press, 2020).

82 Donald J. Savoie, *Power: Where Is It?* (Montreal and Kingston: McGill-Queen's University Press, 2010), 72–5; Savoie, *Whatever Happened to the Music Teacher? How Government Decides and Why* (Montreal and Kingston: McGill-Queen's University Press, 2013), 86.

83 Vanessa MacDonnell, "The Civil Servant's Role in the Implementation of Constitutional Rights," *I-CON: International Journal of Constitutional Law* 13, no. 2 (2015): 383–406.

84 Donald J. Savoie, *Democracy in Canada: The Disintegration of Our Institutions* (Montreal and Kingston: McGill-Queen's University Press, 2019), 309.

85 Jeremy A. Clarke, "Beyond the Democratic Dialogue, and Towards a Federalist One: Provincial Arguments and Supreme Court Responses in

Charter Litigation," *Canadian Journal of Political Science* 39, no. 2 (2006): 293–314.

86 Matthew A. Hennigar, "Exploring Complex Judicial-Executive Interaction: Federal Government Concessions in Charter of Rights Cases," *Canadian Journal of Political Science* 434 (2010): 821–42; Hennigar, "Why Does the Federal Government Appeal to the Supreme Court of Canada in Charter of Rights Cases? A Strategic Explanation," *Law & Society Review* 41, no. 1 (2007): 225–50; Hennigar, "*Reference re Same-Sex Marriage*: Making Sense of the Government's Litigation Strategy," in *Contested Constitutionalism*, ed. James Kelly and Christopher Manfredi (Vancouver: UBC Press, 2009), 209–30.

87 Kate Puddister, *Seeking the Court's Advice: The Politics of the Canadian Reference Power* (Vancouver: UBC Press, 2019); Carissima Mathen, *Courts without Cases: The Law and Politics of Advisory Opinions* (Oxford: Hart Publishing, 2019).

88 Mathen, *Courts without Cases*, 70–4.

89 Puddister, *Seeking the Court's Advice*, 124–32.

90 Mathen, *Courts without Cases*, 74.

91 Puddister, *Seeking the Court's Advice*, 46.

92 Emmett Macfarlane, "Conservative with the Constitution? Moderation, Strategy, and Institutional Distrust," in *The Blueprint: Conservative Parties and Their Impact on Canadian Politics*, ed. J.P. Lewis and Joanna Everitt (Toronto: University of Toronto Press, 2017), 230.

93 Erin Crandall and Andrea Lawlor, "Public Support for Canadian Courts: Understanding the Roles of Institutional Trust and Partisanship," *Canadian Journal of Law and Society* 37, no. 1 (2022): 91–112.

94 Christopher Manfredi, "Conservatives, the Supreme Court of Canada, and the Constitution: Judicial Government Relations, 2006–2015," *Osgoode Hall Law Journal* 52, no. 3 (2015): 951–83.

95 Ibid., 979.

96 Matthew A. Hennigar, "Unreasonable Disagreement? Judicial-Executive Exchanges about Charter Reasonableness in the Harper Era," *Osgoode Hall Law Journal* 54, no. 4 (2017): 1245–73, 1262.

97 Emmett Macfarlane, "'You Can't Always Get What You Want': Regime Politics, the Supreme Court of Canada, and the Harper Government," *Canadian Journal of Political Science* 51, no. 1 (2018): 1–21.

Chapter 2

1 Christopher MacLennan, *Toward the Charter: Canadians and the Demand for a National Bill of Rights, 1929–1960* (Montreal and Kingston: McGill-Queen's University Press, 2003), 148.

2 Section 3(1) of the Canadian Bill of Rights provides: "3 (1) Subject to subsection (2), the Minister of Justice shall, in accordance with such regulations as may be prescribed by the Governor in Council, examine every regulation transmitted to the Clerk of the Privy Council for registration pursuant to the *Statutory Instruments Act* and every Bill introduced in or presented to the House of Commons by a Minister of the Crown, in order to ascertain whether any of the provisions thereof are inconsistent with the purposes and provisions of this Part and he shall report any such inconsistency to the House of Commons at the first convenient opportunity."

3 For more discussion about this requirement, see Janet L. Hiebert, *Charter Conflicts: What Is Parliament's Role?* (Montreal and Kingston: McGill-Queen's University Press, 2002), 4–14.

4 *Robertson and Rosetanni v. The Queen* [1963] S.C.R. 651.

5 Interviews were conducted by Hiebert with several lawyers in the Human Rights Centre at the Department of Justice between 1999 and 2000, on the basis of anonymity. She also had the opportunity for repeated and candid conversations (with attribution granted) with former deputy ministers of justice, John Tait (1994–5) and George Thomson (1998–9), with Edgar Schmidt (2014–15), and former minister of justice Irwin Cotler (2015), as well as interviews conducted on the basis of anonymity with former officials in the department (2014, 2015). Henceforth: Interviews.

6 Elmer A. Driedger, "The Meaning and Effect of the Canadian *Bill of Rights:* A Draftsman's Viewpoint," *Ottawa Law Review* 9 (1977): 306.

7 *Department of Justice Act* R.S., 1985, c. J-2.

8 Alex Stone Sweet, *Governing with Judges: Constitutional Politics in Europe* (Oxford: Oxford University Press, 2000).

9 Interviews.

10 Interviews.

11 These cases included *Singh v. Minister of Employment and Immigration* [1985] 1 S.C.R. 177; *Schacter v. Canada* [1992] 2 S.C.R. 679; and *R v. Oakes* [1986] 1 S.C.R. 103.

12 James B. Kelly, *Governing with the Charter: Legislative and Judicial Activism and Framers' Intent* (Vancouver: UBC Press 2005), 232–4.

13 Mary Dawson, "The Impact of the Charter on the Public Policy Process and the Department of Justice," *Osgoode Hall Law Journal* 30 (1992): 597.

14 Kelly, *Governing with the Charter*, 228.

15 Interviews.

16 Janet Hiebert, *Limiting Rights: The Dilemma of Judicial Review* (Montreal and Kingston: McGill-Queen's University Press, 1996); Emmett Macfarlane, *Governing from the Bench: The Supreme Court of Canada and the*

Judicial Role (Vancouver: UBC Press, 2013). On the inconsistent caselaw on deference under section 1, see also Jula Hughes and Vanessa MacDonnell, "Social Science Evidence in Constitutional Rights Cases in Germany and Canada: Some Comparative Observations," *National Journal of Constitutional Law* 32 (2013): 23–60.

17 Interviews.
18 Interviews.
19 Interviews.
20 Interviews.
21 Interviews.
22 *Edgar Schmidt v. The Attorney General of Canada*, 2016 FC 269.
23 Interviews; Edgar Schmidt, "Worlds in Collision: A Public Lawyer's Challenges When Administrative Directions Seem to Depart from the Law," Presentation to the Canadian Bar Association, New Brunswick Branch, 7 February 2014, Moncton, New Brunswick.
24 Interviews.
25 Interviews.
26 The department subsequently provided a different rationale for the suspension. It told Schmidt that the department required his absence so as to investigate his conduct, and since he was absent from work, and therefore not doing his job, he could not be paid. Interview with Schmidt.
27 Edgar Schmidt and attorney general of Canada. Representations of the Defendant on His Motion, 4 January 2013.
28 Bill Curry, "Judge Raps Justice Officials for Treatment of Whistle-Blower," *Globe and Mail*, 16 January 2013. http://www.theglobeandmail.com/news/politics/judge-raps-justice-officials-for-treatment-of-whistle-blower/article7394559/
29 Edgard Schmidt and attorney general of Canada. Notice of Abandonment, 22 February 2013.
30 Edgar Schmidt and attorney general of Canada, Resondent's Memorandum of Fact and Law.
31 Ibid.
32 Department of Justice, "In Our Opinion: Best Practices for Department of Justice Counsel in Providing Legal Advice," April 2012.
33 Interviews.
34 Interviews.
35 Interviews.
36 Interviews.
37 Interviews.
38 Interviews.
39 Interviews.
40 *Edgar Schmidt v. Canada*, para. 7.

41 Interviews.
42 *Edgar Schmidt v. Canada*, para. 5.
43 *Schmidt v. Canada (Attorney General)*, 2018 FCA 55, para. 141 103–4.
44 *Edgar Schmidt v. Canada*, para. 276.
45 Ibid., paras. 250, 252.
46 Department of Justice, "Legal Risk Management in the Public Sector," 26 November 2007.
47 Department of Justice, "Extracts from 'Effective Communication of Legal Risk,'" 2014.
48 Memorandum of the Appellant at para. 3 and 21, as referred to in the Factum of the Respondent, para. 27.
49 Factum of the Respondent, para. 9.
50 Factum of the Respondent, para. 34.
51 Factum of the Respondent, paras. 34–6.
52 Department of Justice, Effective Communication of Legal Risk, as included in Edgar Schmidt and attorney general of Canada, Statement of Agreed Facts. http://charterdefence.ca/uploads/3/4/5/1/34515720/statement-of-agreed-facts.pdf.
53 *Edgar Schmidt v. Canada*, para. 240.
54 Department of Justice, "In Our Opinion: Best Practices for Department of Justice Counsel in Providing Legal Advice," April 2012.
55 Ibid., para. 243.
56 Ibid., para. 247.
57 Interviews.
58 Emmett Macfarlane, "Conservative with the Constitution? Moderation, Strategy, and Institutional Distrust," in *The Blueprint: Conservative Parties and Their Impact on Canadian Politics*, ed. J.P. Lewis and Joanna Everitt (Toronto: University of Toronto Press, 2017), 233, citing Paul Wells, *Rights Side Up: The Fall of Paul Martin and the Rise of Stephen Harper's New Conservativism* (Toronto: Douglas Gibson, 2006), 231.
59 *Schmidt v. Canada (Attorney General)*, paras. 103–4.
60 Wright, Justice Committee, Evidence, 23 February 2016.
61 Ibid.
62 Christin Schmitz, "Minister Pledges to Reveal Risks in Some Legislation," *Lawyer's Daily*, 16 June 2016.
63 Wright, Justice Committee, Evidence.
64 Ibid.
65 Ibid.
66 Ibid.
67 Murray Rankin, Justice Committee, Evidence, 23 February 2016.
68 Jody Wilson-Raybould, minister of justice, Justice Committee, Evidence, 17 May 2016.

69 Other elements of this commitment were said to include working with the minister of public safety and emergency preparedness to repeal elements of Bill C-51 and introduce measures that respect national security and achieves a better balance between collective security and rights and freedoms; introduce legislation to add gender identity as a prohibited ground of discrimination under the Canadian Human Rights Act, and to list the distinguishing characteristics of "identifiable groups" protected by Criminal Code hate provisions. Minister of justice and attorney general of Canada mandate letter, 13 December 2019. http://pm.gc.ca/eng/minister-justice-and-attorney-general-canada-mandate-letter

70 Justice Committee, Evidence, 18 October 2017.

71 Minister of justice and attorney general of Canada mandate letter.

72 Department of Justice, "Questions and Answers: Cleaning Up the *Criminal Code*, Clarifying and Strengthening Sexual Assault Law, and Respecting the Charter," http://www.justice.gc.ca/eng/csj-sjc/pl/cuol-mgnl/qa2-qr2.html

73 Department of Justice, "Charter Statements," http://www.justice.gc.ca/eng/csj-sjc/pl/charter-charte/index.html.

74 Department of Justice, "Charter Statements."

75 Mark Tushnet, "Policy Distortion and Democratic Debilitation: Comparative Illumination of the Countermajoritarian Difficulty," *Michigan Law Review* 94 (1995): 253.

76 Robert E. Nagel, *Constitutional Cultures: The Mentality and Consequences of Judicial Review* (Berkeley: University of California Press, 1993), 116.

77 Ibid., 120.

78 Hiebert, *Charter Conflicts*, 52–72.

Chapter 3

1 For an excellent analysis of this phenomenon in Canada, See James B. Kelly and Kate Puddister, "Criminal Justice Policy during the Harper Era: Private Member's Bills, Penal Populism and the *Criminal Code* of Canada," *Canadian Journal of Law and Society* 32, no. 3 (2017): 391–415.

2 For a discussion of this phenomenon elsewhere, see Malcolm Dean, "The Origins of Penal Populism," Centre for Crime and Justice Studies, 2012. https://www.crimeandjustice.org.uk/sites/crimeandjustice.org.uk/files/09627251.2012.671022.pdf. Hiebert and Kelly talk about this phenomenon in the context of its impact on legislative rights debates in New Zealand, in *Parliamentary Bills of Rights: The Experiences of New Zealand and the United Kingdom* (Cambridge: Cambridge University Press, 2015), chap. 5.

3 "Harper Announces New Measures to Protect Children and Increase Penalties for Serious Crimes," 8 September 2015. http://www.conservative.ca/harper-announces-new-measures-to-protect-children-and-increase-penalties-for-serious-crimes (page discontinued).

4 Kelly and Puddister, "Criminal Justice Policy."
5 Joe Comartin, Standing Committee on Justice and Human Rights, Evidence, 6 February 2007.
6 Sean Fine, "Stephen Harper's Courts: How the Judiciary Has Been Remade," *Globe and Mail*, 24 July 2015.
7 Paula Mallea, "Tough on Crime, Weak on Results," *The Harper Record 2008–2015*, Canadian Centre for Policy Alternatives, 205.
8 Stephen Harper, House of Commons, 14 February 2007.
9 Emmett Macfarlane, "'You Can't Always Get What You Want': Regime Politics, the Supreme Court of Canada, and the Harper Government," *Canadian Journal of Political Science* 51, no. 1 (2018): 1–21.
10 *R. v. Lloyd* [2016] 1 S.C.R. 130.
11 *R. v. Safarzadeh-Markhali* 2016 SCC 14.
12 Graeme Hamilton, "White Collar Minimums: Some Mandatory Sentences Have Been Struck Down but Stiff Financial Crime Penalties Here to Stay," *Lawyers Weekly*, 26 August 2016. http://www.lawyersweekly.ca.
13 Conservative Party of Canada, "Stand Up for Security," federal election platform, 2006.
14 CBC News, "Toronto Shooting Déjà Vu for Tough-on-Crime Tories," 4 June 2012. http://www.cbc.ca/news/canada/toronto/toronto-shooting-deja-vu-for-tough-on-crime-tories-1.1255129.
15 Tom Flanagan, *Harper's Team: Behind the Scenes in the Conservative Rise to Power*, 2nd ed. (Montreal and Kingston: McGill-Queen's University Press, 2009), 247.
16 Joe Comartin, Standing Committee on Justice and Human Rights, Evidence, 6 February 2007.
17 Paul Wells, "How Stéphane Dion Broke the Liberal Party," *Maclean's*, 20 April 2008. http://www.thecanadianencyclopedia.ca/en/article/how-stephane-dion-broke-the-liberal-party/.
18 Jane Taber, "Liberals' 'Whipped Abstention' Preserves Minority," *Globe and Mail*, 25 October 2007. http://www.theglobeandmail.com/news/national/liberals-whipped-abstention-preserves-minority/article18148212/.
19 Laura Barnett, Robin MacKay, and Dominique Valliquet, "Bill C-2: An Act to Amend the Criminal Code and to Make Consequential Amendments to Other Acts," Library of Parliament, Parliament of Canada, 29 October 2007, LS-565E. https://publications.gc.ca/collections/collection_2008/lop-bdp/ls/392-565-2E.pdf.
20 Legislative Committee on Bill C-2, *First Report*, 20 November 2007.
21 Paula Mallea, *Fearmonger: Harper's Tough-on-Crime Agenda* (Toronto: James Lorimer, 2011), 17.
22 Rob Nicholson, Legislative Committee on Bill C-2, Evidence, 30 October 2007.

23 Andy Rady, Canadian Council of Criminal Lawyers, Legislative Committee on Bill C-2, Evidence, 13 November 2007.

24 Brian Murphy, Legislative Committee on Bill C-2, Evidence, 13 November 2007.

25 Legislative Committee on Bill C-2, Evidence, 13–14 November 2007.

26 Legislative Committee on Bill C-2, Evidence, Isabel Schurman, 14 November 2007; Evan Roitenberg, director, Council of Criminal Defence Lawyers, 13 November 2007.

27 Marlene Jennings, Legislative Committee on Bill C-2, Evidence, 14–15 November 2007.

28 Réal Ménard, Legislative Committee on Bill C-2, Evidence, 13 November 2007.

29 Réal Ménard, Legislative Committee on Bill C-2, Evidence, 15 November 2007.

30 Stanley Cohen, Legislative Committee on Bill C-2, Evidence, 15 November 2007.

31 Réal Ménard, Legislative Committee on Bill C-2, Evidence, 15 November 2007.

32 Stanley Cohen, Legislative Committee on Bill C-2, Evidence, 15 November 2007.

33 *Edgar Schmidt v. The Attorney General of Canada*, 2016 FC 269, para. 250–2.

34 Richard Harris, Legislative Committee on Bill C-2, Evidence, 14 November 2007.

35 Legislative Committee on Bill C-2, Evidence, 20 November 2007.

36 Robert Thibault, *House of Commons Debates*, 23 November 2007.

37 Joe Comartin, *House of Commons Debates*, 23 November 2007.

38 Ibid.

39 Rob Nicholson, *House of Commons Debates*, 23 November 2007.

40 Ibid.

41 Rob Moore, *House of Commons Debates*, 27 November 2007; Joe Comartin, 27 November 2007.

42 Joe Comartin, *House of Commons Debates*, 27 November 2007.

43 Ibid.

44 Robert Thibault, *House of Commons Debates*, 23 November 2007.

45 Carole Freeman, *House of Commons Debates*, 26 November 2007.

46 Standing Senate Committee on Legal and Constitutional Affairs, *Eighth Report*, 12 December 2007.

47 Steven Chase, "Conservative Majority Would Hustle Crime Bill into Law All at Once," *Globe and Mail*, 7 April 2011. http://www.theglobeandmail .com/news/politics/conservative-majority-would-hustle-crime-bills-into -law-all-at-once/article597346/.

48 *R. v. D.B.*, [2008] 2 S.C.R. 3, 2008 SCC 25.

49 Justice Laws Website, Safe Streets and Communities Act. https://laws
    -lois.justice.gc.ca/eng/annualstatutes/2012_1/page-1.html.
50 Robert Nicholson, Justice Committee, Evidence, 6 October 2011.
51 Justice Committee, Evidence, 17 November 2011.
52 Nicholas Bala, Justice Committee, Evidence, 25 October 2011.
53 Michael Jackson, Canadian Bar Association, Justice Committee, Evidence,
    28 October 2011.
54 Catherine Latimer, John Howard Society, Justice Committee, Evidence,
    18 October 2011.
55 Alex Ballingall, "Omnibus Crime Bill C-10 Passed; A Conservative
    Election Promise Kept," *Maclean's*, 13 March 2012. http://www.macleans
    .ca/general/omnibus-crime-bill-c-10-passed-a-conservative
    -election-promise-kept.
56 For a comprehensive discussion of these measures, see Raji Mangat, *More
    than We Can Afford: The Costs of Mandatory Minimum Sentencing*, BC Civil
    Liberties Association, 2014.
57 Ryan Newell, "Making Matters Worse: The Safe Streets and Communities Act
    and the Ongoing Crisis of Indigenous Over-Incarceration," *Osgoode Hall Law
    Journal* 51, no. 1 (2013): 200–1. For a discussion of proportional sentencing, see
    Joshua Sealy-Harrington and David Rennie, "Making Sense of Aboriginal and
    Racialized Sentencing," ABlawg.ca, 5 September 2016. https://ablawg.ca/wp
    -content/uploads/2016/09/Blog_JSH_DR_Laboucan_Kreko_Sept2016.pdf.
58 Canadian Bar Association, "Submission on Bill C-10: Safe Streets and
    Communities Act," October 2011. https://www.cba.org/CMSPages
    /GetFile.aspx?guid=b8cadb63-95fb-47a2-a0f0-2c0f3f63540b.
59 Canadian Bar Association, "10 Reasons to Oppose Bill C-10," *Toronto Star*,
    14 November 2011.
60 Ibid., 23 November 2011.
61 Françoise Boivin, *House of Commons Debates*, 2 December 2011.
62 Irwin Cotler, Justice Committee, Evidence, 23 November 2011.
63 Ibid.
64 Irwin Cotler, *House of Commons Debates*, 2 December 2011.
65 An exception was Elizabeth May (Green Party), who chastised members
    to respect their oath to uphold the constitution: "It seems to be beyond
    our ability to grasp that we are passing a law that is in itself illegal."
    House of Commons Debates, 9 March 2012.
66 Proceedings of the Standing Senate Committee on Legal and
    Constitutional Affairs, issue 14, 24 February 2012.
67 A Liberal senator's proposed amendment to increase judicial discretion
    about when not to impose mandatory minimum punishment was
    defeated. Proceedings of the Standing Senate Committee on Legal and
    Constitutional Affairs, 24 February 2012.

68 *R. v. St-Onge Lamoureux,* 2012 SCC 75, [2012] 3 S.C.R. 187.
69 *R. v. Nur* [2015] 1 S.C.R. 773.
70 *R. v. Lloyd* [2016] 1 S.C.R. 130.
71 Kate Puddister, "How the Canadian Sentencing System Impacts Policy Reform: An Examination of the Harper Era," *Law & Policy* 43, no. 2 (2021): 149–69.
72 *Canada (Attorney General) v. Whaling,* 2014 SCC 20, [2014] 1 S.C.R. 392.
73 *R. v. Smith,* 2015 SCC 34, [2015] 2 S.C.R. 602.
74 *R. v. Boudreault,* 2018 SCC 58, [2018] 3 S.C.R. 599.
75 *R. v. Summers,* [2014] 1 S.C.R. 575; *R. v. Safarzadeh-Markhali,* [2016] 1 S.C.R. 180.
76 Christopher Manfredi, "Conservatives, the Supreme Court of Canada, and the Constitution: Judicial-Government Relations, 2006–2015," *Osgoode Hall Law Journal* 52 (2015): 979.
77 Matthew A. Hennigar, "Unreasonable Disagreement: Judicial-Executive Exchanges about Charter Reasonableness in the Harper Era," *Osgoode Hall Law Journal* 54 (2017): 1262.
78 Macfarlane, "'You Can't Always Get What You Want.'"
79 Hennigar, "Unreasonable Disagreement," 1270.
80 Canadian Press, "Supreme Court Quashes Mandatory Minimum Sentences for Gun Crimes," CBC News, 14 April 2015. https://www.cbc.ca/news/politics/supreme-court-quashes-mandatory-minimum-sentences-for-gun-crimes-1.3031847.
81 Kate Puddister, "Protecting against Cruel and Unusual Punishment: Section 12 of the Charter and Mandatory Minimum Sentences," in *Policy Change, Courts, and the Canadian Constitution,* ed. Emmett Macfarlane (Toronto: University of Toronto Press, 2018), 189–209.
82 Ibid., citing *R. v. Lloyd* at para. 106.
83 Janet L. Hiebert, "Parliamentary Bills of Rights: Have They Altered the Norms for Legislative Decision-Making?" in *Comparative Constitutional Theory,* ed. Gary Jacobson and Miguel Schor (Cheltenham: Edward Elgar Publishing, 2018), 123–43.

Chapter 4

1 *Canada (Attorney General) v. PHS Community Services Society,* 2011 SCC 44, [2011] 3 S.C.R. 134 *[PHS].*
2 Matthew A. Hennigar, "Unreasonable Disagreement? Judicial-Executive Exchanges about Charter Reasonableness in the Harper Era," *Osgoode Hall Law Journal* 54 (2017): 1261.
3 *Vancouver Agreement: 2000–2010 Highlights* (June 2010), 7.
4 *The Vancouver Agreement: An Urban Development Agreement between Canada-British Columbia-Vancouver regarding Economic, Social and Community Development in the City of Vancouver* (9 March 2000), 7.

5 Ibid.

6 *Controlled Drugs and Substances Act*, S.C. 1996, c. 19, 45.

7 *PHS Community Services Society v. Attorney General of Canada*, 2008 BCSC 661; *PHS Community Services Society v. Canada (Attorney General)*, 2010 BCCA 15.

8 *PHS*, para. 152.

9 Ibid., para. 114.

10 Ibid., para. 127.

11 Ibid., para. 150.

12 Ibid., para. 140.

13 Ibid., para. 136.

14 Emmett Macfarlane, "The Dilemma of Positive Rights: Access to Health Care and the Canadian Charter of Rights and Freedoms," *Journal of Canadian Studies* 48, no. 3 (2014): 49–78.

15 See *Gosselin v. Quebec (Attorney General)*, [2002] 4 S.C.R. 429, 2002 SCC 84.

16 See Government of Canada, "Supervised Consumption Sites: Status of Applications," 15 June 2021. https://www.canada.ca/en/health -canada/services/substance-use/supervised-consumption-sites/status -application.html.

17 CTV News, "CMA 'Deeply Concerned' about Tighter Rules for Safe Injection Sites," 6 June 2013. http://www.ctvnews.ca/health/health -headlines/cma-deeply-concerned-about-tighter-rules-for-safe-injection -sites-1.1313766

18 *PHS*, para. 153.

19 Canada, *House of Commons Debates*, 6 May 2008 (Hon. Tony Clement, CPC), 39th Parliament, 2nd Session.

20 Canada, *House of Commons Debates*, 7 February 2008 (Mr. Harold Albrecht, CPC), 39th Parliament, 2nd Session.

21 Canadian Alliance for Social Justice and Family Values Association, "Petition to the House of Commons in Parliament Assembled," 2008.

22 Canada, *House of Commons Debates*, 13 May 2008 (Mr. Maurice Vellacott, CPC), 39th Parliament, 2nd Session.

23 Canada, *House of Commons Debates*, 5 June 2008 (Hon. Tony Clement, CPC), 39th Parliament, 2nd Session.

24 Canada, *House of Commons Debates*, 30 May 2008 (Mr. Steven Fletcher, CPC), 39th Parliament, 2nd Session.

25 Canada, *House of Commons Debates*, 3 October 2011 (Hon. Leona Aglukkaq, CPC), 41st Parliament, 1st Session.

26 Canada, *House of Commons Debates*, 3 October 2011 (Hon. Hedy Fry, Liberal), 41st Parliament, 1st Session.

27 Canada, *House of Commons Debates*, 12 June 2013 (Hon. Leona Aglukkaq, CPC), 41st Parliament, 1st Session.

28 Ibid.

29 Ibid.

30 *PHS*, para. 140.
31 Ibid., para. 153.
32 Canada, *House of Commons Debates*, 18 November 2013 (Ms Megan Leslie, NDP), 41st Parliament, 2nd Session.
33 Canada, *House of Commons Debates*, 8 November 2013 (Ms Hélène Laverdière, NDP), 28 November 2013 (Mr. Glenn Thibeault, NDP), 27 January 2014 (Mr. Raymond Côté, NDP), 41st Parliament, 2nd Session.
34 Canada, *House of Commons Debates*, 4 November 2013 (Mr. Randall Garrison, NDP), 8 November 2013 (Mr. Dany Morin, NDP), 18 November 2013 (Mr. Robert Chisholm, NDP; Mr. Philip Toone, NDP), 21 November 2013 (Mr. Pierre-Luc Dusseault, NDP), 28 November 2013 (Ms Linda Duncan, NDP; Ms Ruth Ellen Brosseau, NDP), 27 January 2014 (Mr. Alexandre Boulerice, NDP), 41st Parliament, 2nd Session.
35 Canada, *House of Commons Debates*, 8 November 2013 (Mr. Murray Rankin, NDP; Hon. Wayne Easter, Liberal; Ms Hélène Laverdière, NDP), 18 November 2013 (Mr. Craig Scott, NDP; Mrs. Sana Hassainia, NDP; Mr. Philip Toone, NDP), 41st Parliament, 2nd Session.
36 *PHS*, para. 152.
37 Canada, *House of Commons Debates*, 18 Nov 2013 (Mr. Craig Scott, NDP), 41st Parliament, 2nd Session.
38 Canada, *House of Commons Debates*, 18 Nov 2013 (Mr. Craig Scott, NDP), 41st Parliament, 2nd Session (emphasis in original).
39 Canada, *House of Commons Debates*, 18 Nov 2013 (Hon. Steven Fletcher, CPC), 41st Parliament, 2nd Session.
40 Canada, Standing Committee on Public Safety and National Security, *Evidence*, 27 October 2014 (Libby Davies, NDP), 41st Parliament, 2nd Session.
41 Canada, Standing Committee on Public Safety and National Security, *Evidence*, 27 October 2014 (Hon. Rona Ambrose), 41st Parliament, 2nd Session.
42 Canada, Standing Committee on Public Safety and National Security, *Evidence*, 27 October, 2014 (Hon. Steven Blaney), 41st Parliament, 2nd Session.
43 Canada, Standing Committee on Public Safety and National Security, *Evidence*, 3 November 2014 (Adrienne Smith), 41st Parliament, 2nd Session.
44 Canada, Standing Committee on Public Safety and National Security, *Evidence*, 3 November 2014 (Donald MacPherson), 41st Parliament, 2nd Session.
45 Emmett Macfarlane, "Positive Rights and Section 15 of the Charter: Addressing a Dilemma," *National Journal of Constitutional Law* 38, no. 1 (2018): 147–68.
46 Canada, *House of Commons Debates*, 31 January 2017 (Hon. Jane Philpott, Lib.), 42nd Parliament, 1st Session.

47 Canada, *House of Commons Debates*, 31 January 2017 (Mr. Raj Grewal), 42nd Parliament, 1st Session.

48 Canada, *House of Commons Debates*, 31 January 2017 (Hon. Michelle Rempel, CPC), 42nd Parliament, 1st Session.

49 Government of Canada, "Apparent Opioid-Related Deaths," (2018) https://www.canada.ca/en/health-canada/services/substance-abuse/prescription-drug-abuse/opioids/apparent-opioid-related-deaths.html [accessed February 1, 2018]

50 Canada, *House of Commons Debates*, 31 January 2017 (Hon. Colin Carrie, CPC; Mr. Don Davies, NDP; Ms Dianne L. Watts, CPC), 42nd Parliament, 1st Session.

51 Canada, *House of Commons Debates*, 31 January 2017 (Hon. Colin Carrie, CPC), 42nd Parliament, 1st Session.

52 Ibid.

53 Canada, *House of Commons Debates*, 31 January 2017 (Mr. Don Davies, NDP), 42nd Parliament, 1st Session (emphasis added).

54 *PHS*, paras. 151–3.

55 It is difficult to ascertain precisely how many of those applications were initiated when the Bill C-2 legislative scheme was still in place. See Government of Canada, "Supervised Consumption Sites: Status of Applications," 15 June 2021. https://www.canada.ca/en/health-canada/services/substance-use/supervised-consumption-sites/status-application.html.

56 Cécile Kazatchkine, Richard Elliott, and Donald MacPherson, *An Injection of Reason: Critical Analysis of Bill C-2* (Toronto: Canadian HIV/AIDS Legal Network and the Canadian Drug Policy Coalition, 2014).

57 Macfarlane, "Positive Rights and Section 15 of the Charter."

58 Anna Junker, "Alberta Harm Reduction Advocated Call on Province to Stop 'Unjust Assault' on Supervised Consumption Sites," *Edmonton Journal*, 30 August 2021. https://edmontonjournal.com/news/local-news/alberta-harm-reduction-advocates-call-on-province-to-stop-unjust-assault-on-supervised-consumption-sites

Chapter 5

1 *Canada (Attorney General) v. Bedford* 2013 SCC 72.

2 *Criminal Code*, R.S.C. 1985, c. C-46: (s. 210); (s. 212 (1) (j)); (s. 213 (1) (c)).

3 *Bedford*, paras. 3, 5, 6.

4 Department of Justice, Canada: Research and Statistics Division, *Online Public Consultation on Prostitution-Related Offences in Canada Final Results*, 2014.

5 Canada, *House of Commons Debates*, 11 June 2014 (Hon. Peter MacKay) 41st Parliament, 2nd Session, 5 p.m.

6 Action Canada, "Statement of Solidarity for Sex Workers' Rights," https://secure.actioncanadashr.org/en/solidarity-sex-workers-rights; Elya M. Durisin, Emily van der Meulen, and Chris Bruckert, eds., *Red Light Labour: Sex Work Regulation, Agency, and Resistance* (Vancouver: UBC Press, 2018).

7 *R. v. Anwar*, 2020 ONCJ 103; *R. v. N.S.* 2021 ONSC 1628. By contrast, an earlier Ontario Superior Court decision, *R. v. Boodhoo, and others*, 2018 ONSC 7205, upheld several provisions of the law.

8 Alyshah Hasham, "Are Canada's Sex Work Laws Unconstitutional? Why That Open Question Has Thrown Ontario Law Enforcement into Chaos," *Toronto Star*, 1 October 2021. https://www.thestar.com/news/gta/2021 /10/01/are-canadas-sex-work-laws-unconstitutional-why-that-open -question-has-thrown-ontario-law-enforcement-into-chaos.html.

9 *Bedford*, para. 1.

10 Ibid., para. 2.

11 Ibid., p. 8.

12 Ibid., p. 5–6.

13 Ibid., para. 87.

14 Ibid., paras. 131, 134.

15 Ibid., paras. 147, 159.

16 Ibid., paras. 154, 155, 156.

17 Ibid., para. 158.

18 Ibid., para. 138.

19 *Criminal Code*, R.S.C. 1985, c. C-46: (s. 212 (1) (*j*)).

20 *Bedford*, para. 137.

21 Ibid., para. 142.

22 Ibid., para. 138.

23 Ibid., p. 11.

24 Ibid., p. 11.

25 Bill C-36, *Protection of Communities and Exploited Persons Act*, 2nd Session, 42nd Parliament, Canada, 2014 (assented to 6 November 2014), 7.

26 Ibid., s. 286.1(1):

27 Ibid., s. 286.5(1).

28 Ibid., s. 286.2(1)(2).

29 Ibid., s. 286.2(4).

30 *Bedford*, p. 10.

31 *An Act to Amend the Criminal Code*, p. 13: 286.2(5). Direct quotation is 286.2(5)(e).

32 Ibid., p. 14.

33 Ibid., s. 213(3) (1.1).

34 Ibid., p. 7.

35 Sean Fine, "Supreme Court Strikes Down Canada's Prostitution Laws," *Globe and Mail*, 20 December 2013. https://www.theglobeandmail.com /news/national/supreme-court-rules-on-prostitution-laws /article16067485/.

36 Palmoa Aguilar, "Government of Canada Launches On-line Consultations to Seek Views on Criminal Code Prostitution-Related Offences," news release, Department of Justice Canada, 17 February 2014. https://www.canada.ca/en/news/archive/2014/02/government -canada-launches-line-consultations-seek-views-criminal-code -prostitution-related-offences.html.

37 Ibid.

38 Canada, Department of Justice, *Online Public Consultation on Prostitution- related Offences in Canada: Final Results*, 2014, p. 5. https://www.justice .gc.ca/eng/rp-pr/other-autre/rr14_09/rr14_09.pdf.

39 Ibid., 2 (emphasis in original).

40 Aguilar, "Government of Canada Launches On-line Consultations."

41 Pacific AIDS Network, "Public Consultations on Prostitution-Related Offences," 6 March 2014. https://pacificaidsnetwork.org/2014/03/06 /public-consultation-on-prostitution-related-offences/.

42 Canadian Press, "Supreme Court Prostitution Ruling Forces Issue on Harper," CBC News, 13 December 2013. https://www.cbc.ca/news/politics /supreme-court-prostitution-ruling-forces-issue-on-harper-1.2472807

43 Canada, *House of Commons Debates*, 11 June 2014 (Hon. Peter MacKay) 41st Parliament, 2nd Session, 4:55 p.m.

44 Ibid.

45 Ibid.

46 Ibid., 5:00 p.m.

47 Ibid., 4:55 p.m.

48 Ibid.

49 *Bedford*, 2013, at para. 165, as cited in Canada, *House of Commons Debates*, 11 June 2014 (Hon. Peter MacKay) 41st Parliament, 2nd Session, 4:55 p.m.

50 Canada, *House of Commons Debates*, 11 June 2014 (Hon. Peter MacKay) 41st Parliament, 2nd Session, 4:55 p.m.

51 Canada, *House of Commons Debates*, 11 June 2014 (Hon. Peter MacKay) 41st Parliament, 2nd Session, 5:00 p.m.

52 Canada, *House of Commons Debates*, 12 June 2014 (Hon. Peter MacKay) 41st Parliament, 2nd Session, 3 p.m.

53 Ibid., 5:00 p.m.

54 Ibid.

55 Ibid.

56 Ibid., 4:55 p.m.

57 Ibid., 5:00 p.m.
58 Ibid.
59 Ibid.
60 *Bedford*, paras. 142, 162 and on p. 10, 11.
61 Canada, *House of Commons Debates*, 11 June 2014 (Hon. Peter MacKay) 41st Parliament, 2nd Session, 5 p.m. (emphasis added).
62 Ibid.
63 Ibid., 5:05 p.m.
64 Ibid.
65 *Bedford*, p. 10.
66 Canada, *House of Commons Debates*, 11 June 2014 (Hon. Peter MacKay) 41st Parliament, 2nd Session, 5:00 p.m.
67 Ibid., 4:55 p.m.
68 Ibid.
69 *Bedford*, p. 10.
70 Canada, *House of Commons Debates*, 11 June 2014 (Françoise Boivin) 41st Parliament, 2nd Session, 5:15 p.m.
71 Ibid.
72 Canada, *House of Commons Debates*, 12 June 2014 (Wayne Easter) 41st Parliament, 2nd Session, 11:55 a.m.
73 Canada, *House of Commons Debates*, 12 June 2014 (Marc-André Morin) 41st Parliament, 2nd Session, 11:55 a.m.
74 Canada, *House of Commons Debates*, 11 June 2014 (Joy Smith) 41st Parliament, 2nd Session, 5:20 p.m.
75 Canada, *House of Commons Debates*, 12 June 2014 (Joy Smith) 41st Parliament, 2nd Session, 1:30 p.m; Canada, *House of Commons Debates*, 12 June 2014 (Bob Dechert) 41st Parliament, 2nd Session, 1:15 p.m.
76 Canada, *House of Commons Debates*, 12 June 2014 (Joy Smith) 41st Parliament, 2nd Session, 1:35 p.m.
77 Canada, *House of Commons Debates*, 12 June 2014 (Sean Casey) 41st Parliament, 2nd Session, 1:40 p.m.
78 Canada, *House of Commons Debates*, 12 June 2014 (Sean Casey) 41st Parliament, 2nd Session, 12:55 p.m.
79 Ibid.
80 Canada, *House of Commons Debates*, 12 June 2014 (Françoise Boivin) 41st Parliament, 2nd Session, 1:40 p.m.; Canada, *House of Commons Debates*, 12 June 2014 (Sean Casey) 41st Parliament, 2nd Session, 1:40 p.m.
81 Canada, *House of Commons Debates*, 12 June 2014 (Joy Smith) 41st Parliament, 2nd Session, 1:20, 1:35, and 1:40 p.m.
82 Ibid.
83 Ibid., 1:00 and 1:05 p.m.
84 Ibid., 12:50 p.m.

85 Ibid., 1:15 p.m.

86 Ibid., 1:05 p.m.

87 Carole Pateman, *The Sexual Contract* (Stanford, CA: Stanford University Press, 1988).

88 Durisin, van der Meulen, and Bruckert, *Red Light Labour*.

89 Canada, *House of Commons Debates*, 12 June 2014 (Françoise Boivin) 41st Parliament, 2nd Session, 11:40 p.m.

90 Ibid.

91 Canada, *House of Commons Debates*, 12 June 2014 (Joy Smith) 41st Parliament, 2nd Session, 1:20 p.m.

92 Canada, *House of Commons Debates*, 12 June 2014 (Joy Smith) 41st Parliament, 2nd Session, 1:30 p.m.

93 Durisin, van der Meulen, and Bruckert, *Red Light Labour*.

94 Canada, *House of Commons Debates*, 12 June 2014 (Sean Casey) 41st Parliament, 2nd Session, 12:55 p.m.

95 Canada, *House of Commons Debates*, 16 June 2014 (Charlie Angus) 41st Parliament, 2nd Session, 3:45 p.m.

96 Genevieve Fuji Johnson, Mary Burns, and Kerry Porth, "A Question of Respect: A Qualitative Text Analysis of the Canadian Parliamentary Committee Hearings on *The Protection of Communities and Exploited Persons Act*," *Canadian Journal of Political Science* 50, no. 4 (2017): 940.

97 Ibid.

98 "A truly progressive society encourages the equality and dignity of women, not the prostitution of women." Canada, *House of Commons Debates*, 12 June 2014 (Joy Smith) 41st Parliament, 2nd Session, 1:35 p.m.

99 MacKay notes, "We feel we have struck the proper balance in the best interests of the public and of prostitutes." Canada, *House of Commons Debates*, 11 June 2014 (Hon. Peter MacKay) 41st Parliament, 2nd Session, 5:20 p.m.

100 Canada, *House of Commons Debates*, 12 June 2014 (Irene Mathyssen) 41st Parliament, 2nd Session, 1:10 p.m.

101 Canada, *House of Commons Debates*, 12 June 2014 (Sean Casey) 41st Parliament, 2nd Session, 1:10 p.m.

102 Canada, *House of Commons Debates*, 12 June 2014 (Françoise Boivin) 41st Parliament, 2nd Session, 1:50 p.m.

103 Canada, *House of Commons Debates*, 12 June 2014 (Irene Mathyssen) 41st Parliament, 2nd Session, 1:10 p.m.

104 Canada, *House of Commons Debates*, 12 June 2014 (Sean Casey) 41st Parliament, 2nd Session, 1:10 p.m.

105 CBC News, "Justin Trudeau Wary of Proposal to Regulate, Tax Prostitution," CBC News, 17 January 2014. https://www.cbc.ca/news/politics/justin-trudeau-wary-of-proposal-to-regulate-tax-prostitution-1.2500357

106 Ibid.
107 David P. Ball, "New Justice Minister Says She'll Listen to Sex Workers on Prostitution Reforms," Tyee.ca, 27 November 2015. https://thetyee.ca /News/2015/11/27/Justice-Minister-on-Sex-Work/.
108 Ibid. See also Action Canada, *Statement of Solidarity for Sex Workers' Rights*.
109 Wilson-Raybould said the Liberal government would ensure that any legislative provisions "are consistent with the commitments that we've made, are consistent with the Charter, and certainly consistent with the values that we generally have as Canadians – values of diversity, of inclusiveness and equality." Cited in Ball, "New Justice Minister Says She'll Listen." Note that, while intent to appeal directly to the Charter is significant, Wilson-Raybould did not name section 7 (or any other section) specifically.
110 Justin Ling, "Governments Have Failed Canada's Sex Workers – and They're Running Out of Patience," *Maclean's*, 6 September 2018. https:// www.macleans.ca/news/canada/governments-have-failed-canadas-sex -workers-and-theyre-running-out-of-patience/.
111 Ibid.
112 Ibid.
113 Kerry Porth and Lyndsay Watson. Pivot Legal Society to Justice Minister David Lametti, 6 December 2019. https://d3n8a8pro7vhmx .cloudfront.net/pivotlegal/pages/3391/attachments/original /1576783192/PCEPA_Review_Lametti_Letter.pdf?1576783192.
114 Sandeep Prasad, "Action Canada's Mandate Letter to the Minister of Justice," Action Canada, 13 December 2019. https://www.action canadashr.org/resources/policy-briefs-submissions/2019-12-17-action -canadas-mandate-letter-minister-justice.
115 Ibid.
116 Charlie Smith, "Liberals Lay Groundwork for Amending Law That Criminalizes Sex in Canada," *Georgia Straight*, 2 July 2020. https://www .straight.com/living/liberals-lay-groundwork-for-amending-law-that -criminalizes-sale-of-sex-in-canada.
117 Ibid.
118 Ibid.
119 Ibid.
120 Canada, *House of Commons Debates: Standing Committee on Justice and Human Rights*, 29 October 2020 (Randall Garrison) 43rd Parliament, 2nd Session, 11:40 a.m.
121 Canada, *House of Commons Debates: Standing Committee on Justice and Human Rights*, 29 October 2020 (David Lametti) 43rd Parliament, 2nd Session, 12:00 p.m.

122 Ibid. "given current events" likely refers to COVID, which is mentioned elsewhere in this (virtual) meeting as a constraint.
123 Lauren Sampson, "The Obscenities of This Country: Canada v. Bedford and the Reform of Canadian Prostitution Laws," *Duke Journal of Gender Law & Policy* 22, no. 1 (2014): 137–72; Michael Plaxton, "First Impressions of Bill C-36 in Light of Bedford," SSRN, 2014. https://papers.ssrn.com/sol3/papers.cfm?abstract_id=2447006; Chris Bruckert, "Protection of Communities and Exploited Persons Act," *Journal of Law & Society* 30, no. 1 (2015): 1–4; Sonia Lawrence, "Expert-Tease: Advocacy, Ideology and Experience in Bedford and Bill C-36," *Canadian Journal of Law & Society* 30, no. 1 (2015): 5–8; Hamish Stewart, "The Constitutionality of the New Sex Work Law," *Alberta Law Review* 54, no. 1 (2016): 69–88; Debra M. Haak, "The Initial Test of Constitutional Validity: Identifying the Legislative Objectives of Canada's New Prostitution Laws," *UBC Law Review* 50, no. 3 (2017): 657–96.
124 Natalie M. Snow, Mollee K. Steely, and Tusty ten Bensel, "The Right to Life, Liberty and Security for Prostitution: *Canada v. Bedford*," *Women & Criminal Justice* (2020), at 7 [published Online First].
125 Ibid.
126 Debra M. Haak, "The Good Governance of Empirical Evidence about Prostitution, Sex Work, and Sex Trafficking in Constitutional Litigation," *Queen's Law Journal* 46, no. 2 (2021): 187–242.
127 *R. v. Boodhoo, and others*, 2018 ONSC 7207.
128 *R. v. Anwar*, para. 1.
129 Ibid., para. 7.
130 *R. v. N.S.* 2021 ONSC 1628, para. 7.
131 Ibid., para. 9.
132 Ibid., paras. 192 and 203.
133 *R. v. N.S.*, 2022 ONCA 160.
134 Ibid., para. 58.
135 Ibid., para. 59.
136 Ibid., para. 63.
137 Jane Sims, "Londoner Joins Court Action to Throw Out Federal Sex Work Law," *London Free Press*, 20 March 2021. https://lfpress.com/news/local-news/londoner-joins-court-action-to-throw-out-federal-sex-work-law.
138 Ibid.
139 Hasham, "Are Canada's Sex Work Laws Unconstitutional?"
140 MacKay notes, "We feel we have struck the proper balance in the best interests of the public and of prostitutes." Canada, *House of Commons Debates*, 11 June 2014 (Hon. Peter MacKay) 41st Parliament, 2nd Session, 5:20 p.m.

141   *R. v. NS*, para. 143.
142   Ibid., para. 150.
143   Ibid., para. 161.
144   Ling, "Governments Have Failed Canada's Sex Workers."
145   Ibid.
146   Ibid.
147   Action Canada, "Statement of Solidarity for Sex Workers' Rights."
148   André Picard, "Canada's New Prostitution Laws May Not Make Sex
      Work Safer: Research," *Globe and Mail*, 26 July 2018. https://www
      .theglobeandmail.com/canada/article-canadas-new-prostitution-laws
      -may-not-make-sex-work-safer-research/.
149   *Bedford v. Canada*, 2010 ONSC 4264; Durisin, van der Meulen, and
      Bruckert, *Red Light Labour*.

Chapter 6

 1   *Carter v. Canada (Attorney General)*, 2015 SCC 5, [2015] 1 S.C.R. 331.
 2   *Carter*, para. 1.
 3   *Rodriguez v. British Columbia (Attorney General)*, [1993] 3 S.C.R. 519.
 4   *Carter*, para. 57.
 5   Ibid., paras. 65–6.
 6   Ibid., para. 46.
 7   Ibid., para. 47.
 8   Ibid., para. 127.
 9   Canada, *House of Commons Debates*, 18 February 2015 (Right Hon. Stephen
     Harper CPC), 41st Parliament, 2nd Session.
10   Dave Snow and Kate Puddister, "Closing a Door but Opening a Policy
     Window: Legislating Assisted Dying in Canada," in *Policy Change, Courts,
     and the Canadian Constitution*, ed. Emmett Macfarlane (Toronto: University
     of Toronto Press, 2018), 47.
11   Eleni Nicolaides and Matthew Hennigar, "*Carter* Conflicts: The Supreme
     Court of Canada's Impact on Medical Assistance in Dying Policy,"
     in *Policy Change, Courts, and the Canadian Constitution*, ed. Emmett
     Macfarlane (Toronto: University of Toronto Press, 2018), 319.
12   Canada, *House of Commons Debates*, 24 February 2015 (Mr. David Wilks
     CPC), 41st Parliament, 2nd Session.
13   Nicolaides and Hennigar, "*Carter* Conflicts," 319.
14   *Carter v. Canada (Attorney General)*, 2016 SCC 4, [2016] 1 S.C.R. 13, para. 2.
15   Bruce Ryder, "Suspending the Charter," *Supreme Court Law Review* 21
     (2003): 267–97; Sarah Burningham, "A Comment on the Court's Decision
     to Suspend the Declaration of Invalidity in *Carter v. Canada*," *Saskatchewan
     Law Review* 78 (2015): 201–7.

16 Robert Leckey, "Assisted Dying, Suspended Declarations, and Dialogue's Time," in "Examining Remedies for Violations of Human Rights." Supplement, *University of Toronto Law Journal* 69, no. S1 (2019): S64–83.

17 Emmett Macfarlane, "Dialogue, Remedies, and Positive Rights: *Carter v. Canada* as a Microcosm for Past and Future Issues under the *Charter of Rights and Freedoms*," *Ottawa Law Review* 49, no. 1 (2017): 107–29.

18 Ibid., 116–19.

19 Kent Roach argues the Court's extension of the suspended declaration, in which it allowed those who met the 2015 decision's threshold for access to seek a court-ordered exemption from the offence, was consistent with a "two-track approach to remedies that allows the courts to give litigants who establish that their rights have been violated effective remedies while deferring to the ability of the legislature to make policy choices in establishing a new and presumably constitutionally compliant regime." Roach acknowledges that this is nonetheless an "onerous" process for affected individuals. Kent Roach, "The Separation and Interconnection of Powers in Canada: The Role of Courts, the Executive and the Legislature in Crafting Constitutional Remedies," *Journal of International and Comparative Law* 5, no. 2 (2018): 331–2.

20 *Canada (Attorney General) v. EF*, 2016 ABCA 155, 34 Atla LR (6th) 1, 403 DLR (4th) 461.

21 Although certain mental illnesses may have severe physical impacts that make a patient eligible. As Grant and Downie have noted, "The patient with refractory anorexia nervosa who lives with enduring, intolerable, and irremediable suffering, and who is in an advanced state of decline, is eligible." D.A. Grant and Jocelyn Downie, "Time to Clarify Canada's Medical Assistance in Dying Law," *Canadian Family Physician* 64 (2018): 641.

22 Ibid.

23 Parliament of Canada, *Medical Assistance in Dying: A Patient-Centred Approach*. Report of the Special Joint Committee on Physician-Assisted Dying (Ottawa: Speaker of the House of Commons, 2016).

24 Ibid., 15.

25 Ibid., 21.

26 Ibid., 24.

27 Ibid., 51–60.

28 Provincial-Territorial Expert Advisory Group on Physician-Assisted Dying, *Final Report*, 30 November 2015, 40.

29 External Panel on Options for a Legislative Response to *Carter v. Canada*, *Consultations on Physician-Assisted Dying: Summary of Results and Key Findings*, 15 December 2015.

30 Ibid., 59.

31 Grégoire Webber, "The Charter Party and the Work of Parliament," *Policy Options*, 27 January 2016. http://policyoptions.irpp.org/2016/01/27/the -charter-party-and-the-work-of-parliament/. Other commentators lament this tendency: see Leonid Sirota, "The Charter Is of No Party," *Policy Options*, 18 January 2016. http://policyoptions.irpp.org/2016/01/28 /the-charter-is-of-no-party/.

32 Emmett Macfarlane, "Dialogue or Compliance? Measuring Legislatures' Policy Responses to Court Rulings on Rights," *International Political Science Review* 34 (2013): 39–56.

33 Liberal Party of Canada, "A New Plan for a Strong Middle Class," 2015, 36.

34 Alysia C. Wright and Jessica C. Shaw, "The Spectrum of End of Life Care: An Argument for Access to Medical Assistance in Dying for Vulnerable Populations," *Medicine, Health Care and Philosophy* 22, no. 2 (2019): 211–19.

35 Scott Y.H. Kim and Trudo Lemmens, "Should Assisted Dying for Psychiatric Disorders Be Legalized in Canada?" *Canadian Medical Association Journal* 188, no. 14 (2016): E337.

36 Ibid.

37 *AC v. Manitoba (Director of Child and Family Services)*, 2009 SCC 30.

38 Dov Kagan, "The Next *Carter*? Medical Assistance in Dying and Mature Minors," *University of Manitoba Journal of Medicine* 1, no. 1 (2018): 4–5; Juliet Guichon, Farah Mohamed, Kim Clarke, and Ian Mitchell, "Autonomy and Beneficence in Assisted Dying in Canada: The Eligibility of Mature Minors," *Alberta Law Review* 54, no. 3 (2017): 793.

39 Guichon et al., "Autonomy and Beneficence," 794.

40 Jocelyn Downie and Jennifer A. Chandler, *Interpreting Canada's Medical Assistance in Dying Legislation* (Institute for Research on Public Policy, March 2018), 11.

41 Ibid., citing *AB v. Canada (Attorney General)*.

42 Firuz Rahimi, "Assisted Death in Canada: An Exploration of the Constitutionality of Bill C-14," *Saskatchewan Law Review* 80 (2017): 457–88; Dianne Pothier, "Doctor-Assisted Death Bill Falls Well within Top Court's Ruling," *Policy Options* 29 April 2016. http://policyoptions.irpp .org/2016/04/29/doctor-assisted-death-bill-falls-well-within-top -courts-ruling/.

43 Carissima Mathen, "A Recent History of Government Responses to Constitutional Litigation," *Constitutional Forum* 25, no. 3 (2016): 106n30.

44 Canada, *House of Commons Debates*, 22 April 2016 (Hon. Jody Wilson-Raybould) 42nd Parliament, 1st Session, 10:05 a.m. (emphasis added).

45 Ibid.

46 Ibid.

47 *Carter*, para. 98.

48 Canada, *House of Commons Debates*, 22 April 2016 (Hon. Jody Wilson-Raybould) 42nd Parliament, 1st Session, 10:05 a.m.

49 Ibid.

50 Ibid., citing *Carter*.

51 Canada, *House of Commons Debates*, 22 April 2016 (Murray Rankin) 42nd Parliament, 1st Session, 10:25 a.m.

52 Canada, *House of Commons Debates*, 2 May 2016 (Robert Aubin) 42nd Parliament, 1st Session, 1:20 p.m.

53 Canada, *House of Commons Debates*, 2 May 2016 (Pierre-Luc Dusseault) 42nd Parliament, 1st Session, 1:55 p.m.

54 Canada, *House of Commons Debates*, 3 May 2016 (Anne Minh-Thu Quach) 42nd Parliament, 1st Session, 10:20 a.m.

55 Canada, *House of Commons Debates*, 3 May 2016 (Don Davies) 42nd Parliament, 1st Session, 10:55 a.m.

56 Ibid., 10:55 a.m., 12:20 p.m.

57 Canada, *House of Commons Debates*, 22 April 2016 (Scott Reid) 42nd Parliament, 1st Session, 10:25 a.m.

58 Canada, *House of Commons Debates*, 22 April 2016 (Michael Cooper) 42nd Parliament, 1st Session, 10:35 a.m.

59 Ibid.

60 Citing *Carter*, para. 105, for example.

61 Canada, *House of Commons Debates*, 2 May 2016 (Garnett Genuis) 42nd Parliament, 1st Session, 12:05 p.m.

62 Canada, *House of Commons Debates*, 2 May 2016 (Rob Oliphant) 42nd Parliament, 1st Session, 12:10 p.m.

63 Canada, *House of Commons Debates*, 2 May 2016 (Garnett Genuis) 42nd Parliament, 1st Session, 12:10 p.m.

64 See, for example, the minister of justice's comments in her appearance before the Justice Committee: Canada, "Evidence of Meeting #10 for Justice and Human Rights," 2 May 2016 (Jody Wilson-Raybould) 42nd Parliament, 1st Session, 4:05 p.m.

65 Ibid. See also Canada, "Evidence of Meeting #10 for Justice and Human Rights," 2 May 2016 (Jane Philpott) 42nd Parliament, 1st Session, 4:20 p.m.

66 Nicolaides and Hennigar, "*Carter* Conflicts," 321.

67 Jocelyn Downie and Daphne Gilbert, "Parliament Should Not Wait to Act on Assisted Dying Ruling," *Policy Options*, 16 September 2019. https://policyoptions.irpp.org/magazines/september-2019/parliament-should-not-wait-to-act-on-assisted-dying-ruling/.

68 Catherine Cullen, "MPs Open Up about Personal Struggles with Assisted Dying Bill," CBC News, 16 May 2016. https://www.cbc.ca/news/politics/assisted-dying-mps-personal-1.3576980.

69 Ibid.
70 Jody Wilson-Raybould, *Indian in the Cabinet* (Toronto: HarperCollins, 2021), 125.
71 Ibid., 128.
72 Canada, *House of Commons Debates*, 10 May 2016 (Justin Trudeau) 42nd Parliament, 1 Session, 2:25 p.m.
73 Canada, Department of Justice. *Legislative Background: Medical Assistance in Dying (Bill C-14, as Assented To on June 17, 2016)*. https://www.justice .gc.ca/eng/rp-pr/other-autre/adra-amsr/p4.html#p4
74 Ibid.
75 See, for example, Evidence of the Justice Committee, Mr. Jean-Pierre Ménard, member, Working Group on the End-of-Life Care, Barreau du Québec, 2 May 2016; Cara Zwibel, director, Fundamental Freedoms Program, Canadian Civil Liberties Association, 3 May; Shanaaz Gokool, chief executive officer, Dying with Dignity Canada, 3 May; Angus Gunn, counsel, Alliance of People with Disabilities Who Are Supportive of Legal Assisted Dying Society, 3 May. For the Senate see, for example, Jocelyn Downie, professor in the Faculties of Law and Medicine at Dalhousie, 5 May 2016; Joseph Arvay, lead counsel in the Carter case, 5 May.
76 Canada, "Evidence of Meeting #13 for Justice and Human Rights," 2 May 2016 (Jocelyn Downie) 42nd Parliament, 1st Session, 8:40 p.m.
77 Emmett Macfarlane, *Constitutional Pariah: Reference re Senate Reform and the Future of Parliament* (Vancouver: UBC Press, 2021); Macfarlane, *The Renewed Canadian Senate: Organizational Challenges and Relations with the Government*, IRPP Study 71 (Montreal: Institute for Research on Public Policy, 2019).
78 Senator Cowen, Proceedings of the Standing Senate Committee on Legal and Constitutional Affairs, Issue 8 Evidence, 4 May 2016.
79 Senator Joyal, Proceedings of the Standing Senate Committee on Legal and Constitutional Affairs, Issue 8 Evidence, 4 May 2016.
80 Catherine Tunney, "Senate Removes Near-Death Requirement from Assisted-Dying Bill," CBC News, 8 June 2016. http://www.cbc.ca/news /politics/bill-c14-senate-amendments-debate-1.3622454.
81 This inference is made from interviews with a public official about the general Charter vetting process who affirms that section 33 is not ever treated as a valid policy option for the federal government.
82 That the addendum was anticipated as a conversation with the Court is suggested by the fact it cites the Court's understanding of dialogue, as explained in *R. v. Mills*, where the Court indicated it must respect Parliament's judgment that a judicial scheme can be improved and that it would be wrong for the Court to "insist on slavish conformity" because this would belie "the mutual respect that underpins" the

judicial–legislative relationship essential to our constitutional democracy. The addendum adds two other statements from the Court in *Mills* to justify the claim that Parliament has a valid role to define legislation, even where it deviates from the Courts, by referring to the Court's reference to *Mills* that that concept of dialogue recognizes the important role Parliament plays representing the interests of vulnerable groups and that the Court does not hold a monopoly on the protection of rights. *Mills*, paras. 55, 58.

83 Peter W. Hogg and Allison A. Bushell, "The Charter Dialogue between Courts and Legislatures (or Perhaps the Charter of Rights Isn't Such a Bad Thing after All)," *Osgoode Hall Law Journal* 35, no. 1 (1997): 75; Christopher P. Manfredi and James B. Kelly, "Six Degrees of Dialogue: A Response to Hogg and Bushell," *Osgoode Hall Law Journal* 37, no. 3 (1999): 513; Matthew A. Hennigar, "Expanding the 'Dialogue' Debate: Canadian Federal Government Responses to Lower Court Charter Decisions," *Canadian Journal of Political Science* 37, no. 1 (2004): 3; Peter W. Hogg, Allison A. Bushell Thornton, and Wade K. Wright, "Charter Dialogue Revisited – Or 'Much Ado about Metaphors,'" *Osgoode Hall Law Journal* 45, no. 1 (2007): 125; Macfarlane, "Dialogue or Compliance"; Macfarlane, "Conceptual Precision and Parliamentary Systems of Rights: Disambiguating 'Dialogue,'" *Review of Constitutional Studies* 17, no. 2 (2012): 73.

84 Hogg and Bushell, "Charter Dialogue between Courts and Legislatures," 98.

85 Macfarlane, "Dialogue, Remedies, and Positive Rights," 113.

86 Examples of "in-your-face" replies include Parliament's reversal of a Supreme Court decision upholding the extreme intoxication defence for perpetrators of sexual assault in *R. v. Daviault*, [1994] 3 S.C.R. 63, 111 DLR (4th) 469 (which effectively involved legislation enacting the dissenting justices' view), and the reversal of a Supreme Court decision on access to sexual assault victims' counselling records in *R. v. O'Connor*, [1995] 4 S.C.R. 411 DLR (4th) 235. In the latter case, the Supreme Court upheld the legislation in *R. v. Mills*, [1999] 3 S.C.R. 668, 180 DLR (4th) 1.

87 Thomas McMorrow, "MAID in Canada: Debating the Constitutionality of Canada's New Medical Assistance in Dying Law," *Queen's Law Journal* 44 (2018): 96, citing Peter W. Hogg and Ravi Amarnath, "Understanding Dialogue Theory," in *The Oxford Handbook of the Canadian Constitution*, ed. Peter Oliver, Patrick Macklem, and Nathalie Des Rosiers (New York: Oxford University Press, 2017), 1053.

88 Ibid., 97.

89 Hogg, Thornton, and Wright, "Charter Dialogue Revisited," 2.

90 Ibid., 31.

91 Nicolaides and Hennigar, "*Carter* Conflicts," 323.
92 Ibid., citing Canada, *House of Commons Debates*, 31 May 2016 (Jody Wilson-Raybould) 42nd Parliament, 1st Session (emphasis added by authors).
93 Canada, *House of Commons Debates*, 13 May 2016 (Jody Wilson-Raybould) 42nd Parliament, 1st Session, 10:30 a.m.
94 Canada, *House of Commons Debates*, 16 June 2016 (Hon. Jody Wilson-Raybould) 42nd Parliament, 1st Session, 10:40 a.m.
95 *Truchon c. Procureur général du Canada*, 2019 QCCS 3792.
96 Ibid., para. 16.
97 Ibid., para. 252.
98 Ibid..
99 Ibid., para. 253.
100 Ibid., paras. 418–22.
101 Ibid., para. 495.
102 Ibid., para. 496.
103 Ibid., para. 497.
104 Ibid., para. 502.
105 Ibid., para. 504, citing *R. v. Mills*, [1999] 3 S.C.R. 668.
106 Ibid., para. 508.
107 Ibid., paras. 518–19.
108 Ibid., para. 674.
109 Ibid., para. 680.
110 Downie and Gilbert, "Parliament Should Not Wait to Act."
111 *Truchon*, para. 744.
112 Canada, *House of Commons Debates*, 26 February 2020 (David Lametti) 43rd Parliament, 1st Session, 4:00 p.m.
113 Ibid., 4:05 p.m.
114 Canada, *House of Commons Debates*, 26 February 2020 (Alistair MacGregor) 43rd Parliament, 1st Session, 4:20 p.m.
115 Canada, *House of Commons Debates*, 26 February 2020 (David Lametti) 43rd Parliament, 1st Session, 4:25 p.m.
116 Ibid., 4:30 p.m.
117 Ibid., 4:25 p.m.
118 Canada, *House of Commons Debates*, 9 October 2020 (Garnett Genius) 43rd Parliament, 1st Session, 10:30 a.m; Canada, *House of Commons Debates*, 9 October 2020 (Michael Cooper) 43rd Parliament, 1st Session, 10:35 a.m.; Canada, *House of Commons Debates*, 9 October 2020 (Rob Moore) 43rd Parliament, 1st Session, 1:45 p.m.
119 Canada, *House of Commons Debates*, 9 October 2020 (Randall Garrison) 43rd Parliament, 1st Session, 1:00 p.m.

120 Canada, *House of Commons Debates*, 9 October 2020 (David Lametti) 43rd Parliament, 1st Session, 10:30 a.m.
121 Canada, *House of Commons Debates*, 9 October 2020 (Rob Moore) 43rd Parliament, 1st Session, 1:50 p.m.
122 Canada, Department of Justice. "Bill C-7: *An Act to Amend the Criminal Code (Medical Assistance in Dying)*," 21 October 2020. https://www .justice.gc.ca/eng/csj-sjc/pl/charter-charte/c7.html.
123 Ibid.
124 Eleni Nicolaides, "*Carter* Compliance: Litigation for Access to Medical Assistance in Dying in Canada," in *Constitutional Crossroads: Reflections on Charter Rights, Reconciliation, and Change*, ed. Kate Puddister and Emmett Macfarlane (Vancouver: UBC Press, forthcoming).
125 Canada, *Senate Debates*, 14 December 2020 (Claude Carignan) 43rd Parliament, 1st Session, 8:30 p.m.
126 See, for example, Canada, *Senate Debates*, 14 December 2020 (Peter Harder) 43rd Parliament, 1st Session, 8:35 p.m.
127 Senate Government Representative Office, "Key Senate Changes Reflected in New Medical Assistance in Dying Law," 17 March 2021. https://senate-gro.ca/news/c7-maid-adopted/.
128 Canadian Press, "Mulroney-Era Documents Reveal Struggle with Abortion Laws," CBC News, 17 November 2013. https://www.cbc.ca /news/politics/mulroney-era-documents-reveal-struggle-with-abortion -laws-1.2430081.
129 Alex Marland, *Whipped: Party Discipline in Canada* (Vancouver: UBC Press, 2020), 311–12.
130 Macfarlane, "Dialogue or Compliance?" 50–1.

Chapter 7

1 Dennis Baker, *Not Quite Supreme: The Courts and Coordinate Constitutional Interpretation* (Montreal and Kingston: McGill-Queen's University Press, 2010), 150.
2 Emmett Macfarlane, *Constitutional Pariah: Reference re Senate Reform and the Future of Parliament* (Vancouver: UBC Press, 2021).
3 It is worth noting that the government had incentives to implement reform, especially to enhance the Senate's legitimacy in the eyes of the public, given the Senate's unpopularity during a recent scandal over expenses. Retaining the status quo thus had risk, given the Liberals would be tied to the actions of any patronage-based appointees in the same way the Conservatives were tied to several senators implicated by the expenses scandal.

4 James B. Kelly and Matthew A. Hennigar, "The Canadian Charter of Rights and the Minister of Justice: Weak-Form Review within a Constitutional Charter of Rights," *International Journal of Constitutional Law* 10, no. 1 (2012): 45.

5 Government of New Zealand, "Briefing to the Incoming Attorney-General," November 2020. https://www.crownlaw.govt.nz/assets /6003883_Crown-Law-Briefing-to-the-Incoming-Attorney-General-2020 -Final.PDF.

6 Prime minister of Canada, "Minister of Justice and Attorney General of Canada Mandate Letter," 12 November 2015. https://pm.gc.ca/en /mandate-letters/2015/11/12/archived-minister-justice-and-attorney -general-canada-mandate-letter.

7 Kelly and Hennigar, "Canadian Charter of Rights," 49.

8 Ibid. See also Adam Dodek, "Separating the Offices of the Attorney General and Minister of Justice," *Slaw*, 5 February 2015. https://www .slaw.ca/2015/02/05/separating-the-offices-of-the-attorney-general-and -minister-of-justice/.

9 Ibid.

10 Office of the Conflict of Interest and Ethics Commissioner, *Trudeau II Report*, August 2019.

11 A. Anne McLellan, *Review of the Roles of the Minister of Justice and Attorney General of Canada*, 28 June 2019, 1.

12 Ibid., 2.

13 Ibid., 29.

14 Adam Dodek, "The Impossible Position: Canada's Attorney-General Cannot Be Our Justice Minister," *Globe and Mail*, 22 February 2019. https://www.theglobeandmail.com/opinion/article-the-impossible -position-canadas-attorney-general-cannot-be-our/.

15 Ibid.

16 Janet L. Hiebert and James B. Kelly, *Parliamentary Bills of Rights: The Experiences of New Zealand and the United Kingdom* (Cambridge: Cambridge University Press, 2015), 109, citing P. Gower, "Finlayson 'Just Doing My Duty' on Crime Bills," *New Zealand Herald*, 4 May 2009.

17 Hiebert and Kelly, *Parliamentary Bills of Rights*, 98–9.

18 Deborah MacNair, "Solicitor-Client Privilege and the Crown: When Is a Privilege a Privilege?" *Canadian Bar Review* 83 (2003): 82: 213–47, citing *R. v. Campbell*, [1999] 1 S.C.R. 565.

19 Ibid., 221.

20 *R. v. Campbell*, para. 50.

21 MacNair, "Solicitor-Client Privilege," 233–4.

22 Adam M. Dodek, "Reconceiving Solicitor-Client Privilege," *Queen's Law Journal* 35 (2010): 493–538.

23 Patrick J. Monahan, "'In the Public Interest': Understanding the Special Role of the Government Lawyer," *Supreme Court Law Review* (2d) 63 (2013): 53.

24 Ibid., 54.

25 Ibid.

26 As the Ministry of Justice website notes, the attorney general retains legal professional privilege in respect of unpublished advice on which he or she has tabled a section 7 (incompatibility) report in Parliament. See New Zealand, Ministry of Justice, *Advice on Consistency of Bills with the Bill of Rights Act*, 8 July 2021. https://www.justice.govt.nz/justice-sector-policy /constitutional-issues-and-human-rights/bill-of-rights-compliance -reports/advice/. For a discussion of the New Zealand bureaucratic vetting process, see Hiebert and Kelly, *Parliamentary Bills of Rights*, 54–61.

27 Hiebert and Kelly, *Parliamentary Bills of Rights*, 293–5.

28 Ibid., 298.

29 Ibid., 299.

30 Ibid., 396.

31 Our thanks to the anonymous reviewer for making this suggestion.

32 Léonid Sirota, "The UK Way," *Double Aspect* blog. 22 July 2021. https:// doubleaspect.blog/2021/07/22/the-uk-way/

33 *R (on the application of SC, CB and 8 children) (Appellants) v Secretary of State for Work and Pensions and others (Respondents)* [2021] UKSC 26.

34 Ibid., para. 180.

35 Ibid., para. 182.

36 Ibid., para. 183.

37 Sirota, "UK Way."

38 *R. v. O'Connor*, [1995] 4 S.C.R. 411; *R. v. Daviault*, [1994] 3 S.C.R. 63.

39 *R. v. Mills*, [1999] 3 S.C.R. 668.

40 *R. v. Brown*, 2022 SCC 18.

41 Tsvi Kahana, "The Notwithstanding Mechanism and Public Discussion: Lessons from the Ignored Practice of Section 33 of the Charter," *Canadian Public Administration* 44, no. 3 (2001): 255–91; Eleni Nicolaides and Dave Snow, "A Paper Tiger No More? The Media Portrayal of the Notwithstanding Clause in Saskatchewan and Ontario," *Canadian Journal of Political Science* 54 (2021): 60–74.

42 *Ford v. Quebec (Attorney General)*, [1988] 2 S.C.R. 712

43 Kahana, "Notwithstanding Mechanism."

44 Richard Albert, "The Desuetude of the Notwithstanding Clause – and How to Revive It," in *Policy Change, Courts, and the Canadian Constitution*, ed. Emmett Macfarlane (Toronto: University of Toronto Press, 2018).

45 *Good Spirit School Division No. 204 v. Christ the Teacher Roman Catholic Separate School Division No. 212*, 2017 SKQB 109.

46 *Saskatchewan v. Good Spirit School Division No. 204*, 2020 SKCA 34.

47 Robert Leckey, "Advocacy Notwithstanding the Notwithstanding Clause," *Constitutional Forum* 28, no. 4 (2019): 2.
48 *Working Families Ontario v. Ontario*, 2021 ONSC 4076.
49 *City of Toronto et al. v. Ontario (Attorney General)*, 2018 ONSC 5151.
50 *Toronto (City) v. Ontario (Attorney General)*, 2019 ONCA 732.
51 Janet Hiebert, "Is it Too Late to Rehabilitate Canada's Notwithstanding Clause?" *Supreme Court Law Review* (2d) (2004) 23: 169–70.
52 Allan Blakeney, premier of Saskatchewan when the Charter was created, thought "the notwithstanding clause would guard against the Charter evolving in a manner that excluded a parliamentary role in defining the scope of protected rights." See Janet L. Hiebert, "Compromise and the Notwithstanding Clause: Why the Dominant Narrative Distorts Our Understanding," in *Contested Constitutionalism: Reflections on the Charter of Rights and Freedoms*, ed. James B. Kelly and Christopher P. Manfredi (Vancouver: UBC Press, 2009), 107–25, at 115–6.
53 Dwight Newman, "Canada's Notwithstanding Clause, Dialogue, and Constitutional Identities," *Constitutional Dialogue: Rights, Democracy, Institutions* (Cambridge: Cambridge University Press, 2019), 214.
54 See Hiebert, "Is It Too Late to Rehabilitate the Notwithstanding Clause?," 172.
55 A majority of the Supreme Court contrasts such policies with those that attempt a balancing act to mediate between different groups in *Irwin Toy Ltd. v. Quebec (Attorney General)*, [1989] 1 S.C.R. 927 at 994.

Conclusion

1 *M. v. H.*, [1999] 2 S.C.R. 3.
2 Trans rights activists have used human rights tribunals to make discrimination claims on the basis of sex or disability, but the Charter has played virtually no role in policy developments to add gender identity and expression to the list of protected grounds in relevant statutes. See Kyle Kirkup, "After Marriage Equality: Courting Queer and Trans Rights," in *Policy Change, Courts, and the Canadian Constitution*, ed. Emmett Macfarlane (Toronto: University of Toronto Press, 2018), 378–94.
3 Ran Hirschl, "The Judicialization of Politics," *The Oxford Handbook of Political Science*. Robert E. Goodin, ed. (Oxford: Oxford University Press, 2011). See also Ran Hirschl, *Towards Juristocracy: The Origins and Consequences of the New Constitutionalism* (Cambridge: Harvard University Press, 2004); Christopher Manfredi, "The Judicialization of Politics: Rights and Public Policy in Canada and the United States," in *Degrees of Freedom: Canada and the United States in a Changing World*, ed. Keith G. Banting, George Hoberg, and Richard Simeon (Montreal and

Kingston: McGill-Queen's University Press, 1997); C. Neal Tate and Thorsten Vallinder, eds., *The Global Expansion of Judicial Power* (New York: New York University Press, 1995); Dave Snow, "The Judicialization of Assisted Reproductive Technology Policy in Canada: Decentralization, Medicalization, and Mandatory Regulation," *Canadian Journal of Law & Society* (2012) 27(2): 169–88.

4 Emmett Macfarlane, "Dialogue or Compliance? Measuring Legislatures' Policy Responses to Court Rulings on Rights," *International Political Science Review* (2013) 34: 39–56.

5 Stephen Gardbaum, *The New Commonwealth Model of Constitutionalism.* (Cambridge: Cambridge University Press, 2013). See also Janet L. Hiebert, "Parliamentary Bills of Rights: An Alternative Model?" *The Modern Law Review* (2006) 69(1): 7–28.

6 Mark Tushnet, *Weak Courts, Strong Rights: Judicial Review and Social Welfare Rights in Comparative Constitutional Law* (Princeton: Princeton University Press, 2008).

7 Mark Tushnet, "New Forms of Judicial Review and the Persistence of Rights- and Democracy-Based Worries," *Wake Forest Law Review* (2003) 38(2): 813–38.

8 *Reference re Same-Sex Marriage*, [2004] 3 S.C.R. 698, 2004 SCC 79. As Kate Puddister writes of the fourth reference question posed to the Supreme Court by the Liberal government under Paul Martin, had the Court "found that the Constitution required governments to provide the right to same-sex marriage, it could have made the court a target for opponents of same-sex marriage, allowing the government to avoid this criticism." See Kate Puddister, *Seeking the Court's Advice: The Politics of the Canadian Reference Power* (Vancouver: UBC Press, 2019) at 94.

9 Elizabeth Goodyear-Grant, J. Scott Matthews, and Janet Hiebert. "The courts/parliament trade-off: Canadian attitudes on judicial influence in public policy," *Commonwealth & Comparative Politics* (2013) 51(3): 377–97.

10 Emmett Macfarlane, ed. *Policy Change, Courts, and the Canadian Constitution* (Toronto: University of Toronto Press, 2018).

11 Alex Marland, *Whipped: Party Discipline in Canada* (Vancouver: UBC Press, 2020).

12 *Carter v. Canada (Attorney General)*, 2015 SCC 5, [2015] 1 S.C.R. 331.

13 *Truchon c. Procureur general du Canada*, 2019 QCCS 3792.

14 Kate Puddister, "How the Canadian Sentencing System Impacts Policy Reform: An Examination of the Harper Era," *Law & Policy* (2021) 43: 149–69.

15 Emmett Macfarlane, "'You Can't Always Get What You Want': Regime Politics, the Supreme Court of Canada, and the Harper Government," *Canadian Journal of Political Science* (2018) 51(1): 1–21, at 13–4.

16 *Reference re Supreme Court Act, ss.5 and 6*, 2014 SCC 21, [2014] 1 S.C.R. 433.

17 For a full account of the Nadon reference and its circumstances, see Carissima Mathen and Michael Plaxton, *The Tenth Justice: Judicial Appointments, Marc Nadon, and the* Supreme Court Act *Reference* (Vancouver: UBC Press, 2020).

18 Emmett Macfarlane, "Conservative with the Constitution? Moderation, Strategy, and Institutional Distrust," in *The Blueprint: Conservative Parties and their Impact on Canadian Politics*, ed. J.P. Lewis and Joanna Everitt (Toronto: University of Toronto Press, 2017).

19 *R. v. Morgentaler*, [1988] 1 S.C.R. 30; *Reference re Same-Sex Marriage*, [2004] 3 S.C.R. 698, 2004 SCC 79.

20 Macfarlane, "'You Can't Always Get What You Want,'" at 14.

21 Puddister, "How the Canadian Sentencing System Impacts Policy Reform."

22 Macfarlane, "'You Can't Always Get What You Want'," at 2.

23 *Canada (Attorney General) v. PHS Community Services Society*, 2011 SCC 44, [2011] 3 S.C.R. 134.

24 Macfarlane, "Dialogue or Compliance?" at 51.

25 Stéphanie Chouinard, "Section 23 of the Charter and Official-Language Minority Instruction in Canada: The Judiciary's Impact and Limits in Education Policymaking," in *Policy Change, Courts, and the Canadian Constitution*, ed. Emmett Macfarlane (University of Toronto Press, 2018); James B. Kelly, "The Charter of the French Language and the Supreme court of Canada: Assessing Whether Constitutional Design Can Influence Policy Outcomes," in *Policy Change, Courts, and the Canadian Constitution*, ed. Emmett Macfarlane (University of Toronto Press, 2018).

26 Emmett Macfarlane, *Governing from the Bench: The Supreme Court of Canada and the Judicial Role* (Vancouver: UBC Press, 2013).

27 Vanessa A. MacDonnell, "The constitution as framework for governance," *University of Toronto Law Journal* (2013) 63(4): 624–652.

28 Ibid, at 653.

29 Ibid.

30 Vanessa MacDonnell, "The New Parliamentary Sovereignty," *Review of Constitutional Studies* (2016) 21(1): 13–36, at 31.

31 *Canada (Attorney General) v. PHS Community Services Society*, 2011 SCC 44, [2011] 3 S.C.R. 134.

32 Ibid., para. 153.

33 Emmett Macfarlane, "The Dilemmas of Positive Rights: Access to Health Care and the Canadian Charter of Rights and Freedoms," *Journal of Canadian Studies* 48, no. 3 (2014): 49–78.

34 *Carter v. Canada (Attorney General)*, 2015 SCC 5, [2015] 1 S.C.R. 331.

35 Kathryn Morrison, *Mature Minor Eligibility for Medical Assistance in Dying (MAiD): An Ethical Analysis* (PhD diss., University of Waterloo, 2021).

36 Emmett Macfarlane, "Dialogue, Remedies, and Positive Rights: *Carter v. Canada* as a Microcosm for Past and Future Issues under the *Charter of Rights and Freedoms*," *Ottawa Law Review* 49, no. 1 (2017): 124.
37 David Lepofsky, "*Carter v Canada (Attorney General)*, The Constitutional Attack on Canada's Ban on Assisted Dying: Missing an Obvious Chance to Rule on the Charter's Disability Equality Guarantee," *Supreme Court Law Review* 76 (2016): 90–1.
38 Brenda Cossman, "Sex Work, Abjection and the Constitution," in *Constitutional Crossroads: Reflections on Charter Rights, Reconciliation, and Change*, ed. Kate Puddister and Emmett Macfarlane (Vancouver: UBC Press, forthcoming).

Selected Bibliography

Albert, Richard. "The Desuetude of the Notwithstanding Clause – and How to Revive It." In *Policy Change, Courts, and the Canadian Constitution*, edited by Emmett Macfarlane, 146–65. Toronto: University of Toronto Press, 2018.

Baker, Dennis. *Not Quite Supreme: The Courts and Coordinate Constitutional Interpretation*. Montreal and Kingston: McGill-Queen's University Press, 2010.

Baker, Dennis, and Rainer Knopff. "*Daviault* Dialogue: The Strange Journey of Canada's Intoxication Defence." *Review of Constitutional Studies* 19, no. 1 (2014): 35–58.

Bakvis, Herman. "Prime Minister and Cabinet in Canada: An Autocracy in Need of Reform?" *Journal of Canadian Studies* 35, no. 4 (2001): 60–79.

Bergman, Gwyneth, and Emmett Macfarlane. "The Impact and Role of Officers of Parliament: Canada's Conflict of Interest and Ethics Commissioner." *Canadian Public Administration* 61, no. 1 (2018): 5–25.

– "Protecting Privacy? Government and Parliamentary Responsiveness to the Privacy Commissioner of Canada." *Canadian Public Administration* 64, no. 3 (2021): 437–57.

Blidook, Kelly. *Constituency Influence in Parliament: Countering the Centre*. Vancouver: UBC Press, 2012.

Brodie, Ian. *At the Centre of Government: The Prime Minister and the Limits on Political Power*. Montreal and Kingston: McGill-Queen's University Press, 2018.

Bruckert, Chris. "Protection of Communities and Exploited Persons Act." *Journal of Law & Society* 30, no. 1 (2015): 1–4.

Burningham, Sarah. "A Comment on the Court's Decision to Suspend the Declaration of Invalidity in *Carter v. Canada*." *Saskatchewan Law Review* 78 (2015): 201–7.

Chouinard, Stéphanie. "Section 23 of the Charter and Official-Language Minority Instruction in Canada: The Judiciary's Impact and Limits in

Education Policymaking." In *Policy Change, Courts, and the Canadian Constitution*, edited by Emmett Macfarlane, 230–49. Toronto: University of Toronto Press, 2018.

Clarke, Jeremy A. "Beyond the Democratic Dialogue, and towards a Federalist One: Provincial Arguments and Supreme Court Responses in Charter Litigation." *Canadian Journal of Political Science* 39, no. 2 (2006): 293–314.

Cossman, Brenda. "Canadian Same-Sex Relationship Recognition Struggles and the Contradictory Nature of Legal Victories." *Cleveland State Law Review* 48 (2000): 49–59.

– "Sex Work, Abjection and the Constitution." In *Constitutional Crossroads: Reflections on Charter Rights, Reconciliation, and Change*, edited by Kate Puddister and Emmett Macfarlane. Vancouver: UBC Press, forthcoming.

Crandall, Erin, and Andrea Lawlor. "Public Support for Canadian Courts: Understanding the Roles of Institutional Trust and Partisanship." *Canadian Journal of Law and Society*, 37, no. 1 (2022): 91–112.

Dawson, Mary. "The Impact of the Charter on the Public Policy Process and the Department of Justice." *Osgoode Hall Law Journal* 30 (1992): 595–603.

Dixon, Rosalind. "The Supreme Court of Canada, Charter Dialogue, and Deference." *Osgoode Hall Law Journal* 47, no. 2 (2009): 235–86.

Docherty, David C. *Mr. Smith Goes to Ottawa: Life in the House of Commons*. Vancouver: UBC Press, 1997.

Dodek, Adam. "Reconceiving Solicitor-Client Privilege." *Queen's Law Journal* 35 (2010): 493–538.

– "Separating the Offices of the Attorney General and Minister of Justice." *Slaw*, 5 February 2015. https://www.slaw.ca/2015/02/05/separating -the-offices-of-the-attorney-general-and-minister-of-justice/.

Downie, Jocelyn, and Jennifer A. Chandler. *Interpreting Canada's Medical Assistance in Dying Legislation*. Montreal: Institute for Research on Public Policy, 2018.

Downie, Jocelyn, and Daphne Gilbert. "Parliament Should Not Wait to Act on Assisted Dying Ruling." *Policy Options*, 16 September 2019. https:// policyoptions.irpp.org/magazines/september-2019/parliament -should-not-wait-to-act-on-assisted-dying-ruling/.

Driedger, Elmer A. "The Meaning and Effect of the Canadian *Bill of Rights*: A Draftsman's Viewpoint." *Ottawa Law Review* 9 (1977): 303–20.

Durisin, Elya M., Emily van der Meulen, and Chris Bruckert, eds. *Red Light Labour: Sex Work Regulation, Agency, and Resistance*. Vancouver: UBC Press, 2018.

Fisher, Louis. *Constitutional Dialogues: Interpretation as Political Process*. Princeton, NJ: Princeton University Press, 1988.

– *Reconsidering Judicial Finality: Why the Supreme Court Is Not the Last Word on the Constitution*. Lawrence: University Press of Kansas, 2019.

Flanagan, Tom. *Harper's Team: Behind the Scenes in the Conservative Rise to Power.* 2nd ed. Montreal and Kingston: McGill-Queen's University Press, 2009.

Fuji Johnson, Genevieve, Mary Burns, and Kerry Porth. "A Question of Respect: A Qualitative Text Analysis of the Canadian Parliamentary Committee Hearings on *The Protection of Communities and Exploited Persons Act.*" *Canadian Journal of Political Science* 50, no. 4 (2017): 921–53.

Gardbaum, Stephen. *The New Commonwealth Model of Constitutionalism: Theory and Practice.* Cambridge: Cambridge University Press, 2013.

Grant, D.A. (Gus), and Jocelyn Downie. "Time to Clarify Canada's Medical Assistance in Dying Law." *Canadian Family Physician* 64 (2018): 641–2.

Greene, Ian, Carl Baar, Peter McCormick, George Szablowski, and Martin Thomas. *Final Appeal: Decision-Making in Canadian Courts of Appeal.* Toronto: Lorimer, 1998.

Godbout, Jean-François. *Lost on Division: Party Unity in the Canadian Parliament.* Toronto: University of Toronto Press, 2020.

Goodyear-Grant, Elizabeth, J. Scott Matthews, and Janet Hiebert. "The Courts/Parliament Trade-off: Canadian Attitudes on Judicial Influence in Public Policy." *Commonwealth & Comparative Politics* 51, no. 3 (2013): 377–97.

Guichon, Juliet, Farah Mohamed, Kim Clarke, and Ian Mitchell. "Autonomy and Beneficence in Assisted Dying in Canada: The Eligibility of Mature Minors." *Alberta Law Review* 54, no. 3 (2017): 775–802.

Haak, Debra M. "The Good Governance of Empirical Evidence about Prostitution, Sex Work, and Sex Trafficking in Constitutional Litigation." *Queen's Law Journal* 46, no. 2 (2021): 187–242.

– "The Initial Test of Constitutional Validity: Identifying the Legislative Objectives of Canada's New Prostitution Laws." *UBC Law Review* 50, no. 3 (2017): 657–96.

Harding, Mark S. *Judicializing Everything? The Clash of Constitutionalism in Canada, New Zealand, and the United Kingdom.* Toronto: University of Toronto Press, 2022.

Hennigar, Matthew A. "Expanding the 'Dialogue' Debate: Canadian Federal Government Responses to Lower Court Charter Decisions." *Canadian Journal of Political Science* 37, no. 1 (2004): 3–21.

– "Exploring Complex Judicial-Executive Interaction: Federal Government Concessions in Charter of Rights Cases." *Canadian Journal of Political Science* 43, no. 4 (2010): 821–42.

– "*Reference re Same-Sex Marriage*: Making Sense of the Government's Litigation Strategy." In *Contested Constitutionalism*, edited by James Kelly and Christopher Manfredi, 209–30. Vancouver: UBC Press, 2009.

– "Unreasonable Disagreement? Judicial-Executive Exchanges about Charter Reasonableness in the Harper Era." *Osgoode Hall Law Journal* 54 (2017): 1245–73.

– "Why Does the Federal Government Appeal to the Supreme Court of Canada in Charter of Rights Cases? A Strategic Explanation." *Law & Society Review* 41, no. 1 (2007): 225–50.

Heichel, Stephan, Christoph Knill, and Sophie Schmitt. "Public Policy Meets Morality: Conceptual and Theoretical Challenges in the Analysis of Morality Policy Change." *Journal of European Public Policy* 20, no. 3 (2013): 318–34.

Hiebert, Janet L. *Charter Conflicts: What Is Parliament's Role?* Montreal and Kingston: McGill-Queen's University Press, 2002.

– "The Charter, Policy, and Political Judgment." In *Policy Change, Courts, and the Canadian Constitution*, edited by Emmett Macfarlane, 81–102. Toronto: University of Toronto Press, 2018.

– "The Charter's Influence on Legislation: Political Strategizing about Risk." *Canadian Journal of Political Science* 51, no. 4 (2018): 727–47.

– "Compromise and the Notwithstanding Clause: Why the Dominant Narrative Distorts Our Understanding." In *Contested Constitutionalism: Reflections on the Charter of Rights and Freedoms*, edited by James B. Kelly and Christopher P. Manfredi, 107–25. Vancouver: UBC Press, 2009.

– "Is It Too Late to Rehabilitate Canada's Notwithstanding Clause?" *Supreme Court Law Review* (2d) 23 (2004): 169–89.

– *Limiting Rights: The Dilemmas of Judicial Review*. Montreal and Kingston: McGill-Queen's University Press, 1996.

– "Parliamentary Bills of Rights: An Alternative Model?" *Modern Law Review* 69, no. 1 (2006): 7–28.

– "Parliamentary Bills of Rights: Have They Altered the Norms for Legislative Decision-Making?" In *Comparative Constitutional Theory*, edited by Gary Jacobson and Miguel Schor, 123–43. Cheltenham, UK: Edward Elgar Publishing, 2018.

Hiebert, Janet L., and James B. Kelly. *Parliamentary Bills of Rights: The Experiences of New Zealand and the United Kingdom*. Cambridge: Cambridge University Press, 2015.

Hirschl, Ran. "The Judicialization of Politics." In *The Oxford Handbook of Political Science*, edited by Robert E. Goodin, 253–74. Oxford: Oxford University Press, 2011.

– *Towards Juristocracy: The Origins and Consequences of the New Constitutionalism*. Cambridge, MA: Harvard University Press, 2004.

Hogg, Peter W., and Ravi Amarnath. "Understanding Dialogue Theory." In *The Oxford Handbook of the Canadian Constitution*, edited by Peter Oliver, Patrick Macklem, and Nathalie Des Rosiers, 1053–74. New York: Oxford University Press, 2017.

Hogg, Peter W., and Allison A. Bushell. "The Charter Dialogue between Courts and Legislatures (or Perhaps the Charter of Rights Isn't Such a Bad Thing after All)." *Osgoode Hall Law Journal* 35, no. 1 (1997): 75–124.

Hogg, Peter W., Allison A. Bushell Thornton, and Wade K. Wright. "Charter Dialogue Revisited – or 'Much Ado about Metaphors.'" *Osgoode Hall Law Journal* 45, no. 1 (2007): 1–65.

Howe, Paul, and Peter H. Russell, eds. *Judicial Power and Canadian Democracy.* Montreal and Kingston: McGill-Queen's University Press, 2001.

Hughes, Jula, and Vanessa MacDonnell. "Social Science Evidence in Constitutional Rights Cases in Germany and Canada: Some Comparative Observations." *National Journal of Constitutional Law* 32 (2013): 23–60.

Huscroft, Grant. "Constitutionalism from the Top Down." *Osgoode Hall Law Journal* 45, no. 1 (2007): 91–104.

Hutchinson, Allan C. *Waiting for Coraf: A Critique of Law and Rights.* Toronto: University of Toronto Press, 1995.

James, Patrick, Donald E. Abelson, and Michael Lusztig, eds. *The Myth of the Sacred: The Charter, the Courts, and the Politics of the Constitution in Canada.* Montreal and Kingston: McGill-Queen's University Press, 2002.

Johnstone, Rachael. "Canadian Abortion Policy and the Limitations of Litigation." In *Policy Change, Courts, and the Canadian Constitution,* edited by Emmett Macfarlane, 336–55. Toronto: University of Toronto Press, 2018.

– *After Morgentaler: The Politics of Abortion in Canada.* Vancouver: UBC Press, 2017.

Johnstone, Rachael, and Emmett Macfarlane. "Public Policy, Rights, and Abortion Access in Canada." *International Journal of Canadian Studies* 51 (2015): 97–120.

Kagan, Doy. "The Next *Carter*? Medical Assistance in Dying and Mature Minors." *University of Manitoba Journal of Medicine* 1, no. 1 (2018): 4–5.

Kahana, Tsvi. "The Notwithstanding Mechanism and Public Discussion: Lessons from the Ignored Practice of Section 33 of the Charter." *Canadian Public Administration* 44, no. 3 (2001): 255–91.

Kam, C.J. *Party Discipline and Parliamentary Politics.* Cambridge: Cambridge University Press, 2009.

Kavanagh, Aileen. "The Lure and the Limits of Dialogue." *University of Toronto Law Journal* 66, no. 1 (2015): 83–120.

Kazatchkine, Cécile, Richard Elliott, and Donald MacPherson. *An Injection of Reason: Critical Analysis of Bill C-2.* Toronto: Canadian HIV/AIDS Legal Network and the Canadian Drug Policy Coalition, 2014.

Kelly, James B. "The Charter of the French Language and the Supreme Court of Canada: Assessing Whether Constitutional Design Can Influence Policy Outcomes." *Policy Change, Courts, and the Canadian Constitution,* edited by Emmett Macfarlane, 250–68. Toronto: University of Toronto Press, 2018.

– *Governing with the Charter: Legislative and Judicial Activism and Framers' Intent.* Vancouver: UBC Press, 2005.

- "Legislative Capacity and Human Rights in the Age of Populism – Two Challenges for Legislated Rights: Discussion of *Legislated Rights – Securing Human Rights through Legislation.*" *Jerusalem Review of Legal Studies* 21, no. 1 (2020): 94–111.

Kelly, James B., and Matthew A. Hennigar. "The Canadian Charter of Rights and the Minister of Justice: Weak-Form Review within a Constitutional Charter of Rights." *International Journal of Constitutional Law* 10, no. 1 (2012): 35–68.

Kelly, James B., and Kate Puddister. "Criminal Justice Policy during the Harper Era: Private Member's Bills, Penal Populism, and the Criminal Code of Canada." *Canadian Journal of Law and Society* 32, no. 2 (2017): 391–415.

Kim, Scott Y.H., and Trudo Lemmens. "Should Assisted Dying for Psychiatric Disorders Be Legalized in Canada?" *Canadian Medical Association Journal* 188, no. 14 (2016): E337.

Kirkup, Kyle. "After Marriage Equality: Courting Queer and Trans Rights." In *Policy Change, Courts, and the Canadian Constitution*, edited by Emmett Macfarlane, 378–94. Toronto: University of Toronto Press, 2018.

Knill, Christoph. "The Study of Morality Policy: Analytical Implications from a Public Policy Perspective." *Journal of European Public Policy* 20, no. 3 (2013): 309–17.

Knopff, Rainer, Rhonda Evans, Dennis Baker, and Dave Snow. "Dialogue: Clarified and Reconsidered." *Osgoode Hall Law Journal* 54 (2017): 609–44.

Koop, Royce, and Amanda Bittner. "Parachuted into Parliament: Candidate Nomination, Appointed Candidates, and Legislative Roles in Canada." *Journal of Elections, Public Opinion and Parties* 21, no. 4 (2011): 431–52.

Lawrence, Sonia. "Expert-Tease: Advocacy, Ideology and Experience in Bedford and Bill C-36." *Canadian Journal of Law & Society* 30, no. 1 (2015): 5–8.

Leckey, Robert. "Advocacy Notwithstanding the Notwithstanding Clause." *Constitutional Forum* 28, no. 4 (2019): 1–8.

- "Assisted Dying, Suspended Declarations, and Dialogue's Time." In "Examining Remedies for Violations of Human Rights." Supplement, *University of Toronto Law Journal* 69, no. S1 (2019): S64–83.

- *Bills of Rights in the Common Law.* Cambridge: Cambridge University Press, 2015.

Lepofsky, David. "*Carter v Canada (Attorney General)*, the Constitutional Attack on Canada's Ban on Assisted Dying: Missing an Obvious Chance to Rule on the Charter's Disability Equality Guarantee." *Supreme Court Law Review* 76 (2016): 89–110.

Lewis, J.P. "Elite Attitudes on the Centralization of Power in Canadian Political Executives: A Survey of Former Canadian Provincial and Federal Cabinet Ministers." *Canadian Journal of Political Science* 46, no. 4 (2013): 799–819.

Longley, Neil. "Legislative Systems with Absolute Party Discipline: Implications for the Agency Theory Approach to the Constituent-Legislator Link." *Public Choice* 97 (1998): 121–40.

MacDonnell, Vanessa. "The Civil Servant's Role in the Implementation of Constitutional Rights." *I-CON: International Journal of Constitutional Law* 13, no. 2 (2015): 383–406.

– "The Constitution as Framework for Governance." *University of Toronto Law Journal* 63, no. 4 (2013): 624–52.

– "The New Parliamentary Sovereignty." *Review of Constitutional Studies* 21, no. 1 (2016): 13–36.

Macfarlane, Emmett. "Conceptual Precision and Parliamentary Systems of Rights: Disambiguating 'Dialogue.'" *Review of Constitutional Studies* 17, no. 2 (2012): 73–100.

– "Conservative with the Constitution? Moderation, Strategy, and Institutional Distrust." In *The Blueprint: Conservative Parties and Their Impact on Canadian Politics*. Edited by J.P. Lewis and Joanna Everitt, 221–41. Toronto: University of Toronto Press, 2017.

– *Constitutional Pariah: Reference re Senate Reform and the Future of Parliament*. Vancouver: UBC Press, 2021.

– "Dialogue or Compliance? Measuring Legislatures' Policy Responses to Court Rulings on Rights." *International Political Science Review* 34 (2013): 39–56.

– "Dialogue, Remedies, and Positive Rights: *Carter v. Canada* as a Microcosm for Past and Future Issues under the *Charter of Rights and Freedoms*." *Ottawa Law Review* 49, no. 1 (2017): 107–29.

– "The Dilemma of Positive Rights: Access to Health Care and the Canadian Charter of Rights and Freedoms." *Journal of Canadian Studies* 48, no. 3 (2014): 49–78.

– *Governing from the Bench: The Supreme Court of Canada and the Judicial Role*. Vancouver: UBC Press, 2013.

– "Judicial Policy Impact in Canada." In *Policy Change, Courts, and the Canadian Constitution*, edited by Macfarlane, 3–18. Toronto: University of Toronto Press, 2018.

– "Positive Rights and Section 15 of the Charter: Addressing a Dilemma." *National Journal of Constitutional Law* 38, no. 1 (2018): 147–68.

– *The Renewed Canadian Senate: Organizational Challenges and Relations with the Government*. IRPP Study 71. Montreal: Institute for Research on Public Policy, 2019.

– "'You Can't Always Get What You Want': Regime Politics, the Supreme Court of Canada, and the Harper Government." *Canadian Journal of Political Science* 51, no. 1 (2018): 1–21.

Macfarlane, Emmett, and Rachael Johnstone. "Equality Rights, Abortion Access, and New Brunswick's Regulation 84–20." *University of New Brunswick Law Journal* 72 (2021): 302–24.

MacLennan, Christopher. *Toward the Charter: Canadians and the Demand for a National Bill of Rights, 1929–1960*. Montreal and Kingston: McGill-Queen's University Press, 2003.

MacNair, Deborah. "Solicitor-Client Privilege and the Crown: When Is a Privilege a Privilege?" *Canadian Bar Review* 82 (2003): 213–47.

Mallea, Paula. *Fearmonger: Harper's Tough-on-Crime Agenda*. Toronto: James Lorimer, 2011.

Mandel, Michael. *The Charter of Rights and the Legalization of Politics in Canada*. Toronto: Thompson Education Publishing, 1994.

Manfredi, Christopher. "Conservatives, the Supreme Court of Canada, and the Constitution: Judicial Government Relations, 2006–2015." *Osgoode Hall Law Journal* 52, no. 3 (2015): 951–83.

– "The Day the Dialogue Died: A Comment on *Sauvé v. Canada*." *Osgoode Hall Law Journal* 45, no. 1 (2007): 105–23.

– *Feminist Activism in the Supreme Court: Legal Mobilization and the Women's Legal Education and Action Fund*. Vancouver: UBC Press, 2004.

– *Judicial Power and the Charter: Canada and the Paradox of Liberal Constitutionalism*. 2nd ed. Oxford: Oxford University Press, 2000.

– "The Judicialization of Politics: Rights and Public Policy in Canada and the United States." In *Degrees of Freedom: Canada and the United States in a Changing World*, edited by Keith G. Banting, George Hoberg, and Richard Simeon, 310–40. Montreal and Kingston: McGill-Queen's University Press, 1997.

Manfredi, Christopher P., and James B. Kelly. "Six Degrees of Dialogue: A Response to Hogg and Bushell." *Osgoode Hall Law Journal* 37, no. 3 (1999): 513–27.

Marland, Alex. *Whipped: Party Discipline in Canada*. Vancouver: UBC Press, 2020.

Mathen, Carissima. *Courts without Cases: The Law and Politics of Advisory Opinions*. Oxford: Hart Publishing, 2019.

– "Dialogue Theory, Judicial Review, and Judicial Supremacy: A Comment on Charter Dialogue Revisited." *Osgoode Hall Law Journal* 45, no. 1 (2007): 125–46.

– "A Recent History of Government Responses to Constitutional Litigation." *Constitutional Forum* 25, no. 3 (2016): 101–8.

McCann, Michael. "Causal versus Constitutive Explanations (or, On the Difficulty of Being So Positive...)." *Law and Social Inquiry* 21 (1996): 457–82.

– "Reform Litigation on Trial." *Law and Social Inquiry* 17, no. 4 (1992): 715–43.

– *Rights at Work: Pay Equity Reform and the Politics of Legal Mobilization*. Chicago: University of Chicago Press, 1994.

McCormick, Peter. *Supreme at Last: The Evolution of the Supreme Court of Canada*. Toronto: Lorimer, 2000.

McMorrow, Thomas. "MAID in Canada: Debating the Constitutionality of Canada's New Medical Assistance in Dying Law." *Queen's Law Journal* 44 (2018): 69–120.

Miller, Mark C. *The View of the Courts from the Hill: Interactions between Congress and the Federal Judiciary.* Charlottesville: University of Virginia Press, 2009.

Miller, Mark C., and Jeb Barnes, eds. *Making Policy, Making Law.* Washington, DC: Georgetown University Press, 2004.

Monahan, Patrick J. "'In the Public Interest': Understanding the Special Role of the Government Lawyer." *Supreme Court Law Review.* (2d) 63 (2013): 43–55.

Mooney, Christopher Z. "The Politics of Morality Policy." *Policy Studies Journal* 27, no. 4 (1999): 675–80.

Morrison, Kathryn. "Mature Minor Eligibility for Medical Assistance in Dying (MAiD): An Ethical Analysis." PhD diss., University of Waterloo, 2021.

Morton, F.L., and Rainer Knopff. *The Charter Revolution and the Court Party.* Toronto: University of Toronto Press, 2000.

Mucciaroni, Gary. "Are Debates about 'Morality Policy' Really about Morality? Framing Opposition to Gay and Lesbian Rights." *Policy Studies Journal* 39, no. 2 (2011): 187–216.

Nagel, Robert E. *Constitutional Cultures: The Mentality and Consequences of Judicial Review.* Berkeley: University of California Press, 1993.

Newell, Ryan. "Making Matters Worse: The Safe Streets and Communities Act and the Ongoing Crisis of Indigenous Over-Incarceration." *Osgoode Hall Law Journal* 51, no. 1 (2013): 199–249.

Newman, Dwight. "Canada's Notwithstanding Clause, Dialogue, and Constitutional Identities." In *Constitutional Dialogue: Rights, Democracy, Institutions,* edited by Geoffrey Sigalet, Grégoire Webber, and Rosalind Dixon, 209–34. Cambridge: Cambridge University Press, 2019.

Nicolaides, Eleni. "*Carter* Compliance: Litigation for Access to Medical Assistance in Dying in Canada." In *Constitutional Crossroads: Reflections on Charter Rights, Reconciliation, and Change,* edited by Kate Puddister and Emmett Macfarlane. Vancouver: UBC Press, forthcoming.

Nicolaides, Eleni, and Matthew Hennigar. "*Carter* Conflicts: The Supreme Court of Canada's Impact on Medical Assistance in Dying Policy." In *Policy Change, Courts, and the Canadian Constitution,* edited by Emmett Macfarlane, 313–35. Toronto: University of Toronto Press, 2018.

Nicolaides, Eleni, and Dave Snow. "A Paper Tiger No More? The Media Portrayal of the Notwithstanding Clause in Saskatchewan and Ontario." *Canadian Journal of Political Science* 54 (2021): 60–74.

Overby, L. Marvin, Christopher Raymond, and Zeynep Taydas. "Free Votes, MPs, and Constituents: The Case of Same-Sex Marriage in Canada." *American Review of Canadian Studies* 41, no. 4 (2011): 465–78.

Overby, L. Marvin, Raymond Tatalovich, and Donley T. Studlar. "Party and Free Votes in Canada: Abortion in the House of Commons." *Party Politics* 4, no. 3 (1998): 381–92.

Parliament of Canada. *Medical Assistance in Dying: A Patient-Centred Approach.* Report of the Special Joint Committee on Physician-Assisted Dying. Ottawa: Speaker of the House of Commons, 2016.

Pateman, Carole. *The Sexual Contract.* Stanford, CA: Stanford University Press, 1988.

Permoser, Julia Mourão. "What Are Morality Policies? The Politics of Values in a Post-Secular World." *Political Studies Review* 17, no. 3 (2019): 310–25.

Plaxton, Michael. 2014. "First Impressions of Bill C-36 in Light of Bedford." (Unpublished, 2014). https://papers.ssrn.com/sol3/papers.cfm ?abstract_id=2447006.

Pothier, Dianne. 2016. "Doctor-Assisted Death Bill Falls Well within Top Court's Ruling." *Policy Options*, 29 April 2016. http://policyoptions.irpp.org/2016 /04/29/doctor-assisted-death-bill-falls-well-within-top-courts-ruling/

Puddister, Kate. "How the Canadian Sentencing System Impacts Policy Reform: An Examination of the Harper Era." *Law & Policy* 43, no. 2 (2021): 149–69.

– "Protecting against Cruel and Unusual Punishment: Section 12 of the Charter and Mandatory Minimum Sentences." In *Policy Change, Courts, and the Canadian Constitution*, edited by Emmett Macfarlane, 189–209. Toronto: University of Toronto Press, 2018.

– *Seeking the Court's Advice: The Politics of the Canadian Reference Power.* Vancouver: UBC Press, 2019.

Rahimi, Firuz. "Assisted Death in Canada: An Exploration of the Constitutionality of Bill C-14." *Saskatchewan Law Review* 80 (2017): 457–88.

Rhodes, R.A., J. Wanna, and P. Weller. *Comparing Westminster.* Oxford: Oxford University Press, 2009.

Riddell, Troy Q. "The Impact of Legal Mobilization and Judicial Decisions: The Case of Official Minority-Language Education Policy in Canada for Francophones outside Quebec." *Law and Society Review* 38 (2004): 583–609.

Roach, Kent. "The Separation and Interconnection of Powers in Canada: The Role of Courts, the Executive and the Legislature in Crafting Constitutional Remedies." *Journal of International and Comparative Law* 5, no. 2 (2018): 315–36.

– *The Supreme Court on Trial: Judicial Activism or Democratic Dialogue.* Rev. ed. Toronto: Irwin Law, 2016.

Rosenberg, Gerald N. *The Hollow Hope: Can Courts Bring About Social Change?* 2nd ed. Chicago: University of Chicago Press, 2008.

– "Positivism, Interpretivism, and the Study of Law." *Law and Social Inquiry* 21 (1996): 435–55.

Ryder, Bruce. "Suspending the Charter." *Supreme Court Law Review* 21 (2003): 267–97.

Sampson, Lauren. "The Obscenities of This Country: Canada v. Bedford and the Reform of Canadian Prostitution Laws." *Duke Journal of Gender Law & Policy* 22, no. 1 (2014): 137–72.

Savoie, Donald J. *Democracy in Canada: The Disintegration of Our Institutions.* Montreal and Kingston: McGill-Queen's University Press, 2019.

– *Governing from the Centre: The Concentration of Power in Canadian Politics.* Toronto: University of Toronto Press, 1999.

– *Power: Where Is It?* Montreal and Kingston: McGill-Queen's University Press, 2010.

– *Whatever Happened to the Music Teacher? How Government Decides and Why.* Montreal and Kingston: McGill-Queen's University Press, 2013.

Sealy-Harrington, Joshua, and David Rennie. "Making Sense of Aboriginal and Racialized Sentencing." *ABlawg.ca*, 5 September 2016. https://ablawg.ca/wp-content/uploads/2016/09/Blog_JSH_DR_Laboucan_Kreko_Sept2016.pdf.

Simpson, Jeffrey. *The Friendly Dictatorship.* Toronto: McClelland & Stewart, 2001.

Sirota, Léonid. "The Charter Is of No Party." *Policy Options*, 28 January 2016. http://policyoptions.irpp.org/2016/01/28/the-charter-is-of-no-party/.

Smith, David E. *Across the Aisle: Opposition in Canadian Politics.* Toronto: University of Toronto Press, 2013.

– *The People's House of Commons: Theories of Democracy in Contention.* Toronto: University of Toronto Press, 2007.

Snow, Dave. "The Judicialization of Assisted Reproductive Technology Policy in Canada: Decentralization, Medicalization, and Mandatory Regulation." *Canadian Journal of Law & Society* 27, no. 2 (2012): 169–88.

Snow, Dave, and Kate Puddister. "Closing a Door but Opening a Policy Window: Legislating Assisted Dying in Canada." In *Policy Change, Courts, and the Canadian Constitution*, edited by Emmett Macfarlane, 40–60. Toronto: University of Toronto Press, 2018.

Snow, Natalie M., Mollee K. Steely, and Tusty ten Bensel. 2020. "The Right to Life, Liberty and Security for Prostitution: *Canada v. Bedford*." *Women & Criminal Justice* [published Online First].

Stewart, Hamish. "The Constitutionality of the New Sex Work Law." *Alberta Law Review* 54, no. 1 (2016): 69–88.

Stone Sweet, Alex. *Governing with Judges: Constitutional Politics in Europe.* Oxford: Oxford University Press, 2000.

Sweet, Martin J. *Merely Judgment: Ignoring, Evading, and Trumping the Supreme Court.* Charlottesville: University of Virginia Press, 2010.

Tate, C. Neal, and Thorsten Vallinder, eds. *The Global Expansion of Judicial Power.* New York: New York University Press, 1995.

Thomas, Paul E.J., and J.P. Lewis. "Executive Creep in Canadian Provincial Legislatures." *Canadian Journal of Political Science* 52 (2019): 363–83.

Thomas, Paul G. "The Influence of Standing Committees of Parliament on Government Legislation." *Legislative Studies Quarterly* 3, no. 4 (1978): 683–704.

Tushnet, Mark. "New Forms of Judicial Review and the Persistence of Rights- and Democracy-Based Worries." *Wake Forest Law Review* 38, no. 2 (2003): 813–38.

– "Policy Distortion and Democratic Debilitation: Comparative Illumination of the Countermajoritarian Difficulty." *Michigan Law Review* 94 (1995): 245–301.

– *Weak Courts, Strong Rights: Judicial Review and Social Welfare Rights in Comparative Constitutional Law.* Princeton, NJ: Princeton University Press, 2008.

Waldron, Jeremy. "The Core of the Case against Judicial Review." *Yale Law Journal* 115 (2006): 1346–1406.

Webber, Grégoire. "The Charter Party and the work of Parliament." *Policy Options*, 27 January 2016. http://policyoptions.irpp.org/2016/01/27/the-charter-party-and-the-work-of-parliament/.

Wright, Alysia C., and Jessica C. Shaw. 2018. "The Spectrum of End of Life Care: An Argument for Access to Medical Assistance in Dying for Vulnerable Populations." *Medicine, Health Care and Philosophy* 22, no. 2 (2019): 211–19.

Zanoni, Marc. "The Supreme Court of Canada, Judicial Remedies, and Punctuated Equilibrium." In *Policy Change, Courts, and the Canadian Constitution*, edited by Emmett Macfarlane, 61–78. Toronto: University of Toronto Press, 2018.

Cases Cited

A.B. v. Canada (Attorney General), 2016 ONSC 1912.

AC v. Manitoba (Director of Child and Family Services), 2009 SCC 30.

Bedford v. Canada, 2010 ONSC 4264.

Canada (Attorney General) v. Bedford 2013 SCC 72.

Canada (Attorney General) v. EF, 2016 ABCA 155, 34 Atla LR (6th) 1, 403 DLR (4th) 461.

Canada (Attorney General) v. PHS Community Services Society, 2011 SCC 44, [2011] 3 S.C.R. 134.

Canada (Attorney General) v. Whaling, 2014 SCC 20, [2014] 1 S.C.R. 392.

Carter v. Canada (Attorney General), 2015 SCC 5, [2015] 1 S.C.R. 331.

Carter v. Canada (Attorney General), 2016 SCC 4, [2016] 1 S.C.R. 13.

Chaoulli v. Quebec (Attorney General), 2005 SCC 35.

City of Toronto et al v. Ontario (Attorney General), 2018 ONSC 5151.

Edgar Schmidt v. The Attorney General of Canada, 2016 FC 269.

Ford v. Quebec (Attorney General), [1988] 2 S.C.R. 712.

Good Spirit School Division No. 204 v. Christ the Teacher Roman Catholic Separate School Division No. 212, 2017 SKQB 109.

Gosselin v. Quebec (Attorney General), [2002] 4 S.C.R. 429, 2002 SCC 84.

Irwin Toy Ltd. v. Quebec (Attorney General), [1989] 1 S.C.R. 927.

M. v. H., [1999] 2 S.C.R. 3.

PHS Community Services Society v. Attorney General of Canada, 2008 BCSC 661.

PHS Community Services Society v. Canada (Attorney General), 2010 BCCA 15.

R. v. Anwar, 2020 ONCJ 103.

R. v. Boodhoo, and others, 2018 ONSC 7205.

R. v. Boudreault, 2018 SCC 58, [2018] 3 S.C.R. 599.

R. v. Brown, 2022 SCC 18.

R. v. Campbell, [1999] 1 S.C.R. 565.

R. v. D.B., [2008] 2 S.C.R. 3, 2008 SCC 25.

R. v. Daviault, [1994] 3 S.C.R. 63.

R. v. Hall, [2002] 3 S.C.R. 309.

R. v. Lloyd [2016] 1 S.C.R. 130.

R. v. Mills, [1999] 3 S.C.R. 668.

R. v. Morales, [1992] 3 S.C.R. 711.

R. v. Morgentaler, [1988] 1 S.C.R. 30.

R. v. N.S. 2021 ONSC 1628

R. v. Nur [2015] 1 S.C.R. 773.

R. v. O'Connor, [1995] 4 S.C.R. 411.

R. v. Oakes [1986] 1 S.C.R. 103.

R. v. Safarzadeh-Markhali 2016 SCC 14.

R. v. Smith, 2015 SCC 34, [2015] 2 S.C.R. 602.

R. v. St-Onge Lamoureux, 2012 SCC 75, [2012] 3 S.C.R. 187.

R. v. Summers, [2014] 1 S.C.R. 575.

R (on the application of SC, CB and 8 children) (Appellants) v. Secretary of State for Work and Pensions and others (Respondents) [2021] UKSC 26.

Reference re Same-Sex Marriage, [2004] 3 S.C.R. 698, 2004 SCC 79.

Reference re Supreme Court Act, ss. 5 and 6, 2014 SCC 21, [2014] 1 S.C.R. 433.

Robertson and Rosetanni v. The Queen [1963] S.C.R. 651.

Rodriguez v. British Columbia (Attorney General), [1993] 3 S.C.R. 519.

Saskatchewan v. Good Spirit School Division No. 204, 2020 SKCA 34.

Sauvé v. Canada (Attorney General), [1993] 2 S.C.R. 438.

Sauvé v. Canada (Chief Electoral Officer), [2002] 3 S.C.R. 519, 2002 SCC 68.

Schachter v. Canada, [1992] 2 S.C.R. 679.

Schmidt v. Canada (Attorney General), 2018 FCA 55.

Singh v. Minister of Employment and Immigration [1985] 1 S.C.R. 177.

Toronto (City) v. Ontario (Attorney General), 2019 ONCA 732.

Truchon c. Procureur général du Canada, 2019 QCCS 3792.

Truchon c. Procureur général du Canada, 2020 QCCS 2019.

Working Families Ontario v. Ontario, 2021 ONSC 4076.

Index